Conrad

Conrad
The Moral World of the Novelist

R. A. Gekoski

BARNES & NOBLE
BOOKS
10 East 53d St., New York 10022
(a division of Harper & Row Publishers, Inc.)

To my Father

Published in the U.S.A. 1978 by
HARPER & ROW PUBLISHERS, INC.
BARNES & NOBLE IMPORT DIVISION

First published in Great Britain 1978 by
Paul Elek Limited, London

Library of Congress Cataloging in Publication Data

Gekoski, R. A.
   Conrad: the moral world of the novelist.

   (Novelists and their world)
   A revision of the author's thesis, University
of Oxford, 1972.
   Bibliography: p.
   Includes index.
   1. Conrad, Joseph, 1857–1924—Philosophy.
I. Title.
PR6005.04Z7255 1978   823'.9'12   78–2118
ISBN 0–06–492348–7

Printed in Great Britain by
Latimer Trend & Company Ltd Plymouth

Contents

Preface

In 1899, Joseph Conrad wrote to the publisher William Blackwood:

> 'To point out to the crowd beauties not manifest to the common eye, to flash the light of one's sympathetic perception upon great, if not obvious, qualities, and even upon generous failings that hold the promise of better things this is indeed a toil worthy of a man's pen, a task that would repay for the time given up, for the strength expended for that sadness that comes of thinking over the sincere endeavour of a soul—for ever debarred from attaining perfection. But the blind distribution of praise or blame, done with a light heart and an empty mind, which is of the very essence of "periodical" criticism seems to me to be a work less useful than skirt-dancing and not quite as honourable as pocket-picking.
>
> There is too a sort of curse upon the critical exercise of human thought. Should one attempt honestly an analysis of another man's production it is ten to one, that one will get the credit for all sorts of motives except for that of sincere conviction . . .'

These are noble ideals, eloquently stated, which set a standard that I am conscious of having failed entirely to live up to in this book. Perhaps it is impossible to do so. My major effort has been to articulate, as clearly as possible, the nature and strength of my admiration for Conrad's work. In the flexibility of his intelligence, and the range of his sympathies, he seems to me not simply a major figure in English fiction, but one of the outstanding talents of our time. In adding yet another critical testimonial to his genius, I am writing for those who admire his work, but even more for those who, though largely unacquainted with it, might yet come to do so. In the interests of readers whose knowledge of Conrad is as yet sketchy, I have included short paraphrases of the novels and stories, where appropriate; I hope that these will not put off more knowledgeable students of his fiction.

In its original form, this work was presented in 1972 as a

D.Phil. thesis at the University of Oxford, and though it has been extensively revised since, I would still like to record especial thanks for the supervision given me by J. I. M. Stewart and John Bayley. At that time I was supported by grants from the Thouron Scholarship Fund and the Danforth Association, without which the work would obviously never have been possible. It has benefited, in the years since then, by the critical guidance of numerous friends and colleagues. I owe particular debts of thanks to Michael Bell, Bernard Bergonzi, Bernard Gekoski, George O'Brien, Wallace Robson, and Jean Rodes, all of whom have saved me, in one way or another, from errors of fact and judgment that had escaped my attention. The same must be said of Jo Smithies and Mike Richards, who more than typed and proof-read the manuscript. All errors that remain are, of course, my own responsibility. To my wife, who has seen me through its many revisions, my warmest gratitude.

R.G.

Publisher's Acknowledgements

Acknowledgement is made to the following for their permission to cite passages from copyright material:

The Trustees of the Joseph Conrad Estate: *Joseph Conrad: Letters to William Blackwood and David S. Meldrum*, edited by W. Blackburn, Duke University Press, 1958; *Conrad's Polish Background: Letters to and from Polish Friends*, edited by Z. Nazder, Oxford University Press, 1964; *Joseph Conrad's Letters to R. B. Cunninghame Graham*, edited by C. T. Watts, Cambridge University Press, London, 1969.

Doubleday & Company, Inc.: *Letters from Conrad, 1895–1924*, edited by E. Garnett, 1928. G. Jean-Aubry, *Joseph Conrad: Life and Letters*, 1927. Also passages from the following by Joseph Conrad: *A Personal Record*, London, 1912; *Under Western Eyes*, 1911; *Chance*, 1913; *Victory*, 1915; *The Shadow Line*, 1917; 'The Secret Sharer'; Author's note (1919) to *An Outcast of the Islands; Notes on Life and Letters*; a letter to Marguerite Poradowska dated 29 October or 5 November 1894 in Yale Library; a letter printed in *The Library of John Quinn*, New York, 1923–24, vol. 1, p. 170; a letter to Marguerite Poradowska quoted by Vernon Young in an article entitled 'Trial by Water', reprinted in *The Art of Joseph Conrad; A Critical Symposium* ed. R. W. Stallman, Michigan, 1960; a letter dated 18 October 1898 in the Pierpont Library, New York.

Edward Arnold (Publishers) Ltd and Harcourt Brace Jovanovich, Inc.: E. M. Forster, *Abinger Harvest* (1936).

Penguin Books Ltd and Dodd, Mead & Company: J. I. M. Stewart, *Joseph Conrad* (Longman, 1968), pp. 84 and 174–5; Copyright © J. I. M. Stewart, 1968; reprinted by permission of Penguin Books Ltd.

Harvard University Press and Oxford University Press: Albert J. Guerard, *Conrad the Novelist*, 1958.

Bowes & Bowes (Publishers) Ltd and Rowman & Littlefield: O. Hewitt, *Conrad: A Reassessment*, 1952, reprinted 1969.

Horizon Press: Irving Howe, *Politics and the Novel*, 1957.

I

Conrad's Moral World

Though widely regarded as a major figure in modern fiction, Joseph Conrad continues to elicit an admiration tinged with a certain wariness, as if, though compelled to respect his achievement, we ought nevertheless to be suspicious of him. This is implicit in much critical discussion of his work; more significantly, it seems to me a constant feature of the response of those of my own colleagues, friends, and students who read him. If Conrad's place in European literature now seems assured, he nevertheless has a smaller, and perhaps less confident, readership than comparable modern classics like Lawrence or Kafka. A colleague recently said to me 'The more I know of Conrad, the less I trust him.' The remark is striking not because it is idiosyncratic, but because it encapsulates a widely held, if not frequently articulated, belief.

Curiously, such reservation generally does not concern the nature of Conrad's limitations. It is universally admitted that his corpus is uneven in quality, and that even his finest works are marred by restriction of vision in important areas. His fictional world is hostile to the intrusion of women and what they bring with them: domesticity or romance, sexuality consummated or repressed. When he writes about romantic attraction he is at best banal, and frequently perverse.[1] In Dickens, a similar problem may be transformed by a sophisticated sentimental aesthetic, while in Conrad we sense rather a blurred incapacity to register the movements of passionate life. His women attain to particularity only in the absence of those fulfilments that sentiment would ascribe to them. Like so many of Conrad's male heroes, they are all defined and particularized with reference to the test which they undergo, rather than by a challenge that they generate themselves. In this sense, Conrad's protagonists are not 'characters' at all; are not memorable as Jude, or Rupert Birkin, or Leopold Bloom are memorable—or, at least, not in the manner that they are. Conrad's heroes seem not to have depths discretely their own; their inner lives consist,

I

in the most dramatic form, of a reflection or enactment of the universe in which they live. The problem of self-knowledge, in Conrad, is conflated with that of knowledge of the world; perception becomes the form of introspection. If Kafka's world of court and castle consists of the projection of a psychology on to a landscape, in Conrad the process is reversed: the psychology of the major characters is the result of an introjected vision of their universe.

Stated this tersely, such a view will not immediately convince, nor is it designed to do so. I wish, instead, simply to indicate the nature of the problem: that it is not Conrad's incapacities that we regret, so much as that what he is good at—the drama of imaginative men struggling with the corrosive effect of truth —should be so difficult to catch hold of.

I should like to put a name to this phenomenon, by recalling a comment from *Under Western Eyes*. Early in that novel, the narrator, perplexed by the foreign psychology of the Russians by whom he is surrounded, seeks a single term to help him to describe 'conditions not easily to be understood ... till some key-word is found.' In his case, that word is 'cynicism', which 'if not truth itself, may perchance hold truth enough to help the moral discovery which should be the object of every tale.'[2] My purpose here is hardly to tell the tale of Conrad, nor is its aim (strictly) a moral one, but I still want that key-word. In considering responses to Conrad's work, the term I wish to invoke is 'obscure'. I need this term in order, like the old teacher of languages, to frame a complicated question as if it were a simple one; but, unlike him, I want it in order to reject it.

That Conrad is 'obscure' is a judgment widely made by critics who both respect and admire his work. Richard Curle, admitting that 'I never felt certain I had pierced to the central core of his thought, where all was fixed and determined',[3] suggests that: 'For though Conrad was, in a way, very, very obscure, nevertheless he was very genuine ... One might wonder what Conrad's final opinions were, but one never doubted that his words, whatever bias they took, were invariably the completely sincere expression of his mood.'[4] It is the 'in a way' that demands clarification, which might in itself necessitate defence of the dubious metaphor of the 'central core'. But if we can dissolve or mitigate the force of Curle's remark, it is not so easy to do away with the unease that it indicates. E. M. Forster, in his essay on Conrad in *Abinger Harvest*, writes:

'What is so elusive about him is that he is always promising to make some general philosophic statement about the universe, and then refraining with a gruff disclaimer ... Is there not also a central obscurity, something noble, heroic, beautiful, inspiring half-a-dozen great books, but obscure, obscure? ... These essays do suggest that he is misty in the middle as well as at the edges; that the secret casket of his genius contains a vapour rather than a jewel; and that we needn't try to write him down philosophically, because there is, in this direction, nothing to write. No creed, in fact. Only opinions, and the right to throw them overboard when facts make them look absurd. Opinions held under the semblance of eternity, girt with the sea, crowned with stars, and therefore easily mistaken for a creed.'[5]

F. R. Leavis, though not unreservedly in agreement with Forster, begins his discussion of Conrad in *The Great Tradition* by citing this passage, on the basis of which, he tells us, he abandoned a projected article entitled 'Conrad, the Soul, and the Universe'. Later in *The Great Tradition* he speaks of Conrad in 'Heart of Darkness' as 'intent on making a virtue out of not knowing what he means',[6] which has something of Forster's flavour about it.

Forster's formulation, while attractive (perhaps it is a little too attractive?), repeats Richard Curle's use of the metaphor of the middle, which I have already suggested to be suspect. Surprisingly, Forster seems to tie his charge of obscurity to the absence of a 'creed' in Conrad. I say 'surprisingly' not because Conrad clearly has a creed (Forster knows this perfectly well; his objection is that Conrad seems unprepared to stick by it), but because it's difficult to see why one is necessary. It is hard to find one in James Joyce; and if Joyce can be called obscure, it is not because of the absence of that creed. It is equally difficult to locate a creed in *A Passage to India*; *Howard's End* might be said to have one, and that may be one of the reasons why it is inferior to *A Passage to India*.

Further, more recent, examples of the charge of obscurity against Conrad can easily enough be marshalled. There is, for instance, Ian Watt's reference to the 'unresolved conflict of attitudes that underlies his obscurity'.[7] But the term 'obscure' may itself, by now, seem a little unclear. The *Oxford English Dictionary* lists seven possibilities, of which the last is most pertinent:

> 'Not manifest to the mind or understanding; imperfectly known or understood; not clear or plain; hidden, doubtful, vague, uncertain. (With regard to words or expressions): Not perspicuous, not clearly expressed; hard to understand.)'

It seems that Forster finds Conrad not difficult but impossible. However, this book will attempt to show that Conrad is not, in any of the senses above, 'obscure'; indeed, his writing and understanding seem to me markedly—though not unfailingly—lucid. But the lucidity of Conrad the writer need not be matched by the clarity of what he writes about: his view of the human condition is that it is, itself, 'obscure': dark, unclear, uncertain. His eye is firmly fixed, but his object wavers; the differing perspectives of his vision register the movement of what he sees.

At the start of 'Heart of Darkness' the narrator makes a remark that seems to me pertinent here:

> 'The yarns of seamen have a direct simplicity, the whole meaning of which lies within the shell of a cracked nut. But Marlow was not typical (if his propensity to spin yarns be excepted), and to him the meaning of an episode was not inside like a kernel but outside, enveloping the tale which brought it out only as a glow brings out a haze, in the likeness of one of these misty haloes that sometimes are made visible by the spectral illumination of moonshine.' (p. 48)

The image of the nut and kernel recalls Forster's similar use of the casket and jewel, and again recalls the question of whether we should be looking inside—towards the 'middle'—for the meaning of Conrad's work. The metaphor of the mist (could this be where Forster gets it?) instead suggests the obscurity of what is seen, not of the perceiving eye. 'As a glow brings out a haze', so too an increase of understanding only reveals the unclarity before it: the more light that is cast, the more mistiness is revealed.

Conrad's first autobiographical volume, *The Mirror of the Sea*, was published in the summer of 1906; in preparing for publication, the publishers Methuen and Company asked Conrad for a statement of his artistic aims. He responded: 'You ask me for something very difficult. Any definition of one's work must be either very intimate or very superficial . . . The intention of temperamental writing is infinitely complex, and to talk about my work is repugnant to me—beyond anything. And what could I say that would be of use to you?'[8]

Conrad's comments on his own work often exhibit both this reluctance to discuss it and a related tendency to disparage it. Of the novels, he once said to Edward Garnett, his first and closest literary friend, 'The *Outcast* is a heap of sand, the *Nigger* a splash of water, *Jim* a lump of clay.'[9] The remark seems radically to undervalue the works. The self-deprecating tone is balanced, however, by the nature of the metaphors: heaps of sand, splashes of water, and lumps of clay, are all evanescent and trivial phenomena, but they are natural ones—they are, in the final analysis, what the world *is*. So too, we can infer, are works of art—at once supremely unimportant and yet, paradoxically, fundamental. This balance between radically opposed points of view, stated in a self-deprecating or ironic manner, is characteristic of Conrad's view of his own work— and is essential, as we shall see, to his vision not only of himself but of man and his place in the natural world.

When we combine this self-reflexive ironic tendency with the natural reticence and politeness that were so characteristic of Conrad, it is easy to understand why some critics have felt that he was an unreliable judge of his own work. In the introduction to his excellent brief study, *Conrad: A Reassessment*, Douglas Hewitt remarks:

'The present study grew very largely from reflection on the marked inferiority of most of Conrad's later works to his earlier ones and on the unhelpfulness of his own comments in prefaces and letters. I was forced to the conclusion that, despite his conscious attention to his craft, he was—particularly after the deterioration set in— far less aware of his real powers than one would expect. If it seems presumptuous to claim to know more about his value than he did himself, I take comfort from a passage in a letter which he wrote to Charles Cassé on 31st January, 1924:

5

"That is the truth as far as I know. *Mais après tout, vous pouvez avoir raison.* Men have but very little self knowledge, and authors especially are victims of many illusions about themselves."[10]

Reflection also had the happy result of persuading me that his best work is not only very different from his account of it, but also very much better.'[11]

We ought to make a distinction between Conrad's evaluations of his novels, and his comments on their technique or meaning. While various personal factors often affected his valuations of his own novels, a careful reading of Conrad's letters, prefaces, and autobiographies, indicates that he was a profound thinker not only about the art of the novel, but about his own works in particular. It is simply not true that Conrad's non-fictional writings are uniformly 'unhelpful' to an understanding of his fiction, although they are not wholly reliable. Conrad's letters are the most useful here, as one might expect; his published autobiographical writings, however, have to be approached with great care. Not only are they factually inaccurate in both trivial and crucial ways, but they are (in places) systematically misleading. (In *A Personal Record* (1912), for instance, Conrad insists that, had he not written in English, he would not have written at all. There is reasonable evidence that this is untrue.) I shall refer to them, however, when they seem appropriate.[12]

The above-cited letter to Methuen and Company contains an intriguing reference to 'temperamental' writing, a term that occurs frequently in Conrad's description of his work. It is not clear to me what this means, nor is Conrad's gloss markedly illuminating: 'There is nothing in me but a turn of mind which, whether valuable or worthless, cannot be imitated.'[13] Now, of course, Conrad can be imitated, if that means 'parodied': Max Beerbohm did it very well in *A Christmas Garland.* (In the stricter sense of 'reproduced', the remark seems no truer of Conrad than of anyone else.) But what is striking is the nature of the equation of identity with mind: 'turn of mind' is not what 'I' consist of, but what 'I' am filled with. To have no 'turn of mind', then, is presumably to be 'hollow at the core'— perhaps as James Wait and Mr Kurtz are?

It seems that the implications of 'temperament' and 'turn of mind' may be worth pursuing. When Conrad published his

6

first novel, *Almayer's Folly*, he was thirty-eight, and the first of his great works, *The Nigger of the 'Narcissus'*, was written at the age of forty. He observed: 'A man of forty unless he is a pathological case must have a formed character, that sort of knowledge of his own weakness which (the knowledge, I mean) is a sort of strength, and also some sense of moral independence and perhaps—surely it is not too much to ask—a certain power of resistance.'[14] *A Personal Record* makes a similar point; it gives 'the vision of a personality; the man behind the books so fundamentally dissimilar as, for instance, "Almayer's Folly" and "The Secret Agent", and yet a coherent, justifiable personality both in its origin and in its action.' (p. xxi.) Neither statement carries much conviction; why, we may wonder, does a personality have to be 'justified'? Why, too, is a 'formed character' based on a 'knowledge of [one's] own weakness'? And—more pertinently—what does this entail with regard to Conrad's fiction?

A letter written in 1918 seems to link 'temperament' not so much to character as to that perceiving eye of which I have been speaking:

'My writing life extends but only over twenty-three years, and I need not point out to an intelligence as alert as yours that all that time has been a time of evolution, in which some critics have detected three marked periods—and that the process is still going on. Some critics have found fault with me for not being constantly myself. But they are wrong. I am always myself. I am a man of formed character. Certain conclusions remain immovably fixed in my mind, but I am no slave to prejudices and formulas, and I shall never be. My attitude to subjects and expressions, the angles of vision, my methods of composition will, within limits, be always changing—not because I am unstable or unprincipled but because I am free. Or perhaps it may be more exact to say, because I am always trying for freedom—within my limits.'[15]

'Temperament', then, is not equivalent to 'conviction' or 'impulse', but to the 'angle of vision' that a man takes upon himself and upon his world. In examining it in this chapter I shall rely largely upon Conrad's non-fictional writings (letters, prefaces, and autobiographical works). There is, of course, no doubt that the novels and stories go deeper, but to extrapolate from the feelings of his narrator (even when he uses an omni-

7

scient one) to those of Conrad himself would be quite unsound. For just as each novel creates its own world, characters, and values, so too the generalizations that it offers are contingent on the particularities of its vision. What is significant about 'art', to Conrad, is that it is not the simple statement of a belief: 'a work of art is very seldom limited to one exclusive meaning and not necessarily tending to a definite conclusion. And this for the reason that the nearer it approaches art, the more it acquires a symbolic character.'[16] This preliminary discussion of Conrad's temperament, then, will rely largely upon his letters exactly because they are not, in the sense above, 'works of art'.

It is commonly recognized that Conrad's writings seem to assert two very different value systems, which have been variously referred to as public and private, social and individual, or committed and alienated. It does not matter greatly which dichotomy one uses, so long as one does not take it too seriously. Unlike (say) D. H. Lawrence's, Conrad's vision is not based on stated polarities; when I refer to Conrad's 'different value systems', I mean that he was deeply attracted by what appear to be contradictory apprehensions about the nature and obligations of human life. The feeling that he is obscure surely arises from this. On the one hand he stresses the private and individual nature of man's existence, the essential isolation of every man (which I shall call his 'vision of personal autonomy'), while on the other, he affirms the public and moral obligations of human existence (which I shall call his 'vision of social responsibility'). Although it is clearly not *logically* necessary that a vision of man as an autonomous being must conflict with a vision of him as a social being, most commentators are agreed that it is very hard to understand how (or even if) Conrad reconciled them.

One of the most interesting critical statements on this aspect of Conrad can be found in Albert Guerard's *Conrad the Novelist*; according to Guerard, we find in Conrad's work:

'A rationalist's declared distrust of the unconscious and rationalist's desire to be a sane orderly novelist—doubled by a powerful introspective drive that took the dreamer deeper into the unconscious than any earlier novelist (except perhaps Dickens);

A declared fear of the corrosive and faith-destroying intellect—doubled by a profound and ironic scepticism;

A declared belief that ethical matters are simple—doubled by an extraordinary sense of ethical complexities;

A declared ethic of simplicity, action, and the saving grace of work—doubled by a professional propensity to passive dreaming;

A declared distrust of generous idealism—doubled by a strong idealism (Conrad in a very modern manner distrusting both the cynical "realist" and the professed "do-gooder" and disliking most intensely the complacency of those in between);

A declared commitment to authoritarian sea-tradition— doubled by a pronounced individualism . . .;

A declared and extreme political conservatism, at once aristocratic and pragmatist—doubled by a great sympathy for the poor and disinherited of the earth (a conflict nominally resolved in the stance of *noblesse oblige*);

A declared fidelity to law as above the individual—doubled by a strong sense of fidelity to the individual, with betrayal of the individual the most deeply felt of all crimes;

Briefly: a deep commitment to order in society and in the self—doubled by an incorrigible sympathy for the outlaw, whether existing in society or the self.'[17]

Guerard declares that we find, in this matrix of 'conflict', the 'psycho-moral foundations of the Conrad "world"'.[18] But how accurately does the word 'conflict' describe the relationship between these two sides of Conrad's temperament? Are what I have called the visions of personal autonomy and social responsibility in irreconcilable opposition, or can they be brought together in terms of some comprehensive understanding?

Guerard believes that the side of Conrad's nature that he calls 'more austere' is predominently found in the letters, prefaces, and autobiographies, while the darker side is generally expressed in the fiction. This is only partially true; in the letters (particularly the early letters)[19] to his closest friends we can get a glimpse of a Conrad darker and more pessimistic than in any of the novels. The most important of these letters form what is virtually a self-contained discourse on metaphysics; written to R. B. Cunninghame Graham during a short period at the end of 1897 and the beginning of 1898, they are indispensable to any student of Conrad's work.[20] In them we get our closest look at Conrad, for it was not yet a time when he needed to censor his letters with the awareness that they were likely to be published. Because they have hitherto not been much discussed,[21] I shall quote from them at length.

'There is a—let us say—a machine. It evolved itself (I am severely scientific) out of a chaos of scraps of iron and behold!—it knits. I am horrified at the horrible work and stand appalled. I feel it ought to embroider—but it goes on knitting. You come and say: "this is all right; it's only a question of the right kind of oil. Let us use this—for instance—celestial oil and the machine shall embroider a most beautiful design in purple and gold." Will it? Alas no. You cannot by any special lubrication make embroidery with a knitting machine. And the most withering thought is that the infamous thing has made itself; made itself without thought, without conscience, without foresight, without eyes, without heart. It is a tragic accident—and it has happened. You can't interfere with it. The last drop of bitterness is in the suspicion that you can't even smash it. In virtue of that truth one and immortal which lurks in the force that made it spring into existence it is what it is—and it is indestructible!

It knits us in and it knits us out. It has knitted time, space, pain, death, corruption, despair and all the illusions and nothing matters. I'll admit however that to look at the remorseless process is sometimes amusing.'[22]

Cunninghame Graham, an idealist of inexhaustible energy and optimism, seems to have replied (his side of the correspondence is lost) that we cannot dwell on the tragic aspect of things, but must go on striving defiantly. Conrad replied:

' "Put the tongue out" why not?[23] One ought to really. And the machine will run on all the same. The question is, whether the fatigue of the muscular exertion is worth the transient pleasure of indulged scorn. On the other hand one may ask whether scorn, love, or hate are justified in the face of such shadowy illusions. The machine is thinner than air and as evanescent as a flash of lightning. The attitude of cold unconcern is the only reasonable one. Of course reason is hateful—but why? Because it demonstrates (to those who have the courage) that we, living, are out of life—utterly out of it. The mysteries of a universe made of drops of fire and clods of mud do not concern us in the least. The fate of a humanity condemned ultimately to perish from cold is not worth troubling about. If you take it to heart it becomes an unendurable tragedy. If you believe in improvement you must weep, for the attained perfection must end in cold, darkness and silence. In a dispassionate view the ardour for reform, improvement for virtue, for knowledge, and even for beauty is only a vain sticking up for appearances as though one were anxious about the cut of one's clothes in a community of blind men. Life knows us not and we do not know life—we don't know even our own thoughts. Half the words we use have no meaning whatever and of the other half each man understands each word after the fashion of his own folly and conceit. Faith is a myth and beliefs shift like mists on the shore; thoughts vanish; words, once pronounced, die; and the memory of yesterday is as shadowy as the hope of tomorrow—only the string of my platitudes seems to have no end. As our peasants say: "Pray, brother, forgive me for the love of God." And we don't know what forgiveness is, nor what love is, nor where God is. *Assez*.'[24]

To this Cunninghame Graham may have responded with a reiterated declaration of faith—towards which Conrad was both strongly attracted and harshly sceptical:

'You with your ideals of sincerity, courage and truth are strangely out of place in this epoch of material preoccupations. What does it bring? What's the profit? What do we get by it? These questions are at the root of every moral, intellectual or political movement. Into the noblest cause men manage to put something of their baseness; and sometimes when I think of You here, quietly you seem to me tragic with your courage, with your beliefs and your hopes. Every cause is tainted: and you reject this one, espouse that other one as if one were evil and the other good while the same evil you hate is in both, but disguised in different words. I am more in sympathy with you than words can express yet if I had a grain of belief left in me I would believe you misguided. You are misguided by the desire of the impossible—and I envy you. Alas! What you want to reform are not institutions—it is human nature. Your faith will never move that mountain. Not that I think mankind intrinsically bad. It is only silly and cowardly. Now *You* know that in cowardice is every evil—especially that cruelty so characteristic of our civilization. But without it mankind would vanish. No great matter truly. But will you persuade humanity to throw away the sword and shield? Can you persuade even me—Who write these words in the fulness of an irresistible conviction? No. I belong to the wretched gang. We all belong to it. We are born initiated, and succeeding generations clutch the inheritance of fear and brutality without a thought, without a doubt without compunction—in the name of God.'[25]

In a letter written eight days later, Conrad further develops this theme:

'Egoism is good, and altruism is good, and fidelity to nature would be the best of all, and systems could be built, and rules could be made—if we could only get rid of consciousness. What makes mankind tragic is not that they are the victims of nature, it is that they are conscious of it. To be part of the animal kingdom under the conditions of this earth is very well—but as soon as you know of your slavery the pain, the anger, the strife—the tragedy begins. We can't return to nature, since we can't change our place in it. Our refuge is in stupidity, in drunkenness of all kinds, in lies, in beliefs, in murder, thieving, reforming—in negation, in contempt—each man according to the promptings of his particular devil. There is no morality, no knowledge and no hope; there is only the consciousness of ourselves which drives us about a world that whether seen in a convex or a concave mirror is always but a vain and fleeting appearance.'[26]

The line of thought is concluded in a letter some time later: 'if this miserable planet had perception, a soul, a heart, it would burst with indignation or fly to pieces from sheer pity.'[27]

The image of the universe as an inexorable and unchanging machine is itself neither tragic nor pessimistic, but primary; it is the foundation on which Conrad's metaphysic is built.

In the absence of the Cunninghame Graham letters it is difficult to assess the intellectual context of Conrad's remarks, which, though rhetorically striking, may seem elusive or arbitrary. They are neither; if Conrad's explication of his position is not systematic, it can (as I will show) be made so.

Thus men, like all the other members of the animal kingdom, are the objects of forces over which no lasting control is possible. Ironically, the quality over which we have traditionally so congratulated ourselves—the ability to think—causes our tragedy: the recognition that human efforts, whatever they aim for or achieve, can come, ultimately, not merely 'to nothing'—the metaphor is too tired—but to nothingness. Men can neither exist with animal passivity and its unconscious acceptance of the immutable in nature, nor can we, through consciousness, ameliorate or transcend our limitations, only regret them. We can see neither the beginning nor the end; there is no certainty save that of eventual annihilation. Thus, the machine and our recognition of its inexorable (hence tragic) operations, combine to mock traditional concepts of 'progress' and 'moral' behaviour.

This is unbearable: conscious of this world in which he is apparently but a momentary and confused visitor, man the thinking animal becomes man the unhappy animal. Though it would ideally be best if this fatal propensity towards thought could be suppressed, men seem inevitably to construct some pattern of value or action designed to give life meaning, to make 'happiness' possible. In this endeavour, be it self-assertive or self-denying, a man must ultimately recognize (if he has the courage) that it is not he that controls life, but life that controls him: 'we, living, are out of life.' Thus we have the primary paradox: although 'every evil' in the civilized world that man creates for himself is caused by his cowardice, it is only through this cowardice that such creation is possible. If we had greater strength, and could confront the facts of our existence, it would issue in despair. Lack of imagination becomes not only itself a virtue, but the basis of virtue itself. The doctrine is not unlike that of original sin: we are ordered to be fruitful and multiply; but we procreate (in a societal sense) only through our fatal weakness, which then plagues our child (the given social or moral system). 'L'homme est un animal méchant. Sa méchanceté doit être organisée. La société est essentiellement criminelle,—ou elle n'existerait pas. C'est l'égoïsme qui sauve tout,—absolument tout,—tout ce que nous abhorrons, tout ce que nous aimons.'[28] There is thus a primary tension between the facts of existence (man in the universe) and the necessities of existence (life in the world).

Since human existence is starkly devoid of any final significance, of transcendental imperative or sanction, talk of 'moral behaviour' becomes nonsensical. All behaviour is equally groundless in the face of man's tragic position; no action is better than any other action: 'There is no morality, no knowledge, and no hope.' But systems of morality cannot be groundless, if only because they can then be seen to be so. In a universe promising only death, 'morality' must inevitably die; all behaviour is finally rendered morally neutral. The mood is that of Matthew Arnold's 'Dover Beach':

'. . . for the world, which seems
To lie before us like a land of dreams,
So various, so beautiful, so new,
Hath really neither joy, nor love, nor light,
Nor certitude, nor peace, nor help for pain;
And we are here as on a darkling plain
Swept with confused alarms of struggle and flight,
Where ignorant armies clash by night.'

Certainty has fled; the speaker is faced with the prospect of a world made tragic by its failure to meet his expectations: his rhetoric and vision dominated by neithers and nors. The Sea of Faith has ebbed, without offering much hope of renewed high tides. If new values are to be found, happiness made possible, then they will have to be projected rather than introjected— made, not found, as the Ten Commandments were found. Thus the crucial sentiment with which the final stanza of 'Dover Beach' opens:

'Ah, love, let us be true
To one another!'

seems to reach towards some significance independent of external nature, some tentative possibility of escape from the shattering bleakness of human existence. Anyone familiar with Conrad's writings will recognize that the vision of personal autonomy, his version of the world of neithers and nors, represents but one aspect of his thought. He was also to enunciate beliefs corresponding to Arnold's desire that we be 'true to one another', which Thomas Moser has characterized in simple terms: 'Humanity is important; fidelity is the highest virtue'—a creed which he refers to as 'stoic humanism'.[29]

Writing to Sir Sidney Colvin in 1917, Conrad tried to characterize the nature of his artistic concern:

'Perhaps you won't find it presumption if, after 22 years of work, I may say that I have not been very well understood. I have been called a writer of the sea, of the tropics, a descriptive writer, a romantic writer—and also a realist. But as a matter of fact all my concern has been with the "ideal" value of things, events and people. That and nothing else. The humorous, the pathetic, the passionate, the sentimental aspects came in of themselves—*mais en vérité c'est les valeurs idéales des faits et gestes humains qui se sont imposés à mon activité artistique.*'[30]

It is hard to understand what Conrad means here by the 'ideal' value of things, for in itself the phrase is so ambiguous as to mean nothing, or everything.[31] This uncertainty of focus is a marked characteristic of what Guerard calls the 'austere' Conrad; expressions of faith, devotion to the simple ethic of Fidelity, are frequently attended by evasive rhetoric and syntactic unclarity, as well as the usage of French, that suggests an uneasy search for an adequate formulation.

This is particularly true of that most frequently examined statement of faith, the 'Familiar Preface' to *A Personal Record*, in which we find one of the most concise presentations of the vision of social responsibility. The memoir is an attempt to give the reader some idea of Joseph Conrad, the private man with that 'coherent, justifiable personality' (p. xxi):

'I have carried my notion of good service from my earlier into my later existence. I, who never sought in the written word anything else but a form of the Beautiful—I have carried over that article of creed from the decks of ships to the more circumscribed space of my desk, and by that act, I suppose, I have become permanently imperfect in the eyes of the ineffable company of pure esthetes.' (p. xvii)

What is being invoked here, quite clearly, is the rigorous code of conduct that rules life at sea; it is *'les valeurs idéales'* that are most important:

'Those who read me know my conviction that the world, the temporal world, rests on a few very simple ideas; so simple that they must be as old as the hills. It rests, notably, among others, on the idea of Fidelity.' (p. xix)

This is a famous stopping-place for critics, many of whom, like Douglas Hewitt, find it strikingly inadequate:

'Faith in Fidelity may be the guiding thread which can lead us through *Chance*, or *Victory*, or *The Rover*, but it is soon lost in 'Heart of Darkness' or *Nostromo* and other works of the same period, where he treats of ideas and beliefs which are very far from simple and to which any naive moralizing is irrelevant. To read them in the light of his later novels, and of his own pronouncements when he had achieved a position of authority as one of the leading novelists of the day, is to miss almost everything which they have to give us.'[32]

Certainly the assertion that the world 'rests . . . on the idea of Fidelity' is strikingly unclear: what is it for the 'world' to 'rest' on an 'idea'? Does it mean that we cannot get along without the 'idea', or without the actions of which it is but the name? Does it mean that the 'world' does 'rest' on the 'idea', or that it should? Does it mean that the 'world' cannot abide without adherence to the 'idea', or that it can only function well with such adherence? Yet it is excessive to claim that 'faith in Fidelity' is of little use in helping us to understand Conrad. Fidelity is not the key to Conrad—he is no more a lock or door than a casket—but how exactly does the importance of fidelity arise, given his metaphysical stance?

I have briefly demarcated what are ostensibly two sides of a paradox, a matrix of apparent conflict out of which emerged the novels and tales of Joseph Conrad. It seems impossible to reconcile these two visions, the one asserting the absolute loneliness and tragedy of the individual in a world without values, the other stressing human solidarity, and demanding self-sacrifice, loyalty to the group, and an unreflective stoicism. The judgment that Conrad is obscure surely arises here. But what must be recognized—this is crucial to an understanding of Conrad—is not only that the two aspects of Conrad's thought are not irreconcilable, but that they are complementary. In short, that the values propounded in the 'Familiar Preface' (and, of course, elsewhere) are a perfectly valid extension of the vision of the early letters to Cunninghame Graham—a vision which, on the surface, appears to render any ethical position irrelevant.

Thus man, when faced with a hostile and unrelenting universe, must come to see that all value systems are equally arbitrary and futile. But this insight does not, in itself, constitute a form of action or dictate a life-style; indeed, it militates against any such choice. It is the given, the primary apprehension out of which all value must flow, and against which any value must ultimately be judged. Clearly, one obvious response to this apprehension is despair, and the result, suicide. Brierly, in *Lord Jim* (1900), and Martin Decoud, in *Nostromo* (1904), fit into this pattern. But most of Conrad's characters, whatever their deepest apprehensions, choose to go on with the painful business of life. Having chosen, not so much to be, as *not* not to be, the question is: how?

In Conradian terms, we need some 'dream' or 'illusion' to follow—if what is 'real' is the meaningless flux of experience, then any attempt to project meaning may *seem* 'real', but can ultimately be seen to be merely a function of the needs of the given individual. Since the recognition of the universe as it really is may well lead to despair, the best way of being would clearly be that in which this recognition was avoided, in which men simply did not think. Thus we sometimes find in Conrad's works what Moser has called 'the simple hero',[33] the man who goes about his work in unreflective commitment to the task itself. Recognizing that Singleton represented such a type in *The Nigger of the 'Narcissus'*, Cunninghame Graham wrote to Conrad suggesting that mankind's ideal product would be a Singleton-with-an-education. Conrad replied:

'You say: "Singleton with an education." Well—yes. Everything is possible, and most things come to pass (when you don't want them). However, I think Singleton with an education is impossible. But first of all—what education? If it is the knowledge how to live my man essentially possessed it. He was in perfect accord with his life. If by education you mean scientific knowledge then the question arises—what knowledge, how much of it—in what direction? Is it to stop at plane trigonometry or at conic sections? Or is he to study Platonism or Pyrrhonism or the philosophy of the gentle Emerson? Or do you mean the kind of knowledge which would enable him to scheme, and lie, and intrigue his way to the forefront of a crowd no better than himself? Would you seriously, of malice prepense cultivate in that unconscious man the power to think? Then he would become conscious—and much smaller—and very unhappy. Now he is simple and great like an elemental force. Nothing can touch him but the curse of decay—the eternal decree that will extinguish the sun, the stars one by one, and in another instant shall spread a frozen darkness over the whole universe. Nothing else can touch him—he does not think.

Would you seriously wish to tell such a man: "Know thyself."

17

Understand that thou art nothing, less than a shadow, more insignificant than a drop of water in the ocean, more fleeting than the illusion of a dream. Would you?'[34]

Singleton thus exists as an ideal type, a symbolic possibility, but no more; as Conrad was later to remark in a letter to Cunninghame Graham, mankind cannot 'get rid of consciousness',[35] and it is impossible to be both educated and unconscious. Singleton is the last survivor of a bygone age, 'a learned and savage patriarch, the incarnation of barbarian wisdom serene in the blasphemous turmoil of the world.'[36] The nostalgia for the 'barbarian'—Rousseau's unconscious, natively wise man—is a noteworthy feature, too, of Melville's remarkably similar story about the Handsome Sailor, Billy Budd. Conrad, like Melville, believed that 'this age of material concern' was particularly and tragically hostile to the survival of the values enacted in the simple hero. But Conrad's position about the human condition is unequivocal; modern man may be less happy, because more conscious, but no return to innocence is possible.

For men such as Singleton, or any of Conrad's more sophisticated 'simple heroes', like Captains Allistoun, McWhirr, and Beard, life is always hard, but never tragic. But whereas they escape tragedy by their unreflective inability to see it (tragedy being not a fact of nature but residing in a certain awareness of nature), there are other characters in Conrad's fiction who are, to a greater or lesser extent, self-aware and reflective, yet who deliberately attempt to *avoid* the consciousness that registers the world as tragic. Winnie Verloc believes that 'life doesn't stand much looking into'; Axel Heyst's doctrine is that 'if you begin to think you will be unhappy.' This clearly will not do, as the fates of Winnie Verloc and Axel Heyst demonstrate. No knowledge of the danger of knowledge allows escape from knowledge: what one might call a paradox of consciousness. To turn one's head away doesn't help; it's what's inside (as the doctor tells Marlow in 'Heart of Darkness') that matters. Such an evasion in fact invites tragedy, which is why Conrad refers to the attitude *itself* as tragic.[37]

A further solution has been felt to be possible. Even if the universe is meaningless, can belief not arise simply from the strength of the desire to have it? The various answers to this question—in Ibsen's 'life-lie', William James's 'Will to Believe', Wallace Stevens's 'Supreme Fiction', or Camus's absurdist philosophy—form an essential part of what we regard as modern thinking. But, to Conrad, there simply can be no self-conscious saving illusion, no belief that contravenes the truth. The truth is what is true, and must be so. And yet values have to be made; the dramatic situation in Conrad, then, has two aspects: (1) the shock of discovering this to be true, and (2) the struggle to preserve values attendant upon this discovery.

It should be clear that the whole question of social cohesion lies in the balance. For if recognition of the ultimate arbitrariness of our values is allowed to express itself at the individual level as nihilism, or at the social level as anarchy, then there is nothing to fall back on. Yet Conrad is quite insistent in his rejection of both of these forms of (what he would regard as) despair; speaking of the role of the author, he makes his attitude towards pessimism explicit:

> 'What one feels so hopelessly barren in declared pessimism is just its arrogance. It seems as if the discovery made by many men at various times that there is much evil in the world were a source of proud and unholy joy . . .
>
> To be hopeful in an artistic sense it is not necessary to think that the world is good. It is enough to believe that there is no impossibility of its being made so.'[38]

We cannot fail to note the discrepancy between such an attitude and the undoubted 'pessimism' of what I have called Conrad's vision of personal autonomy (in which there is *no* possibility of the world being 'made' good).[39] His attitude towards anarchy (which he sees as enacted nihilism) is even less ambiguous; the statement in the Author's Note to *Under Western Eyes* is typical:

> 'The ferocity and imbecility of an autocratic rule rejecting all legality and in fact basing itself upon complete moral anarchism provokes the no less imbecile and atrocious answer of a purely Utopian revolutionism encompassing destruction by the first means to hand, in the strange conviction that a fundamental change of hearts must follow the downfall of any given human institutions. These people are unable to see that all they can effect is merely a change of names.' (p. x)

Social interaction depends upon each member of society, by his recognition of some agreed code and set of sanctions, ceding potential areas of freedom in exchange for those benefits that society alone can offer him—community, stability, variety of comfort. Thus, although society may ultimately be without a secure foundation, although no action may finally be any better than any other action, if we are to live at all then it is necessary to have some stable environment in which to do it. In short, if the universe fails to supply us with a purpose, we must supply it for ourselves, and then face the consequences. An interesting paradox emerges: Conrad's vision both denies and requires moral values. Man is, in this sense, morally a free agent. In Orwellian terms, all values are equal, only some values are more equal than others.

Fidelity to one's fellows, a stern code of conduct, stoical acceptance of life's hardships, and avoidance of introspection (with its morbid possibilities): these are 'saving' graces, for only thus can the anarchic pull be resisted. A man's life is a potentially heroic venture not into, but in, the unknown; as Conrad was to say of Anatole France (and the words seem to apply equally well to himself):

'He feels that men born in ignorance as in the house of an enemy, and condemned to struggle with error and passions through endless centuries, should be spared the supreme cruelty of a hope for ever deferred. He knows that our best hopes are irrealisable; that it is the almost incredible misfortune of mankind, but also its highest privilege, to aspire towards the impossible; that men have never failed to defeat their highest aims by the very strength of their humanity which can conceive the most gigantic tasks but leaves them disarmed before their irremediable littleness. He knows this well because he is an artist and a master; but he knows, too, that only in the continuity of effort there is a refuge from despair for minds less clear-seeing and philosophic than his own. Therefore he wishes us to believe and to hope, preserving in our activity the consoling illusion of power and intelligent purpose. He is a good and politic prince.'[40]

Values are a tonic taken against an incurable, but not untreatable, disease: they will ultimately fail, but are the best medicine available, and the patient must go on with the business of living. The analogy casts Conrad in two roles—the doctor who prescribes the 'remedy', and the patient who takes it. At times in the letters and autobiographical writings it is the doctor, with his weary realism and sharp diagnostic power, that speaks; at other times, the patient, with his will to survive. And Conrad is both of them, they are both right—that human existence seems a tragic joke does not mean that we must give up on life, only that it is altogether too easy to do so.

The best of Conrad's fiction holds the balance between the facts of existence (autonomy and isolation) and the necessities of existence (social responsibilities), and keeps them in greatest tension. He is interested in the riskiness of values. In those situations which call on a man to act both towards his own self-interest (which, from one point of view, is the only genuine interest that he can have) and towards the interests of some given order (which, from another, is equally imperative), lies the ground of the characteristically Conradian moral issue. It is men in such situations who make the really crucial decisions. Many of Conrad's heroes—like Jim or Razumov—are not aware (until it is too late) of the implications of their crucial actions, or of the forces that have produced them. The decision that they make (usually some equivocal form of 'betrayal', since the tension between duty to self and duty to others so often necessitates some betrayal) then forces them, by its consequences, to a vision of what Conrad usually calls 'the abyss'—the terror entailed by a clear understanding of man's tragic isolation. Conrad's 'vulnerable heroes' (to use Moser's term),[41] make decisions that are only marginally errors; Jim's jump or Razumov's betrayal of Haldin are important as acts which respond to the ambiguous or contradictory demands made on the average man.

Conrad is generally insistent that his protagonists are normal men, neither pathological cases nor Henry James's 'fine consciousnesses'. To choose only a few of his heroes: Tom Lingard is one of the 'noisy crowd of men that were so much like himself';[42] Jim is 'one of us';[43] Nostromo is 'a man of the People';[44] Razumov is 'an ordinary young man'.[45] What is interesting about them is that they begin with some illusion of being extraordinary, and come to find, with inevitably tragic results, that they have been wrong. In Conrad's moral world there are no extraordinary men.

In examining the structure of a moral dilemma, rather than postulating any answer to the problem that it poses, he leaves us with some pertinent questions: what is it to 'make' a 'moral' decision? According to what inner knowledge and what values can a man ever choose to act 'correctly'? How can he balance egoism and altruism? Under what circumstances can he atone for a decision imperfectly made or realized? Conrad does *not* offer definitive answers to these questions; indeed, it is essential to his metaphysic that no such definitive answers are tenable. But he is capable at his best of suggesting how various and difficult human existence can be: 'A man's duties are wide and complex: the balance should be held very even.'[46] He is not, as Forster suggests, 'obscure' at the core, but he may well be as oxymoronic as life is paradoxical.

The two visions that I have called 'personal autonomy' and 'social responsibility' are thus interdependent, not only in that the latter flows from the former (not only logically, but to a degree temporally in Conrad's development), but also insofar as they derive their impact and depth of appeal only as they exist in tension with one another, as they pull in apparently different directions. Thus Conrad's assertion of human isolation and universal meaninglessness, taken on its own, leads to a nihilism that he was quick to reject; in the same way, the ethical standards of his assertion of social responsibility, deprived of the darkness of their metaphysical base, become simply naïve moralizing. Only when these two visions exist together, mutually limiting and defining, in conflict and yet interdependent, is the moral situation, of which I have been speaking, created. Conrad put the point rather more cryptically: 'I am proud of my powers of stately invective combined with the art of putting the finger to the nose. It's a fascinating mixture.'[47] It is worth remarking here that this tension leads inevitably to an ironic view of human life. Strictly speaking, Conrad is an ironist, not a sceptic. Though he is 'sceptical', and recommends 'scepticism', there is no thoroughgoing sense in which he is—as, say, Hume was—a philosophical sceptic: uncertain about the capacity of human reason to lead us to the truth, and thus prepared to doubt all conclusions, even his own. But Conrad 'knows' what is true; there is no sense in which he feels that his metaphysic may be overthrown. The tension between facts and necessities of which I have spoken thus becomes the logical ground of irony. It is not my purpose here to discuss the specific ways in which this is manifested—what could be more different than the ironies of *Lord Jim* and those that pervade *The Secret Agent*?—but I would suggest that the ironic tone of much of Conrad's work can finally be traced to his understanding of the conflicting demands that are imposed on individuals. It follows from the dual perspective of his vision that any version of the 'truth' can be ironically balanced—often by the narrator—by a conflicting, and equally viable, version.

Unless we understand the confidence with which Conrad's metaphysic is held—the certainty with which he holds his vision of man's fate—then it is difficult to comprehend the role that he envisages for the novelist. To Conrad, the writer of fiction is not, in the Joycean mode, an artificer—a creator of aesthetic structures satisfying and complex in themselves; rather, the artist is not so much a creator (though he is that) as an 'observer'. This does not transform art into documentary, for the nature of the observed is, to a considerable degree, contingent on the angle(s) of vision from which it is seen— which is what Conrad calls 'temperament'. It would therefore seem that the tension that I have described between truth and value makes for a paradox of a particularly telling kind. If Conrad's commitments are genuinely to the truth as he sees it, then will that truth not be corrosive of value? If the Marlows of his imaginative world are disarmed and disillusioned by their knowledge of the arbitrary quality of our ethical commitments, why should Conrad's readers not be similarly affected? Should they not be left like Singleton, without an education? Why make them conscious? Equally, if, seeking to avoid this conclusion, the novelist should seek simply to reinforce our moral engagements, then will it not be at the expense of what he knows to be true? And, in that case, will his work not become a tract, a sermon, an exhortation—worthy forms, but not art?

> 'A work that aspires, however humbly, to the condition of art should carry its justification in every line. And art itself may be defined as a single-minded attempt to render the highest kind of justice to the visible universe, by bringing to light the truth, manifold and one, underlying its every aspect.'[48]

The artist, then, does not attempt to synthesize the poles of the dialectic of which I have been speaking, but instead to effect a creative release of the sympathies engaged by the 'spectacle' of man's fate. His work—in the attitudes that it both exemplifies and engenders—becomes, itself, a form of 'action' that can stand outside a general scepticism about the efficacy of human action.

> 'The ethical view of the universe involves us at last in so many cruel and absurd contradictions, where the last vestiges of faith, hope, charity, and even of reason itself, seem ready to perish, that I have come to suspect that the aim of creation cannot be ethical at all. I would fondly believe that its object is purely spectacular: a spectacle for awe, love, adoration, or hate, if you like, but in this view—and in this view alone—never for despair! Those visions, delicious or poignant, are a moral end in themselves!'[49]

The term 'moral' is used here in a special sense; it does not signify any given action or point of view, but instead invokes that strictness of intention and clarity of vision that Conrad calls 'sincerity'.

> 'In this view there is room for every religion except for the inverted creed of impiety, the mask and cloak of arid despair; for every joy and every sorrow, for every fair dream, for every charitable hope. The great aim is to remain true to the emotions called out of the deep encircled by the firmament of stars, whose infinite numbers and awful distance may move us to laughter or tears (was it the Walrus or the Carpenter, in the poem, who "wept to see such quantities of sand"?), or again, to a properly steeled heart, may matter nothing at all.'[50]

It is the artist who must transform the universe from an inexplicable nightmare of pain and paradox into a 'spectacle' which is the occasion for awe, compassion, and perhaps even renewed hope. If he is successful, he may present us with that most valuable of all things, an enduring attitude with which to live. Once again, we may turn to Matthew Arnold (a man with many temperamental and artistic affinities with Conrad) for an analogous statement:

> 'We should conceive of poetry worthily, and more highly than it

has been the custom to conceive of it. We should conceive of it as capable of higher uses, and called to higher destinies, than those which in general men have assigned to it hitherto. More and more mankind will discover that we have to turn to poetry to interpret life for us, to console us, to sustain us.'[51]

Conrad would have agreed that it is the 'uses' to which art may be put that provide the artist with his ultimate objectives.

In the Preface to *The Nigger of the 'Narcissus'* (1898), Conrad insists that art, insofar as it consists of the sincere attempt to render the truth as one sees it, is *in itself* good. It is the artist who speaks to the deepest and best emotions in his fellow man, by finding, in the common ground of human experience, the basis for an otherwise inconceivable sense of human solidarity. The following from the Preface is informed by an urgent sense of the *usefulness* of art:

'The changing wisdom of successive generations discards ideas, questions facts, demolishes theories. But the artist appeals to that part of our being which is not dependent on wisdom; to that in us which is a gift and not an acquisition—and, therefore, more permanently enduring. He speaks to our capacity for delight and wonder, to the sense of mystery surrounding our lives; to our sense of pity, and beauty, and pain; to the latent feeling of fellowship with all creation—and to the subtle but invincible conviction of solidarity that knits together the loneliness of innumerable hearts, to the solidarity in dreams, in joy, in sorrow, in aspirations, in illusions, in hope, in fear, which binds men to each other, which binds together all humanity—the dead to the living and the living to the unborn.' (p. viii)

This is perhaps the finest statement of Conrad's art, a transcendent vision resting neither on the awareness of tragedy nor on the absolute need for some arbitrary ethical standard.

The vision of the world as spectacle is finally neither pessimistic nor hopeful:

'In a single-minded attempt of that kind, if one be deserving and fortunate, one may perchance attain to such clearness of sincerity that at last the presented vision of regret or pity, of terror or mirth, shall awaken in the hearts of the beholders that feeling of unavoidable solidarity in mysterious origin, in toil, in joy, in hope, in uncertain fate, which binds men to each other and all mankind to this visible world.' (p. x)

The Preface to *The Nigger of the 'Narcissus'* both exemplifies the tension of which I have been speaking, and also transcends it; the view of art put forward is passionately held, yet coupled with a wry recognition of the futility of things:

'To arrest, for the space of a breath, the hands busy about the work of the earth, and compel men entranced by the sight of distant goals to glance for a moment at the surrounding vision of form and colour, of sunshine and shadows; to make them pause for a look, for a sigh, for a smile—such is the aim, difficult and evanescent, and reserved only for the very few to achieve. But sometimes, by the deserving and the fortunate, even that task is accomplished. And when it is accomplished—behold!—all the truth of life is there: a moment of vision, a sigh, a smile—and the return to an eternal rest.' (p. xii)

Conrad makes an important distinction between 'art' and 'morality', for art consists of the rendering of 'truth', while morality insists upon some arbitrary interpretation and enactment of that truth. 'A good book is a good action. It has more than the force of good example. And if the moralist will say that it has less merit—let him. Indeed, we are not writing for the salvation of our own souls.'[52] The artist examines feeling and attitude, the moralist concentrates primarily on actions. In a universe in which no action is ultimately better than any other, in which 'salvation' is impossible, it is finally only feeling and attitude that are important. If we juxtapose two of Conrad's letters, written twenty-two years apart, we can see that this viewpoint was a constant in his thinking:

'If one looks at life in its true aspect then everything loses much of its unpleasant importance and the atmosphere becomes cleared of what are only unimportant mists that drift past in imposing shapes. When once the truth is grasped that one's own personality is only a ridiculous and aimless masquerade of something hopelessly unknown the attainment of serenity is not very far off. Then there remains nothing but the surrender to one's impulses, the fidelity to passing emotions which is perhaps a nearer approach to truth than any other philosophy of life. And why not? If we are "ever becoming—never being" then I would be a fool if I tried to become this thing rather than that; for I know well that I never will be anything. I would rather grasp the solid satisfaction of my wrong-headedness and shake my fist at the idiotic mystery of Heaven.'[53]

'It is a bitter flavour but bitterness is the very condition of human existence, and mankind generally is neither guilty nor innocent. It simply *is*. That is misfortune enough. Men die and suffer for their convictions and how those convictions are arrived at doesn't matter a bit. That's why, my dear fellow, satire seems to me a vain use of intelligence, and intelligence itself a thing of no great account except for us to torment ourselves with. For directly you begin to use it questions of right and wrong arise and these are things of the air with no connection whatever with the fundamental realities of life. Whereas in the region of feeling there is nothing of the kind. Feelings *are*, and in submitting to them we can avoid neither death nor suffering which are our common lot, but we can bear them in peace.'[54]

By exploring and dramatizing his own feelings (which are presumed, by extension, to be those of other men) the artist cannot enable his reader to transcend mortality, but the truths that he offers him—notably that all men suffer from the same burdens and seek vainly for the same answers—may help him towards 'peace' and stoical acceptance. Thus, the vision of the universe as spectacle does not enable a man to avert the tragic recognition that the values to which he would like to pay absolute service are in fact only arbitrary props—fragments shored up against the ruins—but it may enable him to live with that honour, dignity, and compassion that become the bases of a renewed hope for human intercourse.

Conrad should not be read as a 'moralist', with a 'creed' to offer; rather, he is most profitably understood as an artist profoundly interested in the difficulties inherent in the search for any such 'creed'. The 'obscurity' of which E. M. Forster complains seems to me the result of neither failure of imagination nor failure of understanding. Conrad's finest work finds its power not in the assertion of a unique point of view, but in the tension that it maintains between points of view—between its assertion of certain values, and its sympathy for the transgressors of those values. He is finely conscious of the difficulties inherent in human freedom, of the terrible demands of 'moral' life, of the sorrow lurking behind joy, of the death residing in life and giving it meaning. There is an absence of purpose in

Conrad's novels only if purpose is defined so narrowly as to exclude 'so much insight and compassion as can be expressed in a voice of sympathy and compassion.'

It has not been my purpose in this introductory chapter to provide a methodological model through which all of Conrad can be equally fruitfully approached. Though I have based my remarks largely on Conrad's non-fiction, it would be disingenuous to pretend that I have ignored previous knowledge of his fiction; indeed, the general picture of Conrad's 'temperament' here presented is an attempt to isolate that which is distinctively 'Conradian' in our knowledge of him. I have several times referred to his 'best work' without specifying which novels I include in that category—though it is, of course, on the basis of such valuations that decisions about 'temperament' are made. In the ensuing chapters I shall show that the relative failure of the fiction up to *The Nigger of the 'Narcissus'* (1898) is due to the ill-defined quality of its major moral themes, while the decline in the major late novels—*Chance* (1913) and *Victory* (1915)—can be traced to a slackening of the tensions of which I have been speaking. This leaves *The Nigger of the 'Narcissus'*, 'Heart of Darkness' (1900), *Lord Jim* (1900), *Nostromo* (1904), and (to a degree) *Under Western Eyes* (1911) as examples of that work in which the dialectic between belief and unbelief is best sustained. A separate chapter on *The Secret Agent* (1907) argues that the novel, in spite of its manifest virtues, should not be included in the canon of Conrad's finest work.

2

Almayer's Folly to Tales of Unrest

Almayer's Folly, the first of Conrad's novels, was begun in London some time in September 1889, and was subsequently carried on journeys to the Congo, Switzerland, Poland, Rouen, and then back to England, where it was finally completed on 16 April 1894.[1] Given the literary interests of both the (paternal) Korzeniowski and (maternal) Bobrowski families, and Conrad's own avidity as a reader, it is not startling that he should have used some of the free time generated by a life at sea to try his hand at writing. His memory of the commencement of *Almayer's Folly* typically overestimates the significance of the event: 'There was no vision of a printed book before me as I sat writing at that table, situated in a decayed part of Belgravia. After all these years, each leaving its evidence of slowly blackened pages, I can honestly say that it is a sentiment akin to piety which prompted me to render in words assembled with conscientious care the memory of things far distant and of men who had lived.'[2] Claiming that the writing of the novel 'was not the outcome of a need', Conrad continued: 'Till I began to write that novel I had written nothing but letters, and not very many of these. I never made a note of a fact, of an impression or of an anecdote in my life. The conception of a planned book was entirely outside my mental range when I sat down to write ...'[3] Although it is not true that *Almayer's Folly* was Conrad's first creative effort,[4] his assertion that the wish to write did not entail a further desire to leave the sea for the study is almost certainly true. But he did think enough of his manuscript to seek its publication, and was sufficiently distressed at the continued silence from the publisher Fisher Unwin to suggest to his cousin Marguerite Poradowska, herself a novelist, that they publish the book as a collaboration in French. This plan was quickly abandoned when Unwin, prompted by his reader, Edward Garnett, accepted the novel. Garnett was much taken with the work, not only because of its unique status (its author was a Pole turned English sea captain, writing under the pseudonym of Kamudi),[5] but also because of its undoubted power and exotic flavour.[6] It was published in 1895.

The major thrust of *Almayer's Folly* concerns the tensions that separate a father (Almayer) from the developed womanhood of his half-caste daughter (Nina). Almayer, the personal agent of Lingard and Company, is married to a native woman whom Tom Lingard had imposed on him as the condition of his employment. The marriage, though racially repellent to Almayer, results in the child Nina, on whom Almayer has focused all of his desires for the future. As Nina grows up and develops needs of her own, centred upon the figure of the handsome young trader, Dain Marcola, the resulting conflict with her father leads to his decay and eventual death.

Although Nina has been devoted to her father, she unaccountably leaves him without remorse or misgiving. At the apparent death of Dain, which she has helped to contrive, we see her 'with her heart deeply moved by the sight of Almayer's misery' (p. 103); later she embraces her father, defiantly exclaiming to the Dutch soldiers: 'I hoped to live here without seeing any other white face but this' (p. 141). But once she decides to leave, although she struggles with her mother to be allowed a last look at her sleeping father, she is without sadness at leaving him: 'At the bottom of that passing desire to look again at her father's face there was no strong affection. She felt no scruples and no remorse at leaving suddenly that man whose sentiment towards herself she could not understand, she could not even see.' (p. 151.) A 'savage reversion' is invoked to account for this lack of sympathy, which merely has the effect of cheapening the human value of the scene.

Almayer's love for his daughter is hardly more credible. He has viewed Nina not as a human being, but as an object—the focus of his grandiose dreams of wealth and prestige. He is unaware, in his egoistic simplicity, of whatever turmoil Nina is allowed to reveal. Ultimately we cannot much blame Nina for her decision to abandon the feeble Almayer for the enticing Dain. In a mock address to the long-dead prototype of Almayer, in *A Personal Record*, Conrad says: 'I believed in you in the only way it was possible for me to believe. It was not worthy of your merits? So be it. But you were always an unlucky man,

Almayer. Nothing was ever quite worthy of you. What made you so real to me was that you held this lofty theory with some force of conviction and with an admirable consistency.' (p. 88.) But for Almayer's disintegration, climaxing finally when Nina leaves him, to be of sustained interest, it would be necessary to have seen him, at some former time, with a certain stature—worthy to follow in defeat as in success. But Almayer has from the start been 'weak, irresolute, unhappy' (p. 42), and his acceptance of Lingard's offer of daughter and fortune is regarded not as a tragic compromise, leading inevitably to folly and defeat, but as a natural consequence of a parasitic personality. His self-assessment, after his hopes are quashed by the apparent death of Dain, has a real germ of truth: 'It seemed to him that for many years he had been falling into a deep precipice. Day after day, month after month, he had been falling, falling, falling . . . It struck him as funny.' (p. 99.) The history of a man 'falling, falling, falling' might hold our interest if that fall were from a sufficient height; *Almayer's Folly* presents us with the spectacle of a man falling from a ground-floor window. It is more ludicrous than tragic; what we see is not Almayer's corruption, but merely a sustained reflection of his corruptness.

In the climactic scene, Almayer demands that Nina return home with him. As he raises his pistol to shoot Dain (unambiguously his rival for Nina's love), Nina quickly steps between them. In the ensuing conversation with her father, she tells him:

> 'You told me yesterday . . . that I could not understand or see your love for me: it is so. How can I? No two human beings understand each other. They can understand but their own voices. You wanted me to dream your dreams, to see your own visions—the visions of life amongst the white faces of those who cast me out from their midst in angry contempt. But while you spoke I listened to the voice of my own self; then this man came, and all was still; there was only the murmur of his love.' (p. 179)

But the statement that 'No two human beings understand each other'—with its fundamental Conradian tone—is here only relevant when those human beings are 'savage' and white. Nina correctly charges Almayer with seeking to force her to dream his dreams, but her point is not that he shouldn't have done this, but that it can't be done. It is clear, however, that certain people can dream together, that some people do understand each other: Nina says of her love for Dain, 'I found that we could see through each other's eyes: that he saw things that nobody but myself and he could see' (p. 179). It thus seems that *Almayer's Folly*, which appears to be an exploration of conflict between father and daughter, in which the egoism of the one is balanced by the selfishness of the other, is not about this at all. Ultimately it is a novel about racial conflict and misunderstanding—and the gulf that separates Conrad's 'savages' from his Europeans is so vast that the problems that it creates cannot be called moral issues, but only tragic facts. Things could hardly be other than they are.

Almayer's Folly, however critical of its white men, never attempts to supplant Western culture with Eastern, or even to merge the two. Years later, Conrad was to say: 'A dash of Orientalism on white is very fascinating, at least for me; though I must say that the genuine Eastern had never the power to lead me away from the path of rectitude; to any serious extent—that is.'[7] The curious, indeed slightly offensive, tone of this may help to explain Conrad's treatments of his natives. In a letter to his friend Sir Hugh Clifford (who was an authority on Malayan life) he admitted that he was largely ignorant of Malayan ways: 'I suspect my assumption of Malay colouring for my fiction must be exasperating to those who *know*.'[8] It is exasperating even to those who do not.

Even before *Almayer's Folly* was accepted by Fisher Unwin, Conrad was at work on a short story called 'Two Vagabonds', which subsequently became *An Outcast of the Islands*, published in 1896. This belies the pleasant story that both Conrad and Garnett relate as to the genesis of the novel.[9] Conrad's account is contained in the Author's Note:

> 'A phrase of Edward Garnett's is, as a matter of fact, responsible for this book . . . One evening when we had dined together and he had listened to the account of my perplexities . . . he pointed out that there was no need to determine my future absolutely. Then he added: "You have the style, you have the temperament; why not write another?" . . . Had he said, "Why not go on writing", it is very probable he would have scared me away from pen and ink forever . . . The word "another" did it.' (pp. vi–vii)

Untrue though this may be (it was, after all, written in 1919), it testifies to the warmth of Conrad's feeling for Garnett, and suggests the considerable part that Garnett played in the writing of the novel.[10] That Conrad should have chosen to extend his vision of 'the Eastern Archipelago', of Almayer and Tom Lingard, is regrettable, but by no means surprising.[11] He still intended to return to sea, and would have regarded the idea that he had any literary reputation to develop or protect as absurd. Even so, *An Outcast*, similar as it is to *Almayer's Folly*, is a finer and more complex novel than its predecessor, wider in its concerns, sharper in its moral focus, in all respects more ambitious.

Garnett may not in fact have suggested 'Why not write another?', but *An Outcast*, on first reading, seems altogether too much of 'another'. Written as an inverse-sequel, or pre-history, to *Almayer's Folly*, it is the story of yet another outcast-Dutchman befriended by Tom Lingard, who married a native woman to further his progress, degenerated, and died. Its world is again that of Sambir, peopled by virtually the same cast of Malayans, Arabs, and whites, and cloaked in the same sullen atmosphere of decay. Indeed, if *An Outcast* is but a recasting of *Almayer's Folly*, this time a history of the decline and degradation of Peter Willems, then it suffers from many of the same faults— notably from its lack of a hero of suitable dimension, and from its preconceptions about the inevitability of racial conflict. But unlike *Almayer's Folly*, the moral and psychological concerns of *An Outcast* are firmly centred on its white men. The story is conventionally summarized as follows: Peter Willems, a Dutch youngster who has jumped his ship, is befriended by Tom Lingard, who eventually places him as a clerk with the firm of Hudig and Company. Willems unscrupulously prospers, but is caught allocating company funds towards covering his own speculations, and fired. Rejected by his native wife Joanna (who is, unknown to Willems, Hudig's illegitimate daughter), he decides to commit suicide, but is once again rescued by Lingard, who takes him to Sambir to stay with Almayer. Despised and feared by Almayer (who has his own interests to protect), Willems disconsolately takes to wandering in the jungle. On one of these walks he meets the Arab girl Aissa, for whom he conceives an immediate and overwhelming passion, which is exploited by the natives Babalatchi and Lakamba, who force Willems to guide the ship of Lingard's rival Abdullah up an entrance to the Pantai, known only to Lingard. Returning to Sambir with the repentant Joanna, Lingard finds that Willems has betrayed him. After much procrastination, he announces to the now sated Willems that he is to be abandoned to a lifetime of isolation with Aissa. But Almayer, to whom the continued existence of Willems is a constant threat, directs Joanna to her husband; Aissa, maddened by the sight of this 'other woman', shoots and kills Willems.

As Conrad remarked in a letter to Edward Noble, the deepest concerns of a novel are to be found underlying those actions and events that mark the major turning points in the plot: '... you must treat events only as illustrative of human sensation,—as the outward sign of inward feelings,—of live feelings,—which alone are truly pathetic and interesting. You have much imagination ... Well, that imagination (I wish I had it) should be used to create human souls: to disclose human hearts,—and not to create events that are properly speaking *accidents* only.'[12] The plot of *An Outcast*, even more than that of *Almayer's Folly*, depends largely upon the actions of Tom Lingard; as Albert Guerard has said, 'the historian of Sambir who sought some single explanation for the events of twenty years would find it in Lingard's romantic ego, in his grandiloquent dreams and "infernal charity".'[13] Although this is clearly true, he goes on to add that '*An Outcast of the Islands* is unmistakably about the drifting, dishonest Willems and his slow then sudden deterioration.'[14] There is evidence enough to support this view of the novel—that although Lingard is its most important, and perhaps most interesting, character, it is nevertheless firmly focused on the figure of Willems. Conrad himself never mentions an interest in Lingard as a critical factor in the writing of the book; Garnett reports that: 'Conrad's attitude to *The Outcast* was from the first a strange blend of creative ardour and scepticism. He spoke deprecatingly of his knowledge of Malay life, but all the same the figures of Willems, Joanna and Aissa captivated his imagination. His sardonic interest in Willems' disintegration reflected, I believe, his own disillusionment over the Congo.'[15] It seems strange that the insubstantial and improbable Joanna and the sensual sex-object Aissa should have proven more interesting to Conrad than did Lingard, on whose actions the book depends. Nevertheless, the novel is best understood with the figure of Lingard at its moral centre.

It is, for instance, impossible to account for the length of *An Outcast* (which is more than twice as long as *Almayer's Folly*) if it is simply concerned with Willems, a character whose 'success' is only a function of his arrogant and unscrupulous nature. Writing to Marguerite Poradowska to announce that a certain Mme M. Wood '*M'a volé mon titre*' (that is, 'Two Vagabonds'), Conrad gives a concise description of his hero's character: '*Le motif d'abord c'est une vanité éffrénée, féroce d'un homme ignorant qui a du succès mais n'a ni principes ni d'autre ligne de conduite que la satisfaction de sa vanité.—Aussi il n'est même pas fidèle à soi-même. D'où chute, dégringolade subite jusqu'à l'esclavage physique de l'homme par une femme absolument sauvage. J'ai vu ça!*'[16] From the very first paragraph of the book, outlining his 'little excursion into the wayside quagmires' (p. 3) of morality, Willems is depicted as a shallow and dishonest braggart, a petty tyrant of the most unpleasant type. As with Almayer, his decline, once begun, is inexorable (and, as with Almayer, that decline may be dated from the first meeting with the benevolent Lingard). There is never any doubt that Conrad wishes his reader, from the first, to accept the inevitability of that fate. We are immediately told that Willems 'did not know that his prosperity had touched then its high-water mark, and that the tide was already on the turn' (p. 22). The grave imagery with which he is associated is markedly unambiguous: 'Before going up the steps of his house, he stood awhile, his feet well apart, chin in hand, contemplating mentally Hudig's future partner. A glorious occupation. He saw him quite safe; solid as the hills; deep—deep as an abyss; discreet as the grave.' (p. 11.) Willems's prosperity enables him to take on the sole financial support of his wife and her entire family, a burden that, far from being objectionable, is a welcome verification of his own sense of indispensability:

'It is a fine thing to be a providence, and to be told so on every day of one's life. It gives one a feeling of enormously remote superiority, and Willems revelled in it. He did not analyse the state of his mind, but probably his greatest delight lay in the unexpressed but intimate conviction that, should he close his hand, all those admiring human beings would starve. His munificence had demoralised them. An easy task. Since he descended amongst them and married Joanna they had lost the little aptitude and strength for work they might have had to put forth under the stress of extreme necessity. They lived now by the grace of his will. This was power. Willems loved it.' (pp. 4–5)

But Willems is obviously a vulnerable man; Mr Vinck, his fellow worker, has found him out, and the first chapter ends with his ominous words: 'he is becoming dangerous; he knows too much. He will have to be got rid of' (p. 10), which leads to the image of Willems 'discreet as the grave' (p. 11). The next day he is exposed and fired.

The second chapter introduces Tom Lingard, who briefly indicates his role in Willems's history: 'I picked him up in a ditch, you may say, like a starved cat.' (p. 17.) King Tom, the Rajah Laut, is the most successful trader of the islands, a man who has established his own kingdoms, created his own laws. He is oxymoronically described as a man of complicated simplicity:

> 'Tom Lingard was a master, a lover, a servant of the sea. The sea took him young, fashioned him body and soul; gave him his fierce aspect, his loud voice, his fearless eyes, his stupidly guileless heart. Generously it gave him his absurd faith in himself . . . His greatest pride lay in his profound conviction of its faithfulness—in the deep sense of his unerring knowledge of its treachery.'
> (p. 13)

Thus in the first pages of the novel we have been presented with a parallel between Willems and Lingard, in their roles as dependant and provider. Willems is 'master' of his household, but survives through the charity of Hudig; Lingard is 'master' of men and kingdoms, but 'servant' of the sea. Lingard is, of course, the more impressive figure—he is 'a servant of the sea', while Willems 'was hopelessly at variance with the spirit of the sea'—itself a give-away in Conrad. But, in their position as 'masters', both are men of strong pride, who determine the destiny of others.

Willems is exposed at the beginning of the third chapter, but is able, even in the face of this disaster, to maintain his self-exaltation: 'Idiotic indiscretion; that is how he defined his guilt to himself. Could there be anything worse from the point of view of his undeniable cleverness? What a fatal aberration of an acute mind!' (pp. 22–3.) He accepts blame for what he has done, but only in the most perverse manner: he admits to 'a slight deterioration', but holds to his contempt for other men 'who were merely honest or simply not found out yet.' As he begins to grasp the completeness of his ruin, he has a momentary flash of insight, and for a time he comes 'out of himself' and his concentration on self-interest. But the potential vitality of this recognition, which might spur him towards a new life, is merely demoralizing to Willems, who walks towards the wharves in order to throw himself into the sea.

Once again he is saved by Lingard; the third and fourth chapters deepen the connections between the two men, not only by placing Willems once more into Lingard's hands, but more importantly by stressing their temperamental affinities. Though he has every reason to let Willems kill himself (he is well aware, for instance, that Willems has encouraged him to drunkenly reveal the source of his enormous supply of gutta and rattan), Lingard is nevertheless led by his 'absurd conscience' to take Willems in hand once again: 'We are responsible for one another—worse luck. I am almost ashamed of myself, but I can understand your dirty pride. I can!' (p. 40.) For that pride is but a degraded version of his own, as we are reminded when Lingard describes his relations with the natives of Sambir in terms which echo the description of Willems's relationship with his wife and family:

'D'ye see, I have them all in my pocket. The rajah is an old friend of mine. My word is law—and I am the only trader.' (p. 43)

'You see, Willems, I brought prosperity to that place. I composed their quarrels, and saw them grow under my eyes. There's peace and happiness there. I am more master there than his Dutch Excellency down in Batavia ever will be when some day a lazy man-of-war blunders at last against the river. I mean to keep the Arabs out of it, with their lies and their intrigues. I shall keep the venomous breed out, if it costs me my fortune.' (p. 45)

Lingard's words are immediately followed by a greeting from the ship of the Arab, Abdullah—just as Willems's grandiose reveries had been followed by the voice of Mr Vinck; but Lingard, like Willems, thinks himself inviolable: 'I have the heels of anything that floats in these seas.' (p. 45.) Like Willems, he too takes 'pride' in his benevolence to his 'family'—and it was Leonard, Willems's brother-in-law, who helped to expose him. Pride goes before a fall. Just as Willems has fallen, so too will Lingard—and it is in the nature of this fall that the major interest of the novel lies.[17]

Nevertheless, the story of Willems holds the centre of attention from the start of Chapter 5 (p. 46) to the end of Part II (p. 157). Conrad's letters indicate that he was unhappy with his development of the novel, and in the Author's Note he confesses 'the story itself was never very near my heart' (p. ix). In a letter to Marguerite Poradowska he complains that '*une catastrophe dramatique me manque*',[18] while the letters to Garnett, which give a clear picture of the development of the novel, are insistent in their disparagement of it: 'I dread the moment when you shall see my "Outcast" as a whole. It seems frightful bosh. I never felt like that even in the first days of my "Folly".'[19] During the time that Lingard is absent, Willems's passion for Aissa ripens. Unlike that of Nina and Dain, the passion of Willems and Aissa is from the first associated with death and decay (imaged with omnipresent creepers, parasitic vegetation, and decaying flowers), and is horrifying even to Willems himself. But Guerard is surely wrong to claim that 'The novel's one real area of ambiguity, and of obscure author-involvement, concerns Willems's sexual passion—a passion Conrad here explicitly defines as corrupt'[20]: '. . . that whisper of deadly happiness, so sincere, so spontaneous, coming so straight from the heart—like every corruption. It was the voice of madness, of a delirious peace, of happiness that is infamous, cowardly, and so exquisite that the debased mind refuses to contemplate its termination . . .' (pp. 141–2.) It is clearly not sexual passion that is here defined as corrupt, but the obsessional quality with which it is invested; it is the 'madness' that corrupts—attitude, not act. As Willems is later to say to Lingard: 'It isn't what I have done that torments me. It is the why. It's the madness that drove me to it. It's that thing that came over me.' (p. 270.) Nor is it clear that Willems can be held responsible for this attitude, this madness, for it is a direct result of extreme demoralization and isolation. His sexuality and its madness are always presented as passive and non-volitional:

> 'The next moment he was passing her close, walking rigidly, like a man in a trance. He heard her rapid breathing and he felt the touch of a look darted at him from half-open eyes. It touched his brain and his heart together. It seemed to him to be something loud and stirring like a shout, silent and penetrating like an inspiration. The momentum of his motion carried him past her, but an invisible force made up of surprise and curiosity and desire spun him round as soon as he had passed.' (pp. 68–9)

> 'And Willems stared at her, charmed with a charm that carries with it a sense of irreparable loss, tingling with that feeling which begins like a caress and ends in a blow, in that sudden hurt of a new emotion making its way into a human heart, with the brusque stirring of sleeping sensations awakening suddenly to the rush of new hopes, new fears, new desires—and to the flight of one's own self.' (p. 69)

This is more than sexual passion (Willems is, after all, a sexually experienced man), it involves an absolute loss of control, a loss of self. From this point in the novel, Willems is repeatedly referred to as a 'slave' to his passion and to Aissa: 'his very individuality was snatched from within himself by the hand of a woman . . . All that had been a man within him was gone' (p. 77). But if he cannot really be said to be accountable for his passion (and perhaps by extension, for all its consequences), then to whom can we assign responsibility for his betrayal?

An answer is immediately suggested when Lingard re-enters the action at the start of Part III, which begins with Almayer's bitter words:

> 'Yes! Cat, dog, anything that can scratch or bite; as long as it is harmful enough and mangy enough. A sick tiger would make you happy—of all things. A half-dead tiger that you could weep over and palm upon some poor devil in your power, to tend and nurse for you. Never mind the consequences—to the poor devil. Let him be mangled or eaten up, of course! You haven't any pity to spare for the victims of your infernal charity. Not you!' (p. 161)

Almayer goes on to remind Lingard of a 'half-starved dog'

(Lingard has several times called Willems a 'starved cat') which he had saved, and which subsequently went mad and bit the serang, who died in agony. It seems that not only half-starved dogs can turn on one, for Willems, Almayer reports, has betrayed Lingard by leading the Arabs up the river, as well as by perpetrating various outrages upon himself. Almayer's conclusion is interesting: 'You have no morality.' (p. 162.) Truth has been known to come from mysterious and unworthy agencies; Almayer's diatribe, though prompted by self-interest and humiliation, is nevertheless remarkably to the point. It raises a serious question: how is one to know that a dog is mad—that a man will betray you—before the fact of saving it? This is certainly of general interest with regard to both dogs and men, though there can be no doubt that there was froth on Willems's moral mouth at the very moment that Lingard rescued him.

Lingard is not, of course, open to philosophical discussion with Almayer, whom he complacently regards 'much as a shepherd might look at a pet sheep in his obedient flock turning unexpectedly upon him in enraged revolt' (p. 162). For days he procrastinates, unable to accept a betrayal inexplicable to his simple mind: 'The thing could not be explained. An un-exampled, cold-blooded treachery, awful, incomprehensible. Why did he do it? Why? Why?' (p. 203.) Lingard cannot decide to shoot Willems, for Willems has shown no shame, no acceptance of responsibility for his action. It is in fact not Willems, but Lingard, who feels the lurking unease that as-sociates with guilt—and Willems recognizes this. He sends a note to Lingard: 'Come and see me. I am not afraid. Are you? W.' (p. 203.) The novel works slowly towards its peak as Lingard decides to abandon Willems to his spent passion, to 'leave him his life not in mercy but in punishment' (p. 255). At their climactic confrontation, Lingard (previously 'a man who boasts of never having regretted a single action of his life') recognizes the inescapable truth that he alone is responsible for what has happened to him: 'I am an old fool.'

'He was. The breath of his words, of the very words he spoke, fanned the spark of divine folly in his breast, the spark that made him—the hard-headed, heavy-handed adventurer—stand out from the crowd, from the sordid, from the joyous, unscrupulous, and noisy crowd of men that were so much like himself.' (p. 273)

This is the insight towards which the novel works, and at which it finds its finest moment.[21]

Lingard's confrontation with Willems is also a confrontation with an obscure and deadly aspect of his own behaviour. There is a hint of the tragic in his realization that it was his own distorted sense of responsibility ('infernal charity', 'absurd conscience', 'unreasoning benevolence') which has inevitably led to his betrayal by Willems:

> 'You are my mistake. I shall hide you here . . . Do not expect me to forgive you. To forgive one must have been angry and become contemptuous, and there is nothing in me now—no anger, no contempt, no disappointment. To me you are not Willems, the man I befriended and helped through thick and thin, and thought much of . . . You are not a human being that may be destroyed or forgiven. You are a bitter thought, a something without a body, and that must be hidden. You are my shame.' (p. 275)

But it would be a mistake to take Lingard's recognition for more than it is; he has no doubt learned something, but perhaps only that charity can backfire when misapplied. This is an early and as yet inadequate version of the technique of the 'outcast-double' that Conrad was to use so successfully in works following shortly after *An Outcast*—'Heart of Darkness' and *Lord Jim*—but Lingard is neither as aware as Marlow, nor so haunted as Jim. Conrad had not yet recognized the depth of the insight towards which he was moving. There is some affinity between the egoistic self-exaltation of Lingard and that of Willems, and Lingard comes close to recognizing this, but the identification of his own dark and degraded impulses with those of his antagonist is never made explicit. The larger lesson of the novel is lost to Lingard: the necessary result of that giving which arises from the giver's need to be a providence is the annihilation of the will of the recipient. It is as true of Willems and Almayer with respect to Lingard as it had been with Joanna and her family with respect to Willems: 'His munificence had demoralised them.' If one saves people in the same way that one saves dogs or cats, they are equally likely to bite.

Lingard prescribes for Willems the most appropriate punishment—forced acceptance of the consequences of his own actions. This is a high form of justice, and cannot but be admired. On the other hand, the motives that prompt it are in themselves both inflated and dangerous, and it seems that we must also pass judgment on Lingard. As Thomas Moser has remarked, Conrad is 'a profound psychologist, relentlessly exploring the causes of moral failure and the motives that underlie seemingly praiseworthy actions.'[22] It is through Lingard's actions, which are prompted by his simple idea that 'we are responsible for one another', that the misfortunes of the novel occur.

An Outcast of the Islands should end with Part IV, as the final chapters are largely irrelevant to the thematic texture of the novel. Conrad was himself unhappy with the final part of the book, and never felt that it was suitable:

'I lack the courage to set before myself the task of rewriting the thing. It is not ... a matter of a correction here or there—a matter of changed words—or lines—or pages. The whole conception seems to me wrong. I seem to have seen the wrong side of the situation ... For months I have been afraid of that chapter —and now it is written—and the foreboding is realised in a dismal failure.'[23]

Perhaps the major point of interest about the final scenes is that they call forth one of the worst single bits of writing in all of Conrad's work—Willems's death and final thoughts as rendered by interior monologue: 'His mouth was full of something salt and warm. He tried to cough; spat out ... Who shrieks: In the name of God, he dies!—he dies!—Who dies?—Must pick up—Night!—What? ... Night already ...' (p. 360.)

There is textual evidence to justify the interpretation of *An Outcast* presented here—that it is fundamentally about Tom Lingard, but that Conrad was only imperfectly aware of the possibilities of his material. We have virtually two different novels here, Parts I and II dealing with Willems, III and IV dealing with Lingard. Even in Part V, which clearly seems to indicate the novel's focus, only thirty-three of the seventy-seven pages deal directly with Willems. It is also useful to remember, especially in the light of the interpretation presented here, that the conventional synopsis of the story (as presented in Chapter 1) can, and should be replaced by a summary with Lingard at the centre: 'Tom Lingard, the leading trader of the Eastern Archipelago, places a young Dutch boy, Peter Willems, with the firm of Hudig and Company. When Willems is caught stealing company funds, Lingard takes him to Sambir to stay with Almayer. Etc.' Such a synopsis is true to the deepest concerns of the novel, which are perhaps best stated in the set piece with which Chapter 4 of Part III begins:

'Consciously or unconsciously, men are proud of their firmness, steadfastness of purpose, directness of aim. They go straight towards their desire, to the accomplishment of virtue—sometimes of crime—in an uplifting persuasion of their firmness ... The man of purpose does not understand, and goes on, full of contempt. He never loses his way. He knows where he is going and what he wants. Travelling on, he achieves great length without any breadth, and battered, besmirched, and weary, he touches the goal at last; he grasps the reward of his perseverence, of his virtue, of his healthy optimism: an untruthful tombstone over a dark and soon forgotten grave.' (p. 197)

The words refer to Tom Lingard.

This reading of *An Outcast*, while it may make sense of the novel's underlying concerns, still cannot take away the book's failures. Yet, though blurred in focus, and without the economy and penetration of Conrad's mature works, *An Outcast* is greatly superior to *Almayer's Folly*. The superiority of the one novel over the other is primarily a reflection of the fact that Lingard is a richer and more complex figure than Almayer. As if thinking this very thought, Conrad began yet another novel in the same setting, but this time with Lingard directly in focus. But it was an insight that came too late, and *The Rescuer*, as it was then called, was set aside, and not completed until 1919.

While wrestling unsuccessfully with *The Rescuer* in the years 1896 and 1897, Conrad sought occasional respite by turning to the form of the short story, and produced five of these over the two-year period, while one other attempt, *The Nigger of the 'Narcissus'*, grew into a short novel. The five stories (in order of composition: 'The Idiots', 'An Outpost of Progress', 'The Lagoon', 'The Return', and 'Karain: A Memory') were published as *Tales of Unrest* in 1898.[24] They are by no means the best of Conrad's stories, nor do they best exemplify what I take to be Conrad's central themes (certain of them do this very well, but arguably not so well as other stories, like 'Falk'). But the 'unrest' with which these stories deal is crucial to the understanding of Conrad conveyed in this book, and it is worth paying particular attention to it.

The distinct thematic similarity of the stories is suggested by the word 'unrest': each centres on a character who, safe in a clearly defined understanding of life's regularities and values, is confronted with an experience so traumatic that it destroys belief, and opens up a vista of a universe implacable and terrifying. The result of the shock experienced by a character 'betrayed by his dream, spurned by his illusion'[25] is inevitably the perception—sometimes simply momentary, sometimes leading to suicide or madness—that death is preferable to life.[26] The stories are remarkably grisly, containing sundry unspecified deaths, as well as four murders and three suicides. Indeed, the 'unrest' to which the volume refers is endemic to the human condition, experienced by many, a threat to all.

In 'The Idiots', the shortest and least impressive of the stories, Susan and Jean, a Breton peasant couple, produce as their only offspring four idiot children. Jean, repelled by his children but vainly desirous of an heir to carry on his name and vocation, makes a sexual advance towards his wife, who kills him with a knife, an instinctive defence. A woman of simple and unquestioned piety, Susan is overwhelmed by her vision of a scene consisting of 'four idiots and a corpse', and curses her beliefs:

' "You go and see, mother," retorted Susan, looking at her with blazing eyes. "There's no mercy in heaven—no justice. No! . . . I did not know . . . Haven't I prayed! But the Mother of God herself would not hear me. A mother! . . . Who is accursed—I, or the man who is dead?" ' (p. 75)

Maddened by the thought that Jean's ghost is pursuing her (it is only a fisherman trying to save her as she walks distractedly by the cliffs), she jumps to her death, her final cry echoing straight up to 'the high and impassive heaven' (p. 84).

'An Outpost of Progress', which Conrad described as 'the lightest part of the loot that I carried off from Central Africa',[27] is the best of the stories in the volume, and supplies the first sustained example of that pitiless irony that Conrad could display towards his more inadequate protagonists. Kayerts and Carlier—'two perfectly insignificant and incapable individuals, whose existence is only rendered possible through the high organization of civilized crowds' (p. 89)—are named to command a tiny trading station of the Great Civilizing Company. As the months pass, the men, like Almayer and Willems before them, gradually disintegrate before the malignant hostility of the jungle. Unable to impose any order on their isolated lives, the two men, who 'could only live on condition of being machines' (p. 91), allow their native helpers to be sold into slavery in exchange for six enormous tusks of ivory. They excuse themselves with the assertion that 'there is nobody here' (p. 109) to provide a moral context. They quarrel desperately over their ration of sugar, until Carlier's words luminously define their situation. 'I am hungry—I am sick—I don't joke! I hate hypocrites. You are a hypocrite. You are a slave-dealer. I am a slave-dealer. There's nothing but slave-dealers in this cursed country.' (p. 110.) The two end in a deadly (and hilarious) chase round and round the house, until they collide from exhaustion, and Carlier is killed by an accidental shot from Kayerts's gun. In terms strikingly similar to those used by Raskolnikov in *Crime and Punishment* (not to mention Willems in *An Outcast of the Islands*), Kayerts attempts to rationalize his action:

> 'Incidentally he reflected that the fellow dead there had been a noxious beast anyway; that men died every day in thousands: perhaps in hundreds of thousands—who could tell?—and that in the number, that one death could not possibly make any difference; couldn't have any importance, at least to a thinking creature. He, Kayerts, was a thinking creature. He had been all his life, till that moment, a believer in a lot of nonsense like the rest of mankind—who are fools; but now he thought! He knew! He was at peace; he was familiar with the highest wisdom! (p. 115)

As Kayerts hears the whistle of the trading company steamer, he abandons his 'new wisdom' (p. 114), and runs away to hang himself on a cross which adorns a nearby grave; he is found there by the Managing Director, irreverently sticking out a swollen tongue.[28]

The impact of this story, which is clearly related to those other studies of isolated degeneration, *Almayer's Folly* and *An Outcast of the Islands*, is based on the assumption that human survival is contingent upon a social system in which moral value is generated and preserved. Divorced from that protective shield, and its moral injunctions, a man is lost:

> 'Few men realise that their life, the very essence of their character, their capabilities and their audacities, are only the expression of their belief in the safety of their surroundings. The courage, the composure, the confidence; the emotions and principles; every great and every insignificant thought belongs not to the individual but to the crowd: to the crowd that believes blindly in the irresistible force of its institutions and of its morals, in the power of its police and its opinions.' (p. 89)

It would be well to interject here that 'An Outpost of Progress', like the two novels that precede it, suffers from being based on the degeneration of already contemptible characters. But 'Heart of Darkness', which is an extension of the same theme, is to reinforce the point made in the passage quoted above: that the forces of nature, faced in isolation, may destroy the values and inner stability of the strong as well as of the weak. Conrad continues:

> 'But the contact with pure unmitigated savagery, with primitive nature and primitive man, brings sudden and profound trouble into the heart. To the sentiment of being alone of one's kind, to the clear perception of the loneliness of one's thoughts, of one's sensations—to the negation of the habitual, which is safe, there is added the affirmation of the unusual, which is dangerous; a suggestion of things vague, uncontrollable, and repulsive, whose discomposing intrusion excites the imagination and tries the civilised nerves of the foolish and the wise alike.' (p. 89)

From a reading of the 1897 letters to Cunninghame Graham, it is clear that the 'wrong-headed lucidity' (p. 115) of Kayerts bears a remarkable similarity to some of Conrad's own darkest thoughts. We can, for instance, compare the implication of Kayerts's claim that 'one death could not possibly make any difference', with that of Conrad's own statement that 'there is no morality, no knowledge, and no hope', and conclude that Conrad's treatment of Kayerts is in some sense a reaction to an aspect of his own personality. In his treatment of his most cynical and pessimistic characters, Conrad often sought to distance or to exorcize his own doubt and inclination to despair. We have already noticed, for instance, that even Almayer can be a conveyer of deep truths; in 'An Outpost of Progress' it is Kayerts who is punished fatally for coming too near to the 'truth'. In this way Conrad could distance himself from his *own* 'wrong-headed lucidity'; we shall see this process operating in many of the works, with the extreme example occurring in the treatment of Martin Decoud, in *Nostromo*.

Conrad gave vent to the full depth of his pessimism only in his correspondence with his closest friends, and felt it his clear duty as a public man, and as a writer, to be what he called 'hopeful in an artistic sense'. In 'An Outpost of Progress', Kayerts begins to see the world in terms similar to Conrad's vision of personal autonomy, but he must pay the price of his insight. Thus Almayer, Kayerts, and later Donkin, Decoud, and others, have a propensity for producing truths which, while Conrad might privately have agreed with them, nevertheless become untenable when placed in a certain social context. As he was to assert again and again, there are things more important to a man than truth, though none more important to an artist. The artist may tell us truths, give us a glimpse at unimagined depths to human experience, but even more importantly he reminds us of the personal and social consequences of those truths. In the end, his task is to offer compassion to the suffering, and to suggest the latent bonds of fellowship linking all men.

If this is the purpose of art—as Conrad was to assert in the famous Preface to *The Nigger of the 'Narcissus'*—then it is clear that the major artistic weakness of 'An Outpost of Progress' lies in the ferocity of Conrad's ironic treatment of Kayerts and Carlier, which, like the two novels that precede it, suffers from the unrestrained nature of its condemnation.

'The Lagoon' and 'Karain' are 'very much Malay indeed',[29] both written expressly to sell: Conrad wryly assessed 'The Lagoon's chances for publication in his description of it as 'a tricky thing with the usual forest rivers-stars-wind sunrise, and so on—and lots of second hand Conradese in it. I would bet a penny they will take it.'[30] The stories are now best remembered as having provided the occasion for Max Beerbohm's parody of Conrad in *A Christmas Garland*.

In 'The Lagoon', the Malay, Arsat, sits through the night with a dying woman, recounting to an unnamed white friend the history of his love for her. He and his beloved brother had abducted her as a girl from the service of their ruler; pursued, Arsat had allowed his brother to die alone so that he and the girl might reach safety in a land 'where death is unknown'. But she dies in the morning, allowing Arsat to return to avenge his brother's death. The lesson is apparently that sexual love and brotherhood (in, one notes, a metaphoric sense) often present incompatible demands.

'Karain', written two years later, is, as Conrad remarked, written on the same 'motive' as 'The Lagoon' (that is, betrayal of personal friendship in a Malayan setting) but Conrad goes on to assure us that 'the idea at the back is very different.'[31] The story relates the history of Karain, ruler of three villages on the Eastern Archipelago, a man of 'luxuriant strength' and un-opposed power. Years before, Karain and his best friend, Pata Matara, had gone together on an odyssey of revenge, seeking a Dutchman who had run off with Matara's sister, thus disgracing his family honour. After years of searching, during which Karain is obsessed by a vision of the loveliness of the girl, they finally locate the couple. Matara instructs Karain to kill the man, while he himself murders the sister. Karain instead murders his friend, and is thereafter haunted by his ghost. He finds solace and relief only through the auspices of an old wise man, upon whose death he is once again possessed by the spirit of the dead man. Karain relates this story to three Englishmen aboard a ship which is supplying the natives with contraband guns, and appeals to them for help. He is given 'a charm . . . of great power' (p. 49)—a Jubilee sixpence wrapped in a leather pouch cut from a woman's glove. Wearing this charm around his neck, Karain is freed from his ghost, and regains his self-confidence and authority.

Hollis, the clever young member of the crew who gives Karain the 'charm', offers it to the native while appealing to his friends: 'help me to make him believe—everything's in that.' (p. 50.) Karain does believe, and is saved. The import of this is, if anything, too clear: Karain, haunted by the spectre of death until he becomes 'a slave of the dead', cannot banish his obsession without some stronger power with which to exorcize it. In supplying him with the 'charm', a portrait of the Queen imprinted on an insignificant coin, what Hollis really does is present Karain with a token of belief, a symbol of tradition, order, authority. Karain is, of course, not saved by the 'charm', but by his *belief* in it.[32] Although Jocelyn Baines is a little harsh when he says that 'Conrad gives "Karain" a welcome ironical twist by allowing an English well-wisher cynically to exorcise with a Jubilee sixpenny piece the spirit which is haunting Karain',[33] it is certainly true that Conrad wishes us to recognize the insignificance of the object upon which Karain has based his newfound faith. But is a sixpence any less significant in itself, than a flag or a crucifix? Belief supplies meaning, it does not simply react to it. The sixpence is used here in a conventional symbolic sense (Hollis remarks to his friends: 'She commands a spirit, too—the spirit of her nation') (p. 50), from which the story takes on a deeper resonance, which leads us from Malaya to England.

The full title of the story (which most critics neglect to notice) is 'Karain: A Memory': the coda of the story emphasizes the 'memory' aspect of the tale, by underlining the fundamental idea behind it, and by suggesting that the story must be read as more than an incident in the life of a naïve savage duped by an insignificant trinket.[34]

Years after the events related in the story, the narrator has a chance reunion with one of his shipmates, and the two begin to reminisce about Karain. The shipmate, Jackson, suggests to the narrator his conviction that Karain and his ghost were more 'real' than the frenetic life about them in the Strand. But this assertion of the significance of Karain's experience is immediately countered by the narrator's scepticism, and the story ends with the words: 'I think that, decidedly, he had been too long away from home.' (p. 55.) Thus we have a certain wry tension between two views of Karain's misfortunes: on the one hand, the story is symbolically that of a man exorcizing his fear of death by clinging to a cherished belief; on the other, there is a suggestion that the man is simply fleeing his guilt by clinging to an irrational and insignificant prop. It is perhaps not too much to say that in 'Karain: A Memory' we have (admittedly in an inferior story) a statement of Conrad's view of man's position in the universe—a view at once serious, compassionate, and ironic.

'The Return' is unique among the *Tales of Unrest* both in its setting and its method;[35] based on a background of marital infidelity in middle-class London, it is a psychological study of a man confronted for the first time with the realm of passionate emotion. 'The Return' has received much more critical attention than it would seem to warrant on its merits, especially by critics who like Guerard, Moser, and Meyer are interested in Conrad's inability to write sensibly about the subject of sex. But the story is chiefly interesting for its somewhat startling conclusions about the human condition—conclusions which many critics either misread or neglect altogether.

Alvan Hervey, a prosperous and respectable London businessman, has been married to his eminently suitable wife for five years. Upon his return from work one day, he finds a note from her telling him that she has run away with another man. His frenzied self-pity is shortly interrupted by her abject return. After the usual accusations and defences, Hervey realizes that life can never be the same—that his wife's break of faith has cracked the surface serenity of their life together, and indicated 'the mysterious universe of moral suffering' (p. 133). With this revelation to sustain him, he runs out into the night, never to return.

That the theme of this story is typical of the volume *Tales of Unrest* is clear from the nature of the plot, and is underscored with unambiguous repetitiveness by the text. Shaken from the safety of his innocent view of the universe, Hervey is profoundly shocked by what he sees: 'Life, that to a well-ordered mind should be a matter of congratulation, appeared to him, for a second or so, perfectly intolerable.' (p. 128.) This is a perfect statement of the thematic link of the five stories of this volume, with their movement from naïve certainty to what one might (uneasily) call 'existential' awakening. As Conrad says in the Preface to *The Nigger of the 'Narcissus'*, the shock of awakening need not last more than the 'second' granted to Alvan Hervey; we are allowed, at most, 'a moment of vision, a sigh, a smile—and the return to an eternal rest.' Hervey's vision is indeed of the 'truth of life':

'A dark curtain seemed to rise before him, and for less than a second he looked upon the mysterious universe of moral suffering. As a landscape is seen complete, and vast, and vivid, under a flash of lightning, so he could see disclosed in a moment all the immensity of pain that can be contained in one short moment of human thought. Then the curtain fell again, but his rapid vision left in Alvan Hervey's mind a trail of invincible sadness, a sense of loss and bitter solitude, as though he had been robbed and exiled. For a moment he ceased to be a member of society with a position, a career, and a name attached to all this, like a descriptive label of some complicated compound. He was a simple human being removed from the delightful world of crescents and squares. He stood alone, naked and afraid, like the first man on the first day of evil. There are in life events, contacts, glimpses, that seem brutally to bring all the past to a close. There is a shock and a crash, as of a gate flung to behind one by the perfidious hand of fate. Go and seek another paradise, fool or sage. There is a moment of dumb dismay, and the wanderings must begin again; the painful explaining away of facts, the feverish raking up of illusions, the cultivation of a fresh crop of lies in the sweat of one's brow, to sustain life, to make it supportable, to make it fair, so as to hand intact to another generation of blind wanderers the charming legend of a heartless country, of a promised land, all flowers and blessings . . .' (pp. 133-4)

There is no clearer statement of Conrad's basic novelistic pattern, no clearer definition of what I have called the tension between personal autonomy and social values. The disjunction here between Hervey the respectable member of society and Hervey the man suggests that these two very different beings can never really comfortably come together. Insofar as he knows his fundamental loneliness, a man cannot ever fully believe in his role in a social order. His 'illusions' revealed, the injunction to create new beliefs must now weigh heavily upon him. But the sense of loss and bitterness must remain, for without those illusions life is *not* supportable and *not* fair; thus that vision of the abyss towards which all men wander in their blindness.

Hervey, 'informed of a deadly secret—the secret of a calamity threatening the safety of mankind—the sacredness, the peace of life' (p. 136), nevertheless continues castigating his wife for her infidelity. In the pompous assurance of his own moral uprightness, he berates her for her failure to conform to society's highest norms of conduct:

> 'Yes! Restraint, duty, fidelity—unswerving fidelity to what is expected of you. This—only this—secures the reward, the peace. Everything else we should labour to subdue—to destroy. It's misfortune; it's disease. It is terrible—terrible ... If you don't conform to the highest standards you are no one—it's a kind of death. Didn't this occur to you? You've only to look round you to see the truth of what I am saying.' (pp. 156–7)

But around them is only the image of myriad other Herveys pompously asserting their moral worth, for Conrad has filled the room with mirrors, as if to suggest that the world is filled with identical self-deluded, self-important men. Conrad wrote to Garnett that he 'wanted to produce the effect of insincerity, of artificiality.'[36] Those who feel that Conrad's values are simply 'restraint, duty, fidelity' should reread passages like this in order to appreciate the qualifications, negations, and subtle ironies, with which Conrad accompanies statements of faith.

Hervey rants on, pretentiously reiterating his belief in 'ideal values' ('The ideal must—must be preserved—for others at least') (p. 165), until he comes at last to the logical conclusion of his standards of conduct: 'It seemed to him necessary that deception should begin at home.' (p. 170.) And so Hervey attempts to resume the normal orderliness of life together—respectable, discreet, passionless. He insists on his love for his wife, but she will have none of it: 'You are deceiving yourself. You never loved me. You wanted a wife—some woman—any woman that would think, speak and behave in a certain way—in a way you approved. You loved yourself.' (p. 177.) These honest words provide Hervey with the clue to the 'enigma' over which he has been puzzling:

> 'While she had been speaking he had wandered on the track of the enigma, out of the world of senses into the region of feeling. What did it matter what she had done, what she had said, if through the pain of her acts and words he had obtained the word of the enigma! There can be no life without faith and love—faith in a human heart, love of a human being! That touch of grace, whose help once in life is the privilege of the most undeserving, flung open for him the portals of beyond, and in contemplating there the certitude immaterial and precious he forgot all the

meaningless accidents of existence: the bliss of getting, the delight of enjoying; all the protean and enticing forms of the cupidity that rules a material world of foolish joys, of contemptible sorrows. Faith!—Love!—the undoubting, clear faith in the truth of a soul—the great tenderness, deep as the ocean, serene and eternal, like the infinite peace of space above the short tempests of the earth. It was what he had wanted all his life—but he understood it only then for the first time.' (pp. 177–8)

Thus, while Hervey's first vision is described in terms of the Fall ('Go and seek another paradise'), and is an insight into man's tragic isolation, his second vision is clearly one of an Ascension through 'the portals of beyond' into a contemplation of 'certitude immaterial and precious', and is a vision of Love. Hervey attempts to translate his newfound knowledge into action by making a sexual advance towards his wife, which she repulses with the scream: 'This is odious.' (p. 178.) It thus becomes clear to Hervey that his marriage cannot accommodate the vision of Love and Faith which he has been granted. His response is not anger, but sadness: 'He was saddened by an impersonal sorrow, by a vast melancholy as of all mankind longing for what cannot be attained. He felt his fellowship with every man—even with that man—especially with that man.' (p. 179.) Mrs Hervey, her husband recognizes, has not 'the gift'—she can give neither love nor faith, and only these are important:

'In the pain of that thought was born his conscience; . . . a Divine wisdom springing full-grown, armed and severe out of a tried heart, to combat the secret baseness of motives. It came to him in a flash that morality is not a method of happiness. The revelation was terrible. He saw at once that nothing of what he knew mattered in the least. The acts of men and women, success, humiliation, dignity, failure—nothing mattered. It was not a question of more or less pain, of this joy, of that sorrow. It was a question of truth or falsehood—it was a question of life or death.' (p. 183)

And so, filled with the certainty of this 'truth', Hervey leaves his wife, never to return.

If we compare the thought of the passage quoted above with one of Conrad's letters to Cunninghame Graham, we can understand exactly what it is that makes 'The Return' such an interesting subject for speculation. We may select two passages for comparison:

> 'He saw at once that nothing of what he knew mattered in the least. The acts of men and women, success, humiliation, dignity, failure—nothing mattered.'
>
> '[The knitting machine] has knitted time, space, pain, death, corruption, despair, and all the illusions,—and nothing matters.'[37]

The major difference between the story and the letters lies in the vision of love and faith with which the story ends—a vision noticeably absent in the letters. When we remember that 'The Return' was written between April and September of 1897, while the letters to Cunninghame Graham followed in December and January of 1897 and 1898, it is clear that we cannot lightly ignore the dissimilarity of the two writings. The affirmation of love and faith with which the story ends rings utterly false; perhaps it is intended to do so; in Conrad's best work, 'Divine wisdom' does not even exist, much less spring full-grown out of a heart so inadequate as Alvan Hervey's.

'The Return' is another example in the early works (in fact, *all* of Conrad's prior works with the exception of 'An Outpost of Progress') in which sexual love is related to madness and despair. But for the first time, in 'The Return', it is not sex that is blamed, but the specific relationship of a man and his wife; 'The Return' is unique in that it asserts Love and the emotional life as *positive* values, in its valuation of feeling above acting, a position so unusual in Conrad's early works as to cry out for special mention. 'The Return' is much more than the story of a man passing through a personal 'shadow line': it is the story of a religious conversion of an unmistakably Christian kind. That Conrad intended a degree of satire in the portrayal of Hervey is entirely clear; whether the final vision of the story is analogously ironic I am not certain.[38]

It is difficult to understand why Conrad should have written such a story, but undeniable that he was deeply involved with its progress. 'I feel helpless. That thing has bewitched me. I can't leave it off',[39] he wrote to Garnett on 18 July; on 27 September he wrote 'the work is vile—or else good. I don't know. I can't know';[40] but his final judgment of it is in the Author's Preface: 'my innermost feeling, now, is that "The

Return" is a left-handed production.' (p. viii.) Bernard Meyer has suggested that the story is an expression of Conrad's personal feelings about marriage, brought on with special intensity by the approaching birth of his first son.[41] It is probably more useful to read the story in the light of the previous discussion of Conrad's attempts to exorcize his own pessimism and despair, this time not through the act of self-condemnation by proxy, but by adding on to his own pessimism a veneer of Christian optimism. The story represents an inferior attempt to implement the artistic credo of the Preface to *The Nigger of the 'Narcissus'*; though it is clearly designed as a story 'of the solidarity in mysterious origin, in toil, in joy, in hope, in uncertain faith, which binds men to each other and all mankind to the visible world' (p. x), its affirmation of the transcendental value of Love is totally unconvincing.

Perhaps the difficulty is that 'The Return' was not a story of the binding of men to each other, but the binding of a man to a woman. This was not a congenial theme, as all of Conrad's critics are quick to point out, but it is important to read the story not as a bleak account of impotence and sexual failure, but as an affirmative assertion of transcendental Love and human solidarity. That the story is over-long and badly written, that the vision it upholds is far from convincing, cannot be denied. E. M. Forster sought for a 'creed' in Conrad's works—here is a story in which he would have found one, but at a considerable artistic price.

3

The Nigger of the 'Narcissus'

The Nigger of the 'Narcissus'[1] was conceived as one of the projected volume of short stories, Tales of Unrest, but Conrad became so engrossed in it that it finally became a short novel of 288 pages in first edition (1898). The work is undoubtedly his first masterpiece—a fact of which he was not unaware. Even as he was writing he referred to the book as 'my Beloved Nigger',[2] and at its completion he was sufficiently confident to proclaim 'the book strikes me as good.'[3] Although he was shortly thereafter to mention to Garnett that 'there seems now like a flavour of failure about it',[4] he was no doubt influenced by the inevitably limited popularity of the book, and by the obtuseness of some of his reviewers.[5] His final judgment of The Nigger is accurate and supremely assured:

> 'It is the story by which, as a creative artist, I stand or fall, and which, at any rate, no one else could have written. A landmark in literature, I can safely say, for nothing like it has been done before. I intended to keep it by me for the sake of old associations and then leave it to the Manuscript Department of the British Museum. They preserve many less significant manuscripts there.'[6]

It is not hard to understand why The Nigger of the 'Narcissus' proved to be one of Conrad's easiest books to write. Not only did it treat an aspect of life about which he was supremely knowledgeable, but his feelings about his days at sea were no doubt heightened by an increasing recognition that they were over. In writing about the crew of a merchant ship, Conrad thus had a familiar and deeply respected subject, made more attractive by its ability to function as a collective hero. Two problems were thus circumvented: first, the crew had little of the human inadequacy of Conrad's previous protagonists, and second, this hero could not become involved with a woman. Further, the theme of the 'outcast-double', which is latent in An Outcast of the Islands, could here be extended by allowing

James Wait, primarily, and Donkin, secondarily, to become an aspect of the potential 'self' of the crew in its collective capacity.

The Nigger begins with a series of passages touching the decks and forecastle of the *Narcissus*, which combine in their accuracy of detail and touches of characterization to give a convincingly real picture of a ship and its crew. If the ship and the drama enacted upon its decks are later to be exploited for their symbolic possibilities, it is first necessary that they be made concrete, and only slowly extended to reveal their full resonance. Though only a year had passed between the completion of *An Outcast of the Islands* and the inception of *The Nigger of the 'Narcissus'*, Conrad here reveals a surprising assurance and brilliant economy. This is perhaps most evident in his initial description of the members of the ship's crew: there are the two Norwegians, who 'sat on a chest side by side, alike and placid, resembling a pair of love-birds on a perch' (p. 9); there is the initial description of Donkin—'His neck was long and thin; his eyelids were red; rare hairs hung about his jaws; his shoulders were peaked and drooped like the broken wings of a bird' (p. 10)—which so perfectly suggests the impotent malevolence of the man; there is Podmore, in all his complacent religiosity, 'beaming with the inward consciousness of his faith, like a conceited saint unable to forget his glorious reward' (p. 32).

Into this ship, moored quietly at anchor, its men savouring still their memories of time spent ashore, there come two agents who will threaten it at its most vulnerable spot—in the necessary bond of faith which ties crew and officers together in unspoken battle with the forces of the sea: 'discipline is not ceremonious in merchant ships, where the sense of hierarchy is weak, and where all feel themselves equal before the unconcerned immensity of the sea and the exacting appeal of the work.' (p. 16.) Donkin, the 'votary of change' (p. 14), is from the first a threat to this solidarity. The members of the crew treat him with hearty, if contemptuous, compassion, though they are more than subliminally aware that he is a parasitic menace:

'They all knew him. Is there a spot on earth where such a man is unknown, an ominous survival testifying to the eternal fitness of lies and impudence? . . . The man who can't do most things and won't do the rest. The pet of philanthropists and self-seeking landlubbers. The sympathetic and deserving creature that knows all about his rights, but knows nothing of courage, of endurance, and of the unexpressed faith, of the unspoken loyalty that knits together a ship's company.' (pp. 10–11)

Donkin, 'that filthy object of universal charity' (p. 12), is an unfit object for the compassion that he elicits through his ability to 'conquer the naïve instincts of that crowd' (p. 12). The crew offer him their help not through genuine feelings of pity, nor out of real respect for the hardships that he has suffered, but, as it were, self-indulgently: 'The gust of their benevolence sent a wave of sentimental pity through their doubting hearts. They were touched by their own readiness to alleviate a shipmate's misery.' (p. 12.) Donkin thus feeds off the discontent that he has himself implanted. Having filled the men with a sense of the hardships and indignities of their lot, he is then able to exploit this sentimental self-pity by becoming himself its object. His very degradation furthers his ends, though at the same time it limits the respect that he can genuinely inspire. Even Donkin's first hour on board leads to a fight—the first of a long series of unhappy incidents caused by too much free time—that is only interrupted by the calling of all hands.

James Wait, 'calm, cool, towering, superb' (p. 18), represents a deeper and more insidious threat than does Donkin. His booming statement of his name—'Wait!'—as the crew are first assembled suggests both his disruptive power and burdensome nature.[7] Wait's blackness is insisted upon; though its initial importance is to emphasize his sheer otherness, there is still a suggestion that it connotes some darkness of purpose, some symbolic malevolence:[8] 'He held his head up in the glare of the lamp—a head vigorously modelled into deep shadows and shining lights—a head powerful and misshapen with a tormented and flattened face—a face pathetic and brutal: the tragic, the mysterious, the repulsive mask of a nigger's soul.' (p. 18.) This may sound absolute nonsense to us, but it nonetheless powerfully suggests Wait's impact upon the simple and superstitious members of the crew. One of the most impressionable of them, Podmore (who took his family to church twice each Sunday when ashore), immediately mistakes Jimmy for the Devil.[9]

The first chapter ends with the men assembled below, a curious friendship having sprung up between Jimmy and Donkin, who seem instinctively to recognize in each other a kindred impulse, and with the words of Singleton—'Ships are all right. It is the men in them!'—echoing 'the wisdom of half a century' (p. 24) in vague portent. This leads to the set passage on Singleton and the sailors of his times with which the chapter closes:

> 'But in truth they had been men who knew toil, privation, violence, debauchery—but knew not fear, and had no desire of spite in their hearts. Men hard to manage, but easy to inspire; voiceless men—but men enough to scorn in their hearts the sentimental voices that bewailed the hardness of their fate. It was a fate unique and their own; the capacity to bear it appeared to them the privilege of the chosen! Their generation lived inarticulate and indispensable, without knowing the sweetness of affections or the refuge of a home—and died free from the dark menace of a narrow grave. They were the everlasting children of the mysterious sea. Their successors are the grown-up children of a discontented earth. They are less naughty, but less innocent; less profane, but perhaps also less believing; and if they had learned how to speak they have also learned how to whine. But the others were strong and mute; they were effaced, bowed and enduring, like stone caryatides that hold up in the night the lighted halls of a resplendent and glorious edifice.' (p. 25)

It is not, then, of the crew of the *Narcissus* of whom Conrad spoke when he declared 'I must enshrine my old chums in a decent edifice',[10] but the men of the generation of sailors before them, of whom Singleton (literally now one of a kind) is a last survivor. J. I. M. Stewart has referred to the novel as belonging to the pastoral tradition, and has noticed its insistence on locating in Singleton's generation the fading glories of a Golden Age.[11]

The crew of the *Narcissus* is to be corrupted by 'the grown-up children of the discontented earth': Donkin ('offspring of the ignoble freedom of the slums') (p. 11) and James Wait ('the St Kitt's Nigger'). Thus we are quickly introduced to a major theme—the innocent spitelessness of the sailor contrasted with, and overcome by, the egoistic self-seeking of the landlubber. *The Nigger of the 'Narcissus'* is a chronicle of generations in conflict, of the death of an old and austere way of life at the hands of a new and degraded order.[12] The old generation had as its basis the vision of social responsibility of which I have spoken; its values—stability, loyalty, humility, hard work— had about them a selflessness that was a direct result of the communal impulse that they represented and enforced. The new generation, represented by Wait and Donkin, having lost this communal impulse, are essentially out for themselves. They are in this sense, thoughtful; and a thoughtful man, given the tragic inevitabilities of life, seems destined to become a discontented and self-seeking man. Why, after all, ought one to sacrifice one's self-interest to the pursuit of the unattainable? It is the tension between these two views of life (particularly as that tension is experienced by the members of the crew, swayed first by Singleton and their obligations, then by the inspired rhetoric of Donkin and the sublime egotism of Wait) that motivates and vitalizes the novel.

Chapter 2 begins with the sailing of the *Narcissus*, and the 'dull peace of resumed routine' (p. 29) of the first days at sea. As the ship sets out upon her journey, Conrad begins to extend his vision of her ('that minute world') (p. 31) as microcosm:

'like the earth which had given her up to the sea, she had an intolerable load of regrets and hopes. On her lived timid truth and audacious lies; and, like the earth, she was unconscious, fair to see—and condemned by men to an ignoble fate. The august loneliness of her path lent dignity to the sordid inspiration of her pilgrimage.' (pp. 29–30)

Like the ship itself, James Wait now becomes larger, and more full of meaning; the peace of the early days at sea is disrupted by his mere existence:

'He seemed to hasten the retreat of departing light by his very presence; the setting sun dipped sharply, as though fleeing before our nigger; a black mist emanated from him; a subtle and dismal influence; a something cold and gloomy that floated out and settled on all the faces like a mourning veil. The circle broke up. The joy of laughter died on stiffened lips.' (p. 34)

The astonishingly dense mortuary imagery here makes it all too clear that Wait is to be symbolically associated with death. Insofar as he becomes, in himself, the very presence of Death, it may be said that the reactions of the crew to 'our nigger' are symbolically representative of man's attitude towards death. Wait's power over the crew lies in his claim that he is dying; his consumptive cough terrifies the men into a half-belief that he may be telling the truth, though his voice at other times is a deep and confident baritone ('to hear him speak sometimes you would never think there was anything wrong with that man') (p. 39), and both his physical stature and delight in smoking belie his supposed condition. Jimmy, like Donkin, implants both doubt and pity; he *may* be dying, and if so deserves to be pitied.

What James Wait ultimately exploits is the fear of death of each individual in the crew; his hold over them is relentless because their pity for him (like their pity for Donkin) all too quickly becomes self-pity. Aided by his approaching death, or simply by the possibility that his death may be approaching, Jimmy is able to live a life of complete ease, lording it over the men, causing doubt and disharmony in all quarters:

'We were trying to be decent chaps, and found it jolly difficult; we oscillated between the desire of virtue and the fear of ridicule; we wished to save ourselves from the pain of remorse, but did not want to be made the contemptible dupes of our sentiment. Jimmy's hateful accomplice seemed to have blown with his impure breath undreamt-of subtleties into our hearts. We were disturbed and cowardly.' (pp. 41-2)

What the crew now fears is not that Jimmy may be dying (Wait's symbolic role is already extending; he is becoming what Guerard calls 'something the ship and the men must be rid of before they can complete their voyage'),[13] but that they may think that Jimmy is dying, act accordingly, and then be proven wrong. They are shocked by an interchange between Jimmy and Singleton during dinner, when the old seaman tells Wait 'get on with your dying ... don't raise a blamed fuss with us over that job. We can't help you' (p. 42), but when they are privately reassured by Singleton ('of course he will die') (p. 42) then they are pleased: 'At least we knew our compassion would not be misplaced.' (p. 43.) Donkin quickly reminds them that the fact that Jimmy will die is no more remarkable than the fact that the rest of them will also die; the irony latent in Singleton's words emerges, and unrest is once again rampant:

> 'All our certitudes were going ... We suspected Jimmy, one another, and even our very selves. We did not know what to do. At every insignificant turn of our humble life we met Jimmy overbearing and blocking the way, arm-in-arm with his awful and veiled familiar. It was a weird servitude.' (p. 43)

The second chapter ends with Jimmy enthroned like a black idol in the sanctuary of the sick bay, alternately worshipped and despised by the simple men of the crew:

> 'He fascinated us. He would never let doubt die. He overshadowed the ship. Invulnerable in his promise of speedy corruption he trampled on our self-respect, he demonstrated to us daily our want of moral courage; he tainted our lives.' (pp. 46–7)

Only one thing can now save the ship from the increasing disharmonies that threaten it, and that is some imperious call to action. With the passage around the Cape, and the coming of the storm, the men are at last freed from their tortured doubts by 'the redeeming and ruthless exactions of their glorious and obscure fate' (p. 49). What is 'redeeming' about the toil and hardship imposed by the storm is that they leave scope for nothing but work—no idle whimpering, or (what here amounts to the same thing) sophisticated questioning, no moment of self-pity is allowed in the face of imminent peril: 'We hardly gave a thought to Jimmy and his bosom friend. There was no leisure for idle probing of hearts.' (pp. 52–3.) Here the men confront not the *idea* of death, but death itself.

As the storm rages, Conrad's prose reaches a sustained magnificence rarely met in English literature, encapsulating in its own resonance the sublime terror of the storm:

> 'In the bed-places men lay booted, resting on elbows and with open eyes. Hung-up suits of oil-skin swung out and in, lively and disquieting like reckless ghosts of decapitated seamen dancing in a tempest. No one spoke and all listened. Outside the night moaned and sobbed to the accompaniment of a continuous loud

tremor as of innumerable drums beating far off. Shrieks passed through the air. Tremendous dull blows made the ship tremble while she rolled under the weight of the seas toppling on her deck. At times she soared up swiftly as if to leave this earth for ever, then during interminable moments fell through a void with all hearts on board of her standing still, till a frightful shock, expected and sudden, started them off again with a big thump. After every dislocating jerk of the ship, Wamibo, stretched full length, his face on the pillow, groaned slightly with the pain of his tormented universe. Now and then, for the fraction of an intolerable second, the ship, in the fiercer burst of a terrible uproar, remained on her side, vibrating and still, with a stillness more appalling than the wildest motion. Then upon all those prone bodies a stir would pass, a shiver of suspense. A man would protrude his anxious head and a pair of eyes glistened in the sway of light glaring wildly. Some moved their legs a little as if making ready to jump out. But several, motionless on their backs and with one hand gripping hard the edge of the bunk, smoked nervously with quick puffs, staring upwards; immobilised in a great craving for peace.'
(pp. 54–5)

With the ship perilously positioned on its side, the men sit quietly on the decks awaiting their fate. By cutting the masts the ship can recover its balance, but this Captain Allistoun steadfastly refuses to do; only Donkin objects, and he is brutally silenced.

During the course of the storm Jimmy has been both literally and symbolically forgotten; in the relative calm after the ship settles on its side, however, it is remembered that he is trapped in the sick bay—a cabin virtually inaccessible due to the precarious position of the ship. A party of five men (one of whom is the narrator) volunteers to rescue him; the scene in which Wait is heroically dragged headfirst from the narrow confines of his cabin entails a symbolic rebirth of that complex matrix of darkness and death, doubt and self-pity, that are associated with the nigger. Ironically, the men must risk their lives in order to save that which they most detest. This suggests that whatever it is that Wait represents cannot be hidden away and ignored, but must, at whatever cost, be brought up into the light, and dealt with directly. The men who deliver James Wait from his cabin certainly hate him, and have every reason to wish him dead, but the ethic under which they are

63

operating admits of no exceptions—a shipmate in trouble must be saved, whatever the result:

> 'for though at that time we hated him more than ever—more than anything under heaven—we did not want to lose him. We had so far saved him; and it had become a personal matter between us and the sea. We meant to stick to him. Had we (by an incredible hypothesis) undergone similar toil and trouble for an empty cask, that cask would have become as precious to us as Jimmy was. More precious, in fact, because we would have had no reason to hate the cask. And we hated James Wait.' (p. 72)

The comparison between Jimmy and the empty cask suggests that Wait, like his successor, Mr Kurtz, is 'hollow at the core'.[14]

The standard against which Wait is condemned is succinctly suggested in three separate instances towards the end of Chapter 3. As the crew complain of their physical ailments, and of the captain's callousness during the storm, Mr Baker turns on them with the words: 'Why should he care for you? Are you a lot of women passengers to be taken care of? We are here to take care of the ship—and some of you ain't up to that.' (p. 79.) As the men sit freezing in the howling winds, drenched by the waves, Podmore heroically manages to make some coffee in the shambles of a galley; he emerges, proclaiming: 'As long as she swims I will cook!' (p. 81.) After thirty consecutive hours at the helm, the oldest man on the ship, Singleton, is unremittingly diligent; the chapter ends with the words: 'He steered with care.' (p. 89.) It is against such men, and such sentiments, that James Wait is judged. They are men whose selfless devotion to the work must at all times outweigh considerations of personal need. They are also the most sensitive of the ship's members to the threat represented by James Wait. But the differences in their responses are crucial: Podmore's distrust of Jimmy is merely superstitious; Singleton's, while sharing the superstitious element (and, as we are to see, rightly), is motivated by his unrelentingly selfless vision of life and its obligations; Allistoun, attempting to mediate between Singleton's fierce austerity and the degraded sentimentality of Belfast, tries to deal with Wait compassionately, though he knows him for what he is.

The ending of the storm, with the return to the relative

normalcy of the voyage, presents a striking technical problem, and there is a distinct fall between the climax with which Chapter 3 ends and the opening pages of Chapter 4. Conrad makes the transition deftly, with a set passage that stresses the moral of what has occurred:

'On men reprieved by its disdainful mercy, the immortal sea confers in its justice the full privilege of desired unrest. Through the perfect wisdom of its grace they are not permitted to meditate at ease upon the complicated and acrid savour of existence. They must without pause justify their life to the eternal pity that commands toil to be hard and unceasing, from sunrise to sunset; till the weary succession of nights and days tainted by the obstinate clamour of sages, demanding bliss and an empty heaven, is redeemed at last by the vast silence of pain and labour, by the dumb fear and the dumb courage of men obscure, forgetful, and enduring.' (p. 90)

Two things stand out. First, that the highest form of 'pity' is not that which allows a man to absent himself from work, but that which insists that he immerse himself in it. Second, that justification of human life can only be achieved through this work and the stoical endurance necessary to stick with it. The words of the 'sages' (here represented by Donkin) demanding bliss and heaven (a heaven that the narrator parenthetically describes as empty) must be ceaselessly disavowed.

We can see in this statement an utterly uncompromising assertion of Conrad's vision of social responsibility. James Wait and his accomplice, Death, remind the men that death waits for us all; that, in ultimate terms, all our work comes to nothing. James Wait is relieved from duty because he is dying; Singleton reminds the men that they too are dying. The third term of the latent syllogism is easy to derive; why, then, should they continue to work? Donkin, the Devil's advocate, is able during periods of light work to intensify and make concrete the general metaphysical doubts implanted by Wait. He tells the crew that their lot is unfair, their work menial, their conditions squalid. If it is Jimmy who suggests that Life is Unfair, it is Donkin who makes this terrible truth take root in his reminder to each member of the crew that *his* life is unfair. It is a powerful line of attack:

'We abominated the creature, and could not deny the luminous truth of his convictions. It was all so obvious. We were indubitably good men; our deserts were great and our pay small. Through our exertions we had saved the ship and the skipper would get the credit of it.' (pp. 101–2)

There is a good deal of truth in this. Is it not absurd that a man should risk his life on stormy seas, for poor pay, and in deplorable conditions, in order that some manufacturer might ship his goods across the world? But the crew, inspired by Donkin's democratic doctrines, can see no further than the difference between their lot and that of their officers. Conrad is not sympathetic; their vision is mocked by its final image: 'they dreamed enthusiastically of the time when every lonely ship would travel over a serene sea, manned by a wealthy and well-fed crew of satisfied skippers.' (p. 103.)

The plot proceeds with a telling series of ironies: James Wait, obviously dying, confesses to Donkin that he is shamming—in effect becoming the victim of his own illusion. For while he was convinced that he was well, Jimmy was content to seem ill, but as he becomes increasingly weak, he must in turn deny this for the sake of escaping the death that he had used as an accomplice. Though his hold over the crew remains absolute, it continues to manifest new shifts and directions. When Captain Allistoun, acting out of compassion for a dying man and a dying illusion, insists that Wait remain in the sick bay as a punishment for pretending to be ill, the crew violently object that a sick man is entitled to become well, and that Jimmy should be permitted to return to work. The result of Allistoun's kindly impulse is an abortive mutiny, in which Donkin, naturally enough, plays the major role. In a climactic scene, the captain confronts his rebellious crew with the simple question on which the novel may be said to turn—'What do you want?' (p. 133):

'What did they want? They shifted from foot to foot, they balanced their bodies; some, pushing back their caps, scratched their heads. What did they want? Jimmy was forgotten; no one thought of him, alone forward in his cabin, fighting great shadows, clinging to brazen lies, chuckling painfully over his transparent deceptions. No, not Jimmy; he was more forgotten than if he had been dead. They wanted great things. And suddenly all the simple words they knew seemed to be lost for ever in the immensity of their vague and burning desire. They knew what they wanted, but they could not find anything worth saying.' (p. 134)

Captain Allistoun supplies the answer:

'Tell you what's the matter? Too big for your boots. Think yourselves damn good men. Know half your work. Do half your duty. Think it too much.' (p. 134)

Thinking is thus rhetorically and philosophically opposed to doing.

James Wait clings to his lie, and the crew, now certain that it is a lie, are not yet free. Jimmy, 'absurd to the point of inspiration' (p. 139), continues to elicit a degraded compassion:

'The latent egoism of tenderness to suffering appeared in the developing anxiety not to see him die . . . He was demoralizing. Through him we were becoming highly humanized, tender, complex, excessively decadent: we understood the subtlety of his fear, sympathized with all his repulsions, shrinkings, evasions, delusions—as though we had been over-civilized, and rotten, and without any knowledge of the meaning of life.' (pp. 138–9)

Ironically, and disturbingly, tenderness and compassion have no place in this world. Indeed, the passage comes close to rhetorically equating such values with being civilized itself. But what *is* 'the meaning of life'?—the progress of the story leaves us in no doubt. Singleton's 'completed wisdom' (p. 99) is granted to him in a single flash of immutable truth: 'I am getting old . . . old.' (p. 98.) This man, seemingly indestructible, who 'had never given a thought to his mortal self' (p. 99) (the crime for which Jimmy and Donkin are ultimately convicted), finally recognizes that he, too, must die. The 'meaning of life' is its certain termination in death. The lesson is that in the face of such truth, man must choose to ignore it, and work tirelessly on, surviving through unthinking acceptance.

It may be true that 'The universe conspired with James Wait' (p. 143), but both must be disavowed. Death cannot be avoided, but it need not be unduly pondered; Paul Kirschner notes 'the philosophical inference that all discontent is ultimately an absurd revolt of the self against "what's coming to us all".[15] Until the *Narcissus* is purged of its constant reminder of 'what's coming to us all', discontent will continue to reign, and the ship remain becalmed. This symbolic reading of the action is imaged by Singleton's superstitious theory that the ship will not move until Wait has died and been cast overboard. But Jimmy will not die so long as his shipmates continue to support his life, for he lives on solely as a function of the men's belief in his existence:[16]

> 'There was nothing. No pain. Not now. Perfectly right—but he couldn't enjoy his healthful repose unless someone was by to see it.' (p. 148)

The ship, and the drama enacted upon it, are now, as it were, purely symbolic:

> 'the ship appeared pure like a vision of ideal beauty, illusive like a tender dream of serene peace. And nothing in her was real, nothing was distinct and solid but the heavy shadows that filled her decks with their unceasing and noiseless stir . . .' (p. 145)

It is Donkin, purveyor of degraded truths, who wakens the ship from its nightmare, simply by telling James Wait the truth:

> ' "What? What? Who's a liar? You are—the crowd are—the skipper—everybody. I ain't!"
> "Ye're done!" he cried. "Who's yer to be lied to; to be waited on 'and an' foot like a bloomin' ymperor. Yer nobody. Yer no one at all!" ' (pp. 150–1)

And so James Wait dies, the crew is released from its bondage, the ship from its becalmed state. As James Wait's body is committed to the sea, 'the ship rolled as if relieved of an unfair burden' (p. 160), and the parable enacted upon the decks of the *Narcissus* is ended.

The story draws to a close focused upon the *Narcissus* herself, reminding us once again of her symbolic role. Perhaps absurdly, the ship is likened both to the world in general and to England in particular:

> 'The dark land lay alone in the midst of waters, like a mighty ship bestarred with vigilant lights—a ship carrying the burden of millions of lives—a ship freighted with dross and with jewels, with gold and with steel.' (p. 162)

The final passages of the tale are marred by Conrad's insistence on the austere glories of the sea as contrasted to the filthy degradation of the land (an insistence oddly opposed to the theme of the ship as microcosm); at the end, Conrad ironically focuses on the inversion of value so typical of life on land: here Donkin is full of assurance and poise ('more at home than any of us') (p. 169), while Singleton appears 'a disgusting old brute' (p. 169).[17] The narrator, musing 'Let the earth and the sea each have its own' (p. 172), disengages himself from his shipmates (changing to a first person voice) and bids them farewell:

'The sunshine of heaven fell like a gift of grace on the mud of the earth, on the remembering and mute stones, on greed, selfishness; on the anxious faces of forgetful men. And to the right of the dark group the stained front of the Mint, cleansed by the flood of light, stood out for a moment dazzling and white like a marble palace in a fairy tale. The crew of the "Narcissus" drifted out of sight.' (p. 172)

'Haven't we, together and upon the immortal sea, wrung out a meaning from our sinful lives? Good-bye, brothers! You were a good crowd. As good a crowd as ever fisted with wild cries the beating canvas of a heavy foresail; or tossing aloft, invisible in the night, gave back yell for yell to a westerly gale.' (p. 173)

Writing about *The Nigger* shortly before his death, Conrad was careful to remark the universal theme of the novel:

'In the *Nigger* I give the psychology of a group of men and render certain aspects of nature. But the problem that faces them is not a problem of the sea, it is merely a problem that has arisen on board a ship where the conditions of complete isolation from all land entanglements make it stand out with a particular force and colouring.'[18]

This statement, with its insistence on the metaphoric importance of the ship and the drama enacted upon it, must lead us to the question of whether the moral implications of the novel can profitably be generalized—whether Conrad did 'get through the veil of details at the essence of life.'[19] There is reason to doubt this. The tension between Conrad's glorification of the life at sea ('The true peace of God begins at any spot a thousand miles from the nearest land') (p. 31) and his realistic treatment of his theme is never resolved, and creates what is perhaps the greatest blemish on an otherwise masterful achievement. The reason for this failure must have rested in Conrad's sentimental awareness that his days at sea were over; *The Nigger of the 'Narcissus'* thus became a eulogy to a past increasingly attractive as it became increasingly distant.

In *The Nigger of the 'Narcissus'*, Conrad makes his strongest statement of his vision of social responsibility; the values propounded are those of obedience to authority, work, and stoical acceptance; severely rejected are introspection, concern with the feelings, and metaphysical questioning. It is no accident that Donkin and Wait are most potent in their effect on the crew's senses during the quiet times of the voyage; when there is real work to be done, they are forgotten. 'Grace' (a key word) is won only by an absolute and unquestioned dedication to the group, to human solidarity. Since any fixation on death leads a man to a self-concerned realization that work can but delay the inevitable, introspection becomes dangerous to the very fabric of society. No man deserves to be pitied because he is dying—an insight on the one hand true, and on the other, manifestly unsatisfactory. The code is a hard one, and, like that of *Billy Budd*, admits of no exceptions. The novel thus continues the theme of the self-destructive effects of misplaced pity which we found in *An Outcast of the Islands*, and it suggests, as do Conrad's earlier works, that some characters are irredeemable and unworthy of any attention. Donkin and James Wait cannot be salvaged by compassion, by reason, even by authoritarian discipline—they are not worth the food that sustains them. As Conrad wrote to Marguerite Poradowska: '. . . to return good for evil is not only profoundly immoral but dangerous, in that it sharpens the appetite for evil in the malevolent and develops (perhaps unconsciously) the latent tendency towards hypocrisy in the . . . let us say, benevolent.'[20]

If we do accept the ship as a microcosm of man's social state, we are left with the lesson that men depend absolutely upon one another for the strength to cope with life's hardships, and that the major threat to this necessary solidarity is our potential recognition of the final meaninglessness of things. For as long as the task is *considered* to be meaningful, then it is so; at the point that belief fails, so too does meaning. This is all perfectly clear when aboard ship, where there is a clear-cut goal and equally clear-cut values and relationships, but it is unsatisfactory as a statement of the human condition. When we remember that only seven years later Conrad was to publish *Nostromo*, that epic study of the complexity of 'land entanglements', it is clear that the subject of social cohesion and human interaction is a good deal more complex than it appears in *The Nigger of the 'Narcissus'*.

4
'Heart of Darkness'

'Heart of Darkness' (1900) is one of Conrad's most ambiguous and difficult stories, a tale which has captivated critics with its profuse imagery and philosophical and psychological suggestiveness. It seems almost deliberately constructed in order to provide employment to teachers, critics, and editors of literary casebooks. There are as many 'readings' of the story as its Mr Kurtz has tusks of ivory—many of them gained by similarly 'unsound method'. Its imagery has been described in detail, resonances from Dante, Milton, the Bible, the *Upanishads*, invoked; its philosophical position is argued variously to be Schopenhauerian, Nietzschian, nihilist, existentialist, or Christian; its psychology, Freudian, Jungian, Adlerian, or (more recently) Laingian. That the story has been so comprehensively 'understood' would have surprised Conrad, who was concerned that it might prove elusive even to his most sympathetic readers; he wrote to Cunninghame Graham at the time that the story was being serialized:[1]

> 'There are two more instalments in which the idea is so wrapped up in secondary notions that You—even You!—may miss it. And also you must remember that I don't start with an abstract notion. I start with definite images and as their rendering is true some little effect is produced.'[2]

In 'Heart of Darkness', Conrad takes his deepest look into the human condition, and comes to perhaps his most pessimistic conclusions on the various and incompatible pressures that can be imposed on the human spirit. The readings that the story has given rise to are a testimonial not only to the power and range of its concerns, but to their elusiveness. I shall try, in this chapter, to locate the 'idea' that Conrad tells us lies behind the story, and to discuss at some length the 'secondary notions' with which it is associated.

I have argued that *The Nigger of the 'Narcissus'* treats, in microcosmic terms, the threat to social equilibrium implicit in a recognition of the ultimate futility of life. 'Heart of Darkness' focuses on a similar problem (the image of 'darkness' echoing the resonance of 'blackness' in the previous story), although here what is threatened is not only the group, but also the individual. Whereas Conrad had conveniently circumvented the difficulty of his inadequate protagonists in choosing, for the hero of *The Nigger of the 'Narcissus'*, the entire crew of a ship, in 'Heart of Darkness' the problem is solved—not once, but twice: we not only have the figure of Mr Kurtz, the 'universal genius', but also that of Marlow, in a more complex and morally dynamic role than he previously played in 'Youth'. We cannot, in fact, adequately understand 'Heart of Darkness' if we do not begin by considering in structural terms the relationship that it establishes between Kurtz and Marlow.

We must begin by recognizing that the story is as much about Marlow as about Kurtz. This may seem obvious, but it is nevertheless true that many critics have read 'Heart of Darkness' as if Marlow were simply a means of getting us *to* Kurtz. Such a reading may be implicit in F. R. Leavis's suggestion that 'it is not for nothing that "Heart of Darkness", a predominantly successful tale, is told by the captain of the steamboat—told from that specific and concretely realised point of view.'[3] Such a view fails to account for the tension that Conrad maintains between different points of view, and finally forces the critic to posit artistic flaws (Leavis objects to Conrad's 'making a virtue out of not knowing what he means'[4] and to the 'bad patch'[5] in which Marlow visits Kurtz's Intended) where actually there are virtues. Considered solely as a study of the disintegration of Mr Kurtz, the story is simply a bad one—overlong, digressive, and poorly structured: of its 117 pages, fully twenty-five are set outside Africa, and of those dealing with Africa a great many contain no mention of Kurtz. Indeed, Kurtz's crucial role in the tale lies in his symbolic importance: in the representative quality of his history, in his role as a final incarnation of the darkness itself, and as a potential aspect of Marlow's own self.

We are made aware of Kurtz's symbolic role through the recurrent dream-imagery, which locates him as a phantom in Marlow's dream, as a 'nightmare' from which Marlow only barely manages to awake. This is clear in several places in the story, particularly in the passage in which Marlow turns in frustration to his sceptical audience aboard the ship moored quietly in the Thames:

> ' "I became in an instant as much of a pretence as the rest of the bewitched pilgrims. This simply because I had a notion it would somehow be of help to that Kurtz whom at the time I did not see—you understand. He was just a word for me. I did not see the man in the name any more than you do. Do you see him? Do you see the story? Do you see anything? It seems to me I am trying to tell you a dream—making a vain attempt, because no relation of a dream can convey the dream-sensation, that commingling of absurdity, surprise, and bewilderment in a tremor of struggling revolt, that notion of being captured by the incredible, which is of the very essence of dreams . . ."
>
> He was silent for a while.
>
> ". . . No, it is impossible; it is impossible to convey the life-sensation of any given epoch of one's existence—that which makes its truth, its meaning—its subtle and penetrating essence. We live, as we dream—alone . . ." ' (p. 82)

Insofar, then, as 'Heart of Darkness' is to attempt the impossible —to render the meaning of a dream—we have to remember the context in which the dream is placed. The tale unfolds in layers: first, we have the anonymous 'I' who serves as narrator aboard a ship in the Thames, in the company of the same group who formed the cast of 'Youth'—the Lawyer, the Accountant, the Director, and Marlow; inside this outer frame there is Charley Marlow himself, telling another of his 'inconclusive' stories; within Marlow's tale, too, there are several recognizable layers, for his trip to Africa is framed at the beginning and end by important visits to Brussels, and even his time in Africa is spent on that essential voyage—the trip up the river to pick up Kurtz, and back again. Like a concentric series of ripples caused by a stone thrown into the water, we are presented with an interrelated series of personal and social contexts, all of them affected by the impact of the central agent, Mr Kurtz.

To begin with Marlow.[6] His decision to travel up the Congo[7] is presented to us as the romantic aspiration of a man seeking after the 'glamour' of the mysterious, acting out a childhood (perhaps a childish) wish to seek out 'that blank space of delightful mystery' that deepest Africa represented on the maps of the time. He finds, at the offices of the steamship company in Brussels, an atmosphere reeking with images of death, and is sensitive enough to note the 'ominous' atmosphere; he is far from deterred, however, and leaves Brussels feeling himself involved in a 'commonplace' affair. But it is not long before Marlow's superficial uneasiness gives way to a deeper sense of foreboding. Even during his voyage along the African coast, he is already describing his experience as 'a weary pilgrimage amongst hints for nightmares' (p. 62), a realistic detail with which Conrad is quietly building a major theme of the story. The sight of the French man-of-war, anchored offshore and casually firing again and again into the murky interior of the jungle, is Marlow's first hint of the dark purposelessness ('There was a touch of insanity in the proceeding') (p. 62) with which he is to be confronted. The first white man that Marlow meets at the Central Station is the accountant, a figure ludicrously well groomed amidst the sordid surroundings. Marlow is drawn to the man immediately:

'Yes; I respected his collars, his vast cuffs, his brushed hair. His appearance was certainly that of a hairdresser's dummy; but in the great demoralisation of the land he kept up his appearance. That's backbone. His starched collars and got-up shirt-fronts were achievements of character ... Thus this man had verily accomplished something. And he was devoted to his books, which were in apple-pie order.' (p. 68)

In sharp contrast to the natty, but efficient,[8] figure of the accountant stand those of the Manager and brickmaker of the station. The chief virtue of the former—to which he apparently owes his relatively prosperous position—is his good health. Marlow, appalled by the insensitive immorality of the man, muses:

'Perhaps there was nothing within him. Such a suspicion made one pause—for out there there were no external checks. Once when various tropical diseases had laid low almost every "agent" in the station, he was heard to say, "Men who come out here should have no entrails." ' (p. 74)

This thematic association of success with immorality (imaged, as in *The Nigger of the 'Narcissus'*, by personal emptiness) is repeated with reference to the brickmaker:

> '. . . it seemed to me that if I tried I could poke my forefinger through him, and would find nothing inside but a little loose dirt, maybe.' (p. 81)

The failure of these men may lie in some internal deficiency, but it is manifested in the fact that they do not work:

> 'They beguiled the time by backbiting and intriguing against each other in a foolish kind of way. There was an air of plotting about that station, but nothing came of it, of course. It was as unreal as everything else—as the philanthropic pretence of the whole concern, as their talk, as their government, as their show of work. The only real feeling was a desire to get appointed to a trading-post where ivory was to be had, so that they could earn percentages.' (p. 78)

Marlow is thus disturbed both by the immorality of the Manager, brickmaker and 'pilgrims' who soon join them, and by their 'unreality' (a word repeated several times). This is an odd conjunction; although there is an undeniable air of evil about the Central Station, it cannot dispel the foolish emptiness of the existence led there. It was, of course, from a similar conjunction of evil and absurdity that Conrad produced the gruesome amusement of the murder in 'An Outpost of Progress'. In 'Heart of Darkness', the same point is nicely conveyed in a series of images which link evil with insignificance: there is a 'fiendish' sound about the station, but it is only the buzzing of the flies (p. 69); the Manager is called a 'devil', but he is a 'flabby devil' (p. 72); the brickmaker may be Mephistopheles, but he is a 'papier-mâché Mephistopheles'. It is out of this context of greed and ennui that Marlow's initial interest in Kurtz develops. 'He is a prodigy . . . He is an emissary of pity, and science, and progress, and devil knows what else.' (p. 79.) Intrigued by the brickmaker's description of Kurtz, and finding a solid satisfaction in the daily work of repairing his damaged steamboat, Marlow is able to combat the corrosive effects of life in the wilderness. He begins to see Kurtz as having a certain symbolic importance: 'I was curious to see whether this man, who had come out equipped with moral ideas of some sort, would climb to the top after all and how he would set about his work when there.' (p. 88.)

At this point Marlow begins to make a distinction between two types of 'reality', a subject upon which his thoughts have turned since calling the men of the Central Station 'unreal'. There is, first of all, the reality that Marlow assigns to the mundane efficiency of his everyday tasks, which is later to be described as the 'surface-truth' of life, and associated with the saving illusion of the work ethic. But Marlow is now becoming aware of an insidious force which he locates in (and as) the jungle—though the symbolic nature of that 'darkness' is still being developed—which is also 'real'. The distinction between these two, apparently contradictory, senses of 'reality', and their contrast to the 'unreality' of the Central Station, underlies the following passage:

'I went to work the next day, turning, so to speak, my back on that station. In that way only it seemed to me I could keep my hold on the redeeming facts of life. Still, one must look about sometimes; and then I saw this station, these men strolling aimlessly about in the sunshine of the yard. I asked myself sometimes what it all meant. They wandered here and there with their absurd long staves in their hands, like a lot of faithless pilgrims bewitched inside a rotten fence. The word "ivory" rang in the air, was whispered, was sighed. You would think they were praying to it. A taint of imbecile rapacity blew through it all, like a whiff from some corpse. By Jove! I've never seen anything so unreal in my life! And outside, the silent wilderness surrounding this cleared speck on the earth struck me as something great and invincible, like evil or truth, waiting patiently for the passing away of this fantastic invasion.' (pp. 75–6)

From this point in the story onward, it is to be the tension between these two types of reality—between the reality of ethical imperative and the metaphysical reality of 'the darkness'—that is of crucial interest.

After three months' delay, Marlow at last sets off upriver with the aim of relieving Kurtz at the Inner Station. His voyage is now, clearly, both a literal and a symbolic journey:

'Going up that river was like travelling back to the earliest beginnings of the world, when vegetation rioted on the earth and the big trees were kings . . . There were moments when one's past came back to one, as it will sometimes when you have not a moment to spare to yourself; but it came in the shape of an unrestful and noisy dream, remembered with wonder amongst the overwhelming realities of this strange world of plants, and water, and silence. And this stillness of life did not in the least resemble a peace. It was the stillness of an implacable force brooding over an inscrutable intention. It looked at you with vengeful aspect. I got used to it afterwards; I did not see it any more; I had no time.' (pp. 92-3)

Let us stop to ask the obvious questions. Does 'It was the stillness of an implacable force brooding over an inscrutable intention' simply strain language to the breaking point?—are we to conclude (with F. R. Leavis) that Conrad is intent on 'making a virtue out of not knowing what he means'?

It appears that Conrad is attempting to render some force which exists not only outside, but also inside, the self—a force which will ultimately constitute a threat to Marlow's psychic equilibrium when it comes to be embodied by Mr Kurtz. Its nature is oxymoronic: it is dreamlike, but nevertheless terrifyingly real; it is 'implacable', but 'inscrutable'—that is, incapable of being resisted, but incapable of being identified; it is overwhelming, but can be, if not overcome, at least resisted. It is not enough to locate in this passage the typical late-Victorian shock and horror at the universal human capacity for depravity. For Conrad, the 'horror' cannot be assigned to the fallen nature of man; indeed, our inner darkness simply enacts that of a universe not merely indifferent, but, here, positively malignant. Whether one wishes to invoke Freud's Id, Jung's Shadow (a term explicitly used to describe Kurtz), or Nietzsche's Will to Power, what must be understood is that the 'darkness' is now both external and potentially internal— and that its full fruition constitutes a danger to the equilibrium of the self. This darkness, in its symbolic sense, is not only overwhelmingly powerful, but virtually unknowable, because it almost never manifests itself in unmediated experience. Marlow is sharply aware that he is trying to express the inexpressible; his rhetorical strategy is to invoke its inexpressibility —he constantly turns to his audience, challenging them with the fact that they are simply not equipped with a depth of experience sufficient properly to understand what he is trying to say. In this oblique way, Conrad is able to suggest that which, by its very nature, can be known (except to the exceptional man) only in timorous half-glances.

As the steamship creeps onwards towards Kurtz, the darkness which is externally manifested in the jungle, and internally at some point deep within the self, becomes an increasing threat to Marlow's stability—an ultimate 'reality' seeking to escape both from and into the depths of his being. The process is virtually irresistible, as Marlow has previously suggested with the phrase 'the fascination of the abomination' (p. 50); his narrative conveys an impression of astonishment:

'The steamer toiled along slowly on the edge of a black and incomprehensible frenzy. The prehistoric man was cursing us, praying to us, welcoming us—who could tell? We were cut off from the comprehension of our surroundings; we glided past like phantoms, wondering and secretly appalled, as sane men would be before an enthusiastic outbreak in a madhouse. We could not understand because we were too far and could not remember, because we were travelling in the night of first ages, of those ages that are gone, leaving hardly a sign—and no memories.

The earth seemed unearthly. We are accustomed to look upon the shackled form of a conquered monster, but there—there you could look at a thing monstrous and free.[9] It was unearthly, and the men were—No, they were not inhuman. Well, you know, that was the worst of it—this suspicion of their not being inhuman. It would come slowly to one. They howled and leaped, and spun, and made horrid faces: but what thrilled you was just the thought of their humanity—like yours—the thought of your remote kinship with this wild and passionate uproar. Ugly. Yes, it was ugly enough; but if you were man enough you would admit to yourself that there was in you just the faintest trace of a response to the terrible frankness of that noise, a dim suspicion of there being a meaning in it which you—you so remote from the night of first ages—could comprehend. And why not? The mind of man is capable of anything—because everything is in it, all the past as well as all the future. What was there after all? Joy, fear, sorrow, devotion, valour, rage—who can tell?—but truth—truth stripped of its cloak of time. Let the fool gape and shudder—the man knows, and can look on without a wink. But he must at least be as much of a man as those on the shore. He must meet that truth with his own true stuff—with his own inborn strength. Principles won't do. Acquisitions, clothes, pretty rags—rags that would fly off at the first good shake. No; you want a deliberate belief. An appeal to me in this fiendish row—is there? Very well; I hear; I admit, but I have a voice, too, and for good or evil mine is the speech that cannot be silenced. Of course, a fool, what with sheer fright and fine sentiments, is always safe. Who's that grunting? You wonder I didn't go ashore for a howl and a dance? Well, no—I didn't. Fine sentiments, you say? Fine sentiments, be hanged! I had no time. I had to mess about with white-lead and strips of woollen blanket helping to put bandages on those leaky steam-pipes—I tell you. I had to watch the steering, and circumvent those snags, and get the tin-pot along by hook or by crook. There was surface-truth enough in these things to save a wiser man.' (pp. 96–7)

There are several important distinctions here. First, that it is only the 'man' (as opposed to the 'fool') who is susceptible to the atavistic appeal of savage reversion. The fool will not respond to the call of the savages because he is not aware of its truth, because he has shielded himself from the darkness latent within his own breast. The 'man', on the other hand, is aware of the 'common humanity' that links him with the 'black and incomprehensible frenzy' of the darkness, with the savage and primitive forces within himself. A second distinction, however, exists between the 'man' who, though aware of the appeal of the darkness, resists it, and the 'man' who succumbs—that is, between Marlow and Kurtz. This is further related to a vague and unsatisfactory distinction between principles and beliefs: 'Principles won't do . . . you want a deliberate belief.' Perhaps the two can be distinguished—*Nostromo* tries to do so—but in this context they cannot. We remember Marlow's earlier words:

'The conquest of the earth, which mostly means the taking it away from those who have a different complexion or slightly flatter noses than ourselves, is not a pretty thing when you look into it too much. What redeems it is the idea only. An idea at the back of it; not a sentimental pretence but an idea; and an unselfish belief in the idea—something you can set up, and bow down before, and offer a sacrifice to . . .' (pp. 50–1)

Beliefs can become fetishes, as men (like Kurtz) can become gods. Neither process is salutary.

But there is something more; Marlow finds his security not only in the 'surface-truth' of his daily endeavour, but he is also able to call upon some 'inborn inner strength'. Either a man has such strength, or he doesn't. Those described in terms of hollowness—the Manager, the brickmaker, the 'pilgrims', and, it seems, Kurtz—do not have it; the accountant, the cannibals aboard Marlow's steamship (a neat ironic twist), and Marlow himself, are the fortunate possessors of this asset.

It isn't long before Marlow is telling us that 'as to superstitions, beliefs, and what you may call principles, they are less than chaff in a breeze' (p. 105). Perhaps this indicates that his previous distinction between principles and beliefs was half-hearted, but it also prepares us for what is to come—for the time when only that nebulous 'inborn strength' will allow a man to fight off the call of the darkness. In his description of the agony of that voyage, Marlow asks his listeners: 'Don't you know the devilry of lingering starvation, its exasperating torment, its black thoughts, its sombre and brooding ferocity? Well, I do. It takes a man all his inborn strength to fight hunger properly.' (p. 105.) We are dealing here with a 'hunger' that is not only of the body, but of the soul (hence the repetition of 'all his inborn strength')—a hunger which Conrad associates first with physical starvation, then links to the 'appetite' for ivory, and finally extends to a general and overpowering sense of physical and mental desire, suggested in Kurtz's 'weirdly voracious aspect' (p. 134).

Chapter 3 begins with Marlow's encounter with Kurtz's Russian disciple—an incident of some importance in delaying, and setting the tone for, Marlow's approaching meeting with Kurtz. The Russian sees Kurtz as a noble soul, entitled by his innate qualities to the magisterial enactment of his own desires. This view—balancing that of Kurtz as a merely lawless ivory hunter—places him (in Nietzsche's phrase) 'beyond good and evil'—'You can't judge Mr Kurtz as you would an ordinary man' (p. 128)—and implicitly poses one of the story's major questions: how *is* Kurtz to be judged? The desire to answer this question underlies Marlow's anticipation of the much delayed meeting with Kurtz, who has just returned from a long journey with another gigantic lot of ivory. This 'appetite for more ivory', which we have seen to be linked to a less easily satisfied spiritual hunger, is soon associated with the colour of the skeleton heads with which Kurtz adorns his house. Marlow is not so much shocked by the sight of the heads, as by what they reveal about the state of mind of Mr Kurtz:

'They only showed that Mr Kurtz lacked restraint in the gratification of his various lusts, that there was something wanting in him—some small matter which, when the pressing need arose, could not be found under his magnificent eloquence. Whether he knew of this deficiency himself I can't say. I think the knowledge came to him at last—only at the very last. But the wilderness had found him out early, and had taken on him a terrible vengeance for the fantastic invasion. I think it had whispered to him things about himself which he did not know, things of which he had no conception till he took counsel with this great solitude —and the whisper had proved irresistibly fascinating. It echoed loudly within him because he was hollow at the core . . .' (p. 131)

The symbolic association of the ivory with the heads outside Kurtz's house is then extended until it suggests the very essence of Kurtz himself; Marlow's first description of the man neatly combines the two images:

'I could see the cage of his ribs all astir, the bones of his arm waving. It was as though an animated image of death carved out of old ivory had been shaking its hand with menaces at a motionless crowd of men made of dark and glittering bronze. I saw him open his mouth wide—it gave him a weirdly voracious aspect, as though he had wanted to swallow all the air, all the earth, all the men before him.' (p. 134)

But we are never to know the secret of Mr Kurtz's degradation, nor the nature of the 'abominable satisfactions' in which he has immersed himself. This is only mildly frustrating, certainly not an artistic failure. Nothing is so uninteresting (as any reader of Sade will know) as a detailed description of abominable satisfactions.

The Manager of the Central Station, impressed yet disturbed by the huge amounts of ivory that Kurtz has collected, expresses to Marlow the opinion that the ivory trade will be ruined by Kurtz's 'unsound method' (p. 137). This phrase, glibly bypassing all of the unspeakable evils which Kurtz has perpetrated, appals Marlow. It is at this point that his identification with Kurtz first becomes explicit, for in his assertion that Kurtz is nevertheless 'a remarkable man' (p. 137) he chooses to side with him against the Manager and his fellow 'fools'. The decision is embodied in the phrase 'a choice of nightmares' (p. 137), by which Marlow attempts to justify his sympathy with the full-blooded egoism of Kurtz rather than with the nasty equivocation of the 'pilgrims' and their like. But really he is responding not so much to Kurtz as to what Kurtz may be said to represent:

> 'I had turned to the wilderness really, not to Mr Kurtz, who, I was ready to admit, was as good as buried. And for a moment it seemed to me as if I also were buried in a vast grave full of unspeakable secrets. I felt an intolerable weight oppressing my breast, the smell of the damp earth, the unseen presence of victorious corruption, the darkness of an impenetrable night . . .'
> (p. 138)

The threat that Kurtz represents becomes increasingly real to Marlow as his knowledge of the man (and, by extension, of himself), and his distance from the saving grace of everyday work, increase. He recognizes that only he can seek Kurtz out after his remarkable escape:

> 'I did not betray Mr Kurtz—it was ordered I should never betray him—it was written I should be loyal to the nightmare of my choice. I was anxious to deal with this shadow by myself alone,—and to this day I don't know why I was so jealous of sharing with anyone the peculiar blackness of that experience. (pp. 141–2)

Like that of James Wait at the end of *The Nigger of the 'Narcissus'*, Kurtz's role is now almost purely symbolic: he, too, is a 'blackness' that must somehow be resisted.

As Marlow blindly searches the jungles, recognizing (perhaps a bit conveniently) that he is confusing the beating of drums with that of his heart, he comes upon an ill and desperate Kurtz crawling back towards the savage enclave of which he is the adored leader. This ultimate struggle of will between Marlow and Kurtz can easily be misunderstood. Jocelyn Baines, for instance, asserts that Marlow 'is even able to wrest Kurtz from the grasp of the wilderness when he is drawn back to it',[10] which greatly oversimplifies the scene. Marlow does make the statement ('You will be lost . . . utterly lost') (p. 143) that sways Kurtz in his tortured conflict, but it is Kurtz alone who finally resists the virtually irresistible call of the darkness, and allows himself to be led back to 'civilization'. Had he chosen to 'make a row', Kurtz would have been heard, and rescued, by the natives. But he does not do so, and this is perhaps the basis of his final triumph, and of Marlow's fidelity to his memory.

In his description of their struggle, Marlow gives us the key to the puzzling and terrifying character of Kurtz:

> 'I had to deal with a being to whom I could not appeal in the name of anything high or low. I had, even like the niggers, to invoke him—himself—his own exalted and incredible degradation. There was nothing either above or below him, and I knew it. He had kicked himself loose of the earth. Confound the man! he had kicked the very earth to pieces. He was alone, and I before him did not know whether I stood on the ground or floated in the air. I've been telling you what we said—repeating the phrases we pronounced—but what's the good? They were common everyday words—the familiar, vague sounds exchanged on every waking day of life. But what of that? They had behind them, to my mind, the terrific suggestiveness of words heard in dreams, of phrases spoken in nightmares. Soul! If anybody has ever struggled with a soul, I am the man. And I wasn't arguing with a lunatic either. Believe me or not, his intelligence was perfectly clear—concentrated, it is true, upon himself with horrible intensity, yet clear; and therein was my only chance—barring of course, the killing him there and then, which wasn't so good, on account of the unavoidable noise. But his soul was mad. Being alone in the wilderness, it had looked within itself, and, by heavens! I tell you, it had gone mad. I had—for my sins, I suppose—to go through the ordeal of looking into it myself. No eloquence could have been so withering to one's belief in mankind as his final burst of sincerity. He struggled with himself, too. I saw it,—I heard it. I saw the inconceivable mystery of a soul that knew no restraint, no faith, and no fear, yet struggling blindly with itself.' (pp. 144–5)

Several phrases early in the passage—'a being to whom I could not appeal in the name of anything high or low', 'There was nothing either above or below him', 'He had kicked himself loose from the earth', and particularly, 'He was alone'—suggest that Kurtz cannot be taken simply as a symbol of transcendental evil;[11] it is now clear that Kurtz's fate is of general interest because it is a consequence of his isolation, of his absolute freedom. He is a fully autonomous man, attempting to generate and enact his own moral truths, confronting the results of his freedom. In this passage we find the germinal 'idea' of the story (to which Conrad had referred in his letter to Cunninghame Graham) most clearly embodied: that 'safety' and 'value' are illusions that can only be generated and preserved within a given society, while any attempt to place oneself outside these artificial, but necessary, moral structures will drive any *man* into a perilous condition of 'excited imagination'. The Manager of the Central Station and the other 'fools' of the story can never descend to the 'heart of darkness' because they have no 'imagination'. What makes Kurtz remarkable is not only that he has lived in the darkness, but also chosen to leave it. *It* never leaves him, nor any man who has confronted it. We are never told the grounds on which Kurtz makes his final choice, and we may perhaps be left wondering why it is that Kurtz, who had been described as 'hollow at the core' (p. 131), could suddenly become capable of his final, remarkable, victory.

It seems there are different kinds of hollowness, differently resonant. The Manager and brickmaker are simply void; Kurtz's hollowness contains the nothingness of his universe. Like E. M. Forster's Marabar Caves, Kurtz echoes the final meaninglessness of all things.

That Kurtz's soul should become the theatre in which this 'boum' echoes is not because he is immoral, but the reverse: he is the prototype of the idealistic man. His pamphlet (written for the International Society for the Suppression of Savage Customs) is charged with naïve eloquence about the role of the white man in raising the natives to a 'civilized' state, and presents what is at first glance an appealing moral position, faintly similar to Kipling:

'He began with the argument that we whites, from the point of development we had arrived at, "must necessarily appear to them (savages) in the nature of supernatural beings—we approach them with the might as of a deity", and so on, and so on. "By the simple exercise of our will we can exert a power for good practically unbounded," etc., etc.' (p. 118)

By taking advantage of conditions which allow him to assume

the role of the benevolent deity, the white man can exercise his unlimited power towards good—or any other end that he chooses. Yet the assumption that a man in a state of absolute freedom will do good is nonsense; at the very 'heart of darkness' every man desires, like Kurtz, to 'take a high seat among the devils of the land.' Hence we have Kurtz's final scrawl at the bottom of his pamphlet, 'Exterminate all the brutes!' (p. 118). Kurtz's fate is that of any man who attempts to take upon himself the entire structure of morality.

The Nigger of the 'Narcissus' refers to 'the latent egoism of tenderness to suffering', a theme that is extended in 'Heart of Darkness' to include the perception that altruism may ultimately be no more than egoistic self-glorification. A pitier always has a certain sense of superiority to the pitied, and this lurking wisp of self-congratulation seems inevitably to lead, in Conrad's vision, either to a feeling of self-pity or an assertion of the will to power. In *The Nigger of the 'Narcissus'*, the men's pity for Jimmy and Donkin leads them to identify with the sufferings of the men whose cause they have taken up; in 'Heart of Darkness', Kurtz's assumption of the 'white man's burden' is merely the pretext for an overwhelming desire for dominance.

When Kurtz dies on the steamer taking him down the Congo, his last words, 'The horror! The horror!', impressive and even terrifying as they are, are nevertheless thoroughly ambiguous. They might represent Kurtz's final desire to return to the scene of those abominable satisfactions, be his judgment on the unworthiness of his end, a comment on the human condition, or a vision of eternal damnation. Marlow, however, is certain of his own interpretation; he sees Kurtz's last words as a confession, as a final attempt at self-purification: 'a judgment upon the adventures of his soul upon this earth' (p. 150):

> 'This is the reason why I affirm that Kurtz was a remarkable man. He had something to say. He said it. Since I had peeped over the edge myself, I understand better the meaning of his stare, that could not see the flame of the candle, but was wide enough to embrace the whole universe, piercing enough to penetrate all the hearts that beat in the darkness. He had summed up—he had judged. "The horror!" ' (p. 151)

At the 'heart of darkness', it seems, there is a piercing clarity—a vision of man's fate so unendurable that it can only remain nameless:

> 'He was a remarkable man. After all, this was the expression of some sort of belief; it had candour, it had conviction, it had a vibrating note of revolt in its whisper, it had the appalling face of a glimpsed truth—the strange commingling of desire and hate . . . It is his extremity that I seem to have lived through. True, he had made that last stride, he had stepped over the edge, while I had been permitted to draw back my hesitating foot. And perhaps in this is the whole difference; perhaps all the wisdom, and all truth, and all sincerity, are just compressed into that inappreciable moment of time in which we step over the threshold of the invisible. Perhaps! I like to think my summing-up would not have been a word of careless contempt. Better his cry—much better. It was an affirmation, a moral victory paid for by innumerable defeats, by abominable terrors, by abominable satisfactions. But it was a victory! That is why I have remained loyal to Kurtz to the last . . .' (pp. 151-2)

Kurtz's final vision, then, is one both of the human predicament and of his own experience—is both general and particular, as J. I. M. Stewart points out:

> 'Kurtz's evil courses—and this is the final terror of the fable—have brought him to the heart of an impenetrable darkness in which it is yet possible to *see* more than can be seen in daylight by those to whom no such journey had befallen. Kurtz's last words are a statement of the widest generality. They define one tenable view of man's situation in an alien universe. Alternatively, they define the only sense of himself that man can bring back from a wholly inward journey: that into the immense darkness, the unmeaning anarchy, of his own psyche.'[12]

In the light of this interpretation of Kurtz's final words, then, it seems that we must go back and re-evaluate exactly what Marlow meant when he indicted Kurtz as 'hollow at the core'. If Kurtz's fate is, as it seems, of universal significance, then to what extent can his degradation be said to be due to his inner hollowness? Marlow's remark that Kurtz's final words were an affirmation and a victory seems to contradict an earlier assertion that Kurtz was 'hollow at the core'. We appear to have two conflicting strands operating in 'Heart of Darkness': one which makes a distinction between those men who are 'hollow' and those who have 'inborn strength', while the other seems to regard Kurtz as a remarkable man who has made a journey into the self which few men could have endured. We may perhaps be left with the thought that the judgments that one makes about autonomous individuals are very different from the judgments that one makes about individuals as they relate to some social organization. Kurtz's egoism may damn him, but he is a remarkable man. Again, we turn to Nietzsche for a key to the enigma of Kurtz:

> 'Something might be true although at the same time harmful and dangerous in the highest degree; indeed, it could pertain to the fundamental nature of existence that a complete knowledge of it would destroy one—so that the strength of a spirit could be measured by how much "truth" it could take, more clearly, to what degree it *needed* it attenuated, veiled, sweetened, blunted, and falsified.'[13]

Kurtz—like his successor, Martin Decoud of *Nostromo*—sees too much, too clearly, to live through the experience.

After Kurtz's death, Marlow spends a long period hovering between life and death, undergoing the spiritual agony of a man whose illusions have been painfully shattered by viewing (and vicariously participating in) Kurtz's tragedy. Upon his return to Brussels, Marlow feels a different person from the young man he had been some months before.[14] An initiate into the deepest knowledge, he is contemptuous of the unthinking smugness of 'civilized' man. There is one question left to be answered: given that Marlow has had a vision of the 'truth', what is he to do with it?

The answer lies in the scene in which Marlow visits Kurtz's Intended, in which his obligation to his 'choice of nightmares' is finally clarified. Conrad once said that his method aimed at using a final incident to clarify his themes. As an example he cited: 'the last pages of "Heart of Darkness" where the interview of the man and the girl locks in—as it were—the whole 30000 [sic] words of narrative description into one suggestive view of a whole phase of life, and makes of that story something quite on another plane than an anecdote of a man who went mad in the Centre of Africa.'[15] As Marlow enters the house of

Kurtz's fiancée, he feels as if the spectre of Kurtz and his savage followers enters with him, seeking admittance into the world of commonplace truths and assured safety: 'It was a moment of triumph for the wilderness, an invading and vengeful rush which, it seemed to me, I would have to keep back alone for the salvation of another soul.' (p. 156.) As he listens to her eloquent descriptions of Kurtz's goodness and love, it becomes clear to Marlow that her capacity to believe in Kurtz, to cling to her false image of his worth, is the sustaining force of her existence. Pressed to confirm her glorification of Kurtz in his own words, Marlow is faced with a critical moral dilemma. He has previously given his opinion on the subject of lying in unequivocal terms: 'You know I hate, detest, and can't bear a lie, not because I am straighter than the rest of us, but simply because it appals me. There is a taint of death, a flavour of mortality in lies—which is exactly what I hate and detest in the world—what I want to forget.' (p. 82.) If Marlow tells Kurtz's Intended the truth of his experience with Kurtz, her 'mature capacity for fidelity, for belief, for suffering' (p. 157)—the 'few simple notions' on which *society* is based—will collapse, and the darkness that Marlow is seeking to contain within himself will have triumphed. Thus when pressed to confirm the genius and benevolence of Kurtz, he responds in terms which, while not untrue, are ambiguous. He makes three specific comments on what the girl takes to be Kurtz's virtues: he tells her that 'We shall always remember him'; that 'his words will remain'; and that 'his example, too' (p. 160) will remain. She takes these remarks as laudatory, but Marlow (and of course the reader) recognizes their ironic tone. At the very end of his visit, Marlow is forced into a position in which an absolute lie seems necessary. Seeking 'something to live with', the grief-stricken girl pleads with Marlow to reveal Kurtz's last words; he responds 'the last word he pronounced was—your name' (p. 161). She is sustained in her illusion, and will be able to carry on with life sustained by her own 'life-lie'. The darkness is exorcized with this lie.

If it is a lie. A final ironic possibility remains—Marlow's remark may be ambiguous in the same way as his previous assertions: the 'horror' and the name of Kurtz's Intended may be identical. But she is never to know this, can never know it.

And so 'Heart of Darkness' ends with the suggestion that truth is unendurable in the context of everyday life, that what one needs in order to maintain an assurance of safety and comfort is some sustaining illusion to which one can be faithful. The story closes with the anonymous narrator—his voice recognizably muted and chastened—looking over the quiet reaches of the Thames, and assuring us that it, too, 'seemed to lead into the heart of an immense darkness' (p. 162).

Lord Jim

Immediately upon completion of 'Heart of Darkness', Conrad set to work on *Lord Jim*, which he envisaged as a short story of some 20,000 words, called 'Jim', based solely on the *Patna* incident. Like *An Outcast of the Islands*—a novel in many respects an *Ur-Jim*—the story grew and grew, until when it was completed in mid-July 1900 it had reached 140,000 words. From its first appearance in book form,[1] it was criticized as essentially a short story that had got beyond its author's control;[2] Conrad's response to this charge—'I am not so sure about that'[3] —was based on his belief that the moral problems involved in the *Patna* incident were a sufficient pivot for a 'free and wandering tale'.[4] Thus the full title of the novel became *Lord Jim: A Tale*. Yet he was never really satisfied with the book, feeling particularly that there was a structural flaw in the insufficient formal connection between the *Patna* story and the later events in Patusan: a flaw that he was later to refer to as 'the plague spot' of the novel.[5]

Lord Jim is yet another trip into the 'heart of darkness', and once again deals with a romantic idealist whose dreams are shattered, yet who goes on to seek, and ambiguously to win, a final redemption at death. But Jim, though he shares certain qualities with both Peter Willems and Mr Kurtz, is a further development in Conrad's maturing use of the hero. Jim is neither a petty scoundrel, like Willems, nor a degraded genius, like Kurtz; he is the first of a series of Conrad's 'simple and sensitive' protagonists: he is 'one of us'.[6] The fact of Jim's apparent soundness makes the threat to human solidarity that he represents more insidious than that of those men who are in some way outside of the confines or conventions of ordinary society—'outlaws' like Willems, Donkin, James Wait, and Kurtz. Jim threatens society from the inside, as Marlow recognizes:

'I tell you I ought to know the right kind of looks. I would have trusted the deck to that youngster on the strength of a single glance, and gone to sleep with both eyes—and, by Jove! it wouldn't have been safe. There are depths of horror in that thought. He looked as genuine as a new sovereign, but there was some infernal alloy in his metal.' (p. 45)

As Jim is a different kind of character from Kurtz, so too is the Marlow of *Lord Jim* a changed man from the Marlow of 'Heart of Darkness'; superficially, he is the same teller of 'inconclusive' tales, but there is a crucial difference between the 'inconclusive' nature of 'Heart of Darkness' and that of *Lord Jim*. Although 'Heart of Darkness' ends with an ambiguous tension between its vision of the 'hollow' Kurtz, 'grubbing for ivory in the wretched bush', and the 'remarkable' Kurtz, who achieves a 'moral victory', nevertheless Marlow tells the tale from an assured, perhaps even an enlightened (he is constantly associated with images of the Buddha), point of view: he is relating something that he has learned. In *Lord Jim*, however, Marlow has none of this self-assurance: he wavers, changes his mind, contradicts himself, compulsively seeks out advice and guidance, and seems uncertain of the 'lesson' lurking ambiguously in his material.

The effect of Marlow's uncertainty and ceaseless questioning is eventually to implicate and actively to involve the reader in the psychological and moral difficulties of the novel. Several critics have, however, felt that Marlow's uneasiness before the spectacle of Jim is simply a reflection of Conrad's uncertainty with regard to his material. Douglas Hewitt tells us that:

'The effect of muddlement which is so commonly found in *Lord Jim* comes, in short, from this—that Marlow is himself muddled. We look to him for a definite comment, explicit or implicit, on Jim's conduct and he is not able to give it . . . But the muddlement goes farther than this. I have so far begged the question by saying "Marlow, Conrad's mouthpiece". In fact the confusion seems to extend to Conrad's conception of the story . . . There is, very clearly, a conflict in his own mind; he raises the issue of the sufficiency of the "few simple notions you must cling to if you want to live decently", but he does not, throughout the book, face it consistently.'[7]

Jocelyn Baines voices a similar doubt when he tells us that 'one may be tempted to wonder whether even Conrad himself was always quite clear as to what he was trying to say or, in this case, whether there was not some unresolved ambiguity in his own attitude to the events described.'[8] Thus there seems to be some feeling that *Lord Jim* is artistically compromised because it never finally makes its choice, never resolves its pervasive uncertainty. Conrad appears to be having it both ways: condemning Jim, and yet sympathizing with, and even exonerating, him.

Yet I have been maintaining that it is not a weakness, but a virtue, of much of Conrad's writing that, rather than expressing a philosophy of life (as Mr Hewitt and Mr Baines would apparently wish in the case of *Lord Jim*), it consists of an exploration of the difficulties inherent in the search for such a philosophy. If *Lord Jim* is morally ambiguous, it is so because its subject is moral ambiguity. Marlow's understanding of his involvement with Jim, and what Jim represents, does not lead to any given moral truths, but rather indicates the lurking paradoxes that underlie *any* given moral stance.

One's first impression of *Lord Jim* is that it is curiously independent of the story on which it is based. On first reading, the opening chapters are largely incomprehensible, for they give us a detailed rendering of the reactions of various characters to a fact which is intentionally—it seems, almost perversely—held back by the author. Indeed we have already been told of Jim's curious conduct as a water-clerk, heard the proceedings of the Court of Inquiry, and been a party to Marlow's compulsive musings, before we are told the nature of Jim's disgrace, what the Court is inquiring about, and why Marlow is so intrigued by the whole affair. It is in fact not until page 83 that we find out that the *Patna* did not sink—a bit of information that Conrad offers with characteristic casualness in a conversation between Jim and Marlow: ' "So that old bulkhead held out after all," I remarked, cheerfully. "Yes," he murmured, "it held. And yet I swear to you I felt it bulge under my hand." "It's extraordinary what strains old iron will stand sometimes," I said.' It is even possible that the reader may miss the significance of this, and have to wait until page 97 to be told that 'These sleeping pilgrims were destined to accomplish their whole pilgrimage to the bitterness of some other end.' The confusion that this structural withholding engenders is, of course, essential to the novel's moral strategy, insofar as it makes the reader incapable of making his own initial judgment on Jim. When the time to make that judgment finally arrives, it is already too late—the novel's pervasive rhythm of uncertainty is established, the reader by now wary of making any unambiguous response. What would have been easy is now difficult.

Jim's failure on board the *Patna* has its inevitable consequences: his certificate is cancelled, and he is left to face his disgrace and ruin. But the moral problems that his experience brings to the fore are generally lost on him, for he is too intimately involved in his disgrace to be interested in the implications of his moral failure. Thus Conrad returns to using Marlow as a commentator on the causes, effects, and possible interpretations of Jim's allegedly cowardly behaviour. During the course of his careful analysis of Jim's history (most of Part I of the novel), Marlow is exposed to a vision of man's fate which threatens to overwhelm his previous allegiance to the 'few simple notions' that form the basis of human social interaction. Just as Jim's idealized conception of himself is tried by the nightmarish quality of his experience on board the *Patna*, so too are Marlow's simple ideals of human conduct tested by his mature understanding of the implications of Jim's jump.

The standards against which Jim is judged are themselves simple enough—they are exactly those which condemn the malingering of James Wait and the agitation of Donkin: the rigorous ideals of courage, fidelity, and hard work. These values are first made explicit by Big Brierly, the apparent epitome of the traditions of the sea:

'This is a disgrace. We've got all kinds amongst us—some anointed scoundrels in the lot; but, hang it, we must preserve professional decency or we become no better than so many tinkers going about loose. We are trusted. Do you understand?— trusted! Frankly, I don't care a snap for all the pilgrims that ever came out of Asia, but a decent man would not have behaved like this to a full cargo of old rags in bales. We aren't an organised body of men, and the only thing that holds us together is just the name for that kind of decency. Such an affair destroys one's confidence.' (pp. 67–8)

This statement can be taken as a comment on morality in general. Brierly's point is that social stability (men being 'held together') rests on certain essential canons of trust and decency. Marlow several times echoes this thought, but like Brierly, he often ends his affirmation in doubt and uncertainty—a doubt that is the unfortunate legacy of Jim's unsettling act of cowardice. When Jim tells him that there 'was not the thickness of a sheet of paper between the right and wrong of this affair' (p. 130), Marlow responds 'How much more did you want?'

> ' "It is difficult to see a hair at midnight," I put in, a little viciously I fear. Don't you see what I mean by the solidarity of the craft? I was aggrieved against him, as though he had cheated me—me!—of a splendid opportunity to keep up the illusion of my beginnings, as though he had robbed our common life of the last spark of its glamour.' (p. 131)

After Jim's certificate is cancelled by the Court of Inquiry, Marlow muses upon the justice of the verdict:

> 'The real significance of crime is in its being a breach of faith with the community of mankind, and from that point of view he was no mean traitor . . .' (p. 157)

This sentiment is repeated later in the narrative:

> 'Woe to the stragglers! We exist only insofar as we hang together. He had straggled in a way; he had not hung on . . .' (p. 223)

Judging by the values that underlie such assertions, there can be no doubt as to Jim's guilt: 'He was guilty, too. He was guilty—as I told myself repeatedly—guilty and done for.' (p. 152.) It seems that there can be no excuse for Jim.

If Jim has contravened a certain explicit code of ethical standards, if he is thus guilty, what then is all the fuss about? His significance must rest on more than the simple fact of his crime—a crime that is, after all, shared by the other officers of the *Patna*. But he is different from them; they are (in the terms used in 'Heart of Darkness') 'fools', men recognized by Brierly as 'anointed scoundrels'. Jim, after all, is 'one of us'; if he can fail, what then are we to think of our cherished values of honour, decency, and fidelity? If Jim can fail, so can we all:

'Nothing more awful than to watch a man who has been found out, not in a crime but in a more than criminal weakness. The commonest sort of fortitude prevents us from becoming criminals in a legal sense; it is from weakness unknown, but perhaps suspected, as in some parts of the world you suspect a deadly snake in every bush—from weakness that may lie hidden, watched or unwatched, prayed against or manfully scorned, repressed or maybe ignored more than half a lifetime, not one of us is safe.' (pp. 42–3)

A disturbing thought; if social equilibrium depends on strict adherence to our 'few simple notions', and yet every man has within him weaknesses which can make it impossible for him to act according to those notions, then things are precariously balanced indeed.

Jim's experience forces Marlow to reconsider the nature of his standards—and thinking (as we remember from *The Nigger of the 'Narcissus'*) is inevitably a destructive process:

'Hang ideas! They are tramps, vagabonds, knocking at the back door of your mind, each taking a little of your substance, each carrying away some crumb of that belief in a few simple notions you must cling to if you want to live decently and would like to die easy.' (p. 43)

'Imagination, the enemy of men' (p. 11) is unleashed; Marlow begins to recognize that reality against which his 'few simple notions' are so inadequate a protection. When experiences such as Jim's obtrude—as they inevitably seem to do—the serenity of one's simple view of life is broken, and a turbulent and hostile universe is revealed: we have yet another view of the 'heart of darkness':

'For a moment I had a view of the world that seemed to wear a vast and dismal aspect of disorder, while, in truth, thanks to our unwearied efforts, it is as sunny an arrangement of small conveniences as the mind of man can conceive. But still—it was only a moment: I went back into my shell directly. One *must*—don't you know?—though I seemed to have lost all my words in the chaos of dark thoughts I had contemplated for a second or two beyond the pale.' (p. 313)

What Marlow sees during this momentary peep out of the shell is enough to change his opinion about the nature of things:

> 'It seemed to me I was being made to comprehend the Inconceivable—and I know of nothing to compare with the discomfort of such a sensation. I was made to look at the convention that lurks in all truth and on the essential sincerity of falsehood . . . as if the obscure truth involved were momentous enough to affect mankind's conception of itself . . .' (p. 93)

It is altogether too easy to read this passage superficially, to miss the import of the phrase 'the convention that lurks in all truth and on the essential sincerity of falsehood'. It seems that 'truth' is merely an agreed formula, of no intrinsic importance, and that what we reject as 'falsehood' may, however base the action in which it issues, arise from motives of no mean kind.

This postulates a universe in which the basic fact is not human solidarity, but human loneliness:

> 'It is when we try to grapple with another man's intimate need that we perceive how incomprehensible, wavering, and misty are the beings that share with us the sight of the stars and the warmth of the sun. It is as if loneliness were a hard and absolute condition of existence; the envelope of flesh and blood on which our eyes are fixed melts before the outstretched hand, and there remains only the capricious, unconsolable, and elusive spirit that no eye can follow, no hand can grasp.' (pp. 179–80)

We thus have two starkly contrasted views of reality: there is the everyday world, associated with light, words, and 'a few simple notions'; underlying that 'conventional' world, however, a 'deeper' reality exists, associated with darkness, loneliness, and absolute egoism. *Lord Jim* suggests that moral culpability exists only in the first of them.

Conrad had previously used the 'deep hole' or 'abyss' as an image of that reality that man confronts only at the risk of his 'few simple notions'. Kurtz, for instance, finds the final truth of life in the depths of the 'abyss' into which he descends, and over the edge of which Marlow is allowed to peek. Jim's initiation into life's deep and turbulent reality is similarly imaged: 'There was no going back. It was as if I had jumped into a well—into an everlasting deep hole . . .' (p. 111.) In Marlow's statement that Jim 'had tumbled from a height he could never scale again' (p. 112), he refers not so much to the irredeemable quality of Jim's disgrace, as to the corrosive effect of the knowledge that the disgrace entails. Marlow, through and with Jim, peers into the same darkness: 'Yet for all that the great plain on which men wander amongst graves and pitfalls remained very desolate under the impalpable poesy of its crepuscular light, overshadowed in the centre, circled with a bright edge as if surrounded by an abyss full of flames.' (p. 215.) The thoughts triggered by Jim's jump imaginatively reveal to Marlow a reality different from, and deeper than, the reality of his everyday world. At which point, the question of Jim's guilt takes on new dimensions. Only if we are sure of our standards can we confidently judge transgression. If, as our deepest truth, we substitute an idea of man's ultimate loneliness and alienation from other human beings, for our previous ideal of human solidarity based on '*les valeurs idéales*', then all concepts of human responsibility are changed. This accounts—in a schematic way—for Marlow's confused attitude to Jim.

If we re-examine the circumstances of Jim's jump in this light, he becomes much more sympathetic to us. At the most superficial level, it is necessary to remember the mitigating circumstances of his failure. Unlike the other officers of the *Patna*, Jim's first impulse is not simply to save his own skin; his paralysis is at least partially due to the hopelessness of the situation: the bulkheads cannot fail to burst, any alarm will produce a stampede amongst the pilgrims, there are far too few lifeboats, and a squall is moving quickly towards the *Patna*. The ship simply must sink at any moment. It seems as if Jim's choice is only whether eight hundred pilgrims will drown, or eight hundred pilgrims and himself. Even so, Jim might have stayed on board had not circumstances ironically contrived against him. Mistaking the cries of the unworthy Captain and his officers as pleas for him to join them in their lifeboat, he finally jumps. But the jump itself is not willed, it simply happens: 'I had jumped . . . It seems.' (p. 111.) It seems more appropriate to say that Jim 'is jumped'. Furthermore, while the other officers of the *Patna* make their escape upon learning that the ship did not sink, Jim stays to face the consequences of his action. Thus his behaviour, while impossible to condone, is nevertheless easy to sympathize with.

Conrad goes further, introducing deeper reasons to lessen Jim's disgrace. The first of these lies in Marlow's vision of universal loneliness, in which there is the clear implication that, in the last analysis, one's duties are to one's self. This is not to imply that they should be—they should not—but simply that they are. The phrase 'in the last analysis', as it is used here, indicates why Conrad was so deeply suspicious of 'ideas' and 'Imagination': both tend to reveal unpleasant, and corrosive, truths. Even the French Lieutenant whom Marlow meets is inclined to admit the universality of cowardice: the primitive urge to save one's skin. This may explain Jim's having passively found himself in the water, rather than actively jumping, as if an unconscious life-force had exerted itself on his behalf.

Once we recognize this instinct of self-preservation, and the way in which it isolates the individual in moments of crisis, then a second factor emerges to illuminate Jim's history. According to conventional notions of duty and honour, Jim is as guilty as are the other officers of the *Patna*; such is the inevitable verdict of the Court of Inquiry, which cancels the certificates of all the officers. But just as Kurtz may be of greater stature than the 'pilgrims' and 'flabby devils' of 'Heart of Darkness' (though his crime is greater than theirs), so too is Jim a man and not a fool. It is men like Jim, who is 'one of us', who remind us that we are all (at least potentially) guilty, that any of us might jump from some *Patna*. In judging him, we must accept that we judge ourselves. No consideration is likelier to lead to a lenient verdict.

The third factor in the re-examination of Jim's case lies in the possibility of atonement on his part. Jim, unlike the other officers of the *Patna*, both accepts and believes in the standards by which he is judged. His character could hardly be called irretrievably corrupt. His motives, like those of Kurtz, are essentially those of an 'idealised selfishness', but could not be called wicked. Following his trial, Jim is obsessed with the thought that he may never get a chance to atone for his behaviour, never be able to realize the ideal picture of himself that he cannot abandon. Marlow is far from sympathetic to this aspect of him ('the idea obtrudes itself that he made so much of his disgrace, while it is the guilt alone that matters') (p. 177) but nevertheless he, too, ponders the possibility of

99

some redemptive experience for Jim. Although Jim has twice been betrayed—and become a betrayer—through his romantic self-glorification, he retains his belief that he needs but one more chance to prove his value. The second half of the novel, in which Jim becomes Lord Jim, is the chronicle of that chance.

Before proceeding to a brief discussion of the Patusan episode, let us look once more at the possible mitigating factors that lead us to view Jim in a sympathetic light. Although Conrad is sensitive to the ambiguities exposed by Jim's betrayal, he nevertheless does not wish absolutely to condone Jim's behaviour. Far from it. Having established the standard necessary to social cohesion ('we exist only insofar as we hang together'), and having revealed, through the implications of Jim's failure, a deeper view of reality in which Jim cannot be said to be in any way unique in his failure, Conrad uses Part I of *Lord Jim* to expose Marlow (and the reader) to a variety of possible points of view on Jim's story. These are modulated so that Marlow (and the reader) continue to vacillate between outright condemnation of Jim and the desire to excuse him. Those passages that relate to the *Patna*'s sneaking officers, and those regarding Chester and Captain Robinson, who wish to use Jim ('He's no good, is he?') (p. 166) as an overseer on their inaccessible guano island, serve to heighten our empathy for Jim, and to underscore a certain fineness in his nature. On the other hand, those sections in which the two Malay steersmen (who stood at the tiller of the *Patna* as it was being abandoned) give their testimony at the Court of Inquiry, and those relating the story of the heroism of Little Bob Stanton (who drowned trying to save a panicky lady's-maid on board a sinking ship), serve to highlight the values against which Jim is judged.

Two major commentators on Jim's disaster, Big Brierly and the anonymous French Lieutenant, might easily be taken, like the Malay steersmen and Little Bob Stanton, as simple examples of men in whom the values and traditions of the sea are honourably embodied. In neither case is this true. In the case of Big Brierly, who 'had never in his life made a mistake' (p. 57) (at least, that anyone knew of), and who served on the Court of Inquiry that judged Jim, it ironically turns out that Jim is not to be judged by Brierly's impeccable standards, but Brierly by Jim's somewhat tarnished moral nature. It appears that

Brierly, like Jim, has committed some major moral failure,[9] but that, unlike Jim, he has failed to face the consequences. Jim, at least, is entitled to say 'I may have jumped, but I don't run away' (p. 154); Brierly is not. The only way, then, in which Brierly's character may mark as a standard against which to judge Jim lies in his suicide. But it is clearly not an action that Conrad could be said to suggest as a viable alternative for Jim; aside from which, it is a suicide prompted by the example of Jim's moral courage in facing the consequences of his failure.

The case of the French Lieutenant, while similar, nevertheless goes more deeply into the matter. This man, who stayed on board the damaged *Patna* as she was being towed into port, admits to Marlow that:

> '. . . there is a point—there is a point—for the best of us—there is somewhere a point when you let go everything (*vous lâchez tout*). And you have got to live with that truth—do you see? Given a certain combination of circumstances, fear is sure to come. Abominable funk . . . Man is born a coward (*L'homme est né poltron*). It is a difficulty—*parbleu*! It would be too easy otherwise. But habit—habit—necessity—do you see?—the eye of others—*voilà*. One puts up with it.' (pp. 146–7)

It appears that the French Lieutenant, too, has experienced the 'abominable funk' to which he refers, and can only conclude 'one does not die of it.' The proper response to this universal cowardice, however, lies in the imperative to strengthen one's obedience to the 'few simple notions'; there is the need for 'honour':

> 'I contended that one may get on knowing very well that one's courage does not come of itself (*ne vient pas tout seul*). There's nothing much in that to get upset about. One truth the more ought not to make life impossible . . . But the honour—the honour, monsieur! . . . The honour . . . that is real—that is! And what life may be worth when . . . when the honour is gone—*ah ça! par exemple*—I can offer no opinion—because—monsieur—I know nothing of it.' (p. 148)

What is interesting is Marlow's reaction to this sentiment:

> 'Hang the fellow! he had pricked the bubble. The blight of futility that lies in wait for man's speeches had fallen upon our

conversation, and made it a thing of empty sounds. "Very well," I said, with a disconcerted smile, "but couldn't it reduce itself to not being found out?" He made as if to retort readily, but when he spoke he had changed his mind. "This, monsieur, is too fine for me—much above me—I don't think about it." ' (pp. 148–9)

Nowhere in *Lord Jim* is it clearer that Marlow is not Conrad's mouthpiece. Bent on his defence of Jim, Marlow here attempts to reject the common sense of the French Lieutenant—who is stating the one position in the novel with which Conrad would unequivocally have agreed—and to substitute the cynical notion that 'honour' might just be a state of 'not being found out'. This idea is, of course, true in a world in which all of us share Jim's guilt, in which the Brierlys are but shams masquerading as honourable men. But the French Lieutenant is speaking of everyday reality, and attempting to reject the level of consciousness from which Marlow is speaking. Yes, he would admit, it is true that 'man is born a coward', but this truth must make us reinforce our notion of 'honour', and remind us to stop asking too many questions: 'This, monsieur, is too fine for me—much above me—I don't think about it.'

Marlow, then, like the men of the crew of the *Narcissus*, is becoming 'highly humanized, tender, complex, excessively decadent . . . and without any knowledge of the meaning of life.'[10] Like the crew of the *Narcissus* in relation to James Wait, like the former Marlow in relation to Kurtz, he is held in a 'weird servitude' by Jim, who so confuses and disorientates him that he is incapable of recognizing the 'simple' truth when he is confronted with it. For there are two kinds of 'truth' available: the simple, with its notions of honour and fidelity, and the 'complex', with its loneliness and amorality. In his search for knowledge, man must accept the 'complex' truth as the deepest reality; in his search for peace, man must accept the 'simple' truth as his saving illusion. In Marlow, Conrad creates a character who wants both knowledge and peace. The impression with which we are left is that the two needs are incompatible; the final emotion, that doubt that accompanies any intensive look into the conflicting demands of self and society that may confront the individual.

Part II of *Lord Jim* attempts to supply an answer to the

apparently insurmountable difficulties set up by the clash between man's fundamental egoism and the imperative to 'hang together'. Jim is sent to Patusan by Marlow's friend Stein, to head an obscure trading station. Stein, as interested in specimens of humanity as he is in his rare and beautiful collection of butterflies, gives an immediate diagnosis of Jim's character: ' "He is romantic—romantic," he repeated. "And that is very bad, very bad ... Very good, too," he added.' (p. 216.) He offers an analogy that has troubled many readers of *Lord Jim*:

'A man that is born falls into a dream like a man who falls into the sea. If he tries to climb out into the air as inexperienced people endeavour to do, he drowns—*nicht war*? ... No! I tell you! The way is to the destructive element submit yourself, and with the exertions of your hands and feet in the water make the deep, deep sea keep you up. So if you ask me—how to be? ... I will tell you! For that, too, there is only one way ... And yet it is true—it is true. In the destructive element immerse ... That was the way. To follow the dream, and again to follow the dream—and so— *ewig—usque ad finem* ...' (pp. 214–15)

This is not very clear. The most likely interpretation[11] is that Jim, in order to overcome his disgrace, must follow his own 'dream' of heroic responsibility by submitting to it entirely, rather than rejecting or attenuating it, though this may entail his own destruction. In the terms that I have been using, it is only by accepting his autonomy—his ultimate loneliness in the water—that a man can buoy himself up. If he attempts to struggle with his fate, by trying to locate some firm ground on which he can secure himself (I think the metaphysical impli- cation is clear), he can only fail. If, however, he not only accepts, but actively 'submits himself' to his relation with the potentially destructive element, then perhaps he may succeed. But what does 'success' mean here? Certainly not escape from mortality, nor even the attainment of peace. Perhaps all that he can finally attain is freedom from the terrible conflict and uncertainty that come from ceaseless struggling against the facts of nature. If we accept that we are alone, that life is hard, that there is no ground beneath our feet, then perhaps we can find ourselves in equilibrium with the facts of our existence. Thus, the primary tension between the facts and necessities of existence can be transcended if the primary *necessity* becomes acceptance of the *facts*. *Lord Jim* leaves us with this question: has Jim managed this synthesis between the demands of his ego and those of his conscience, or has he merely continued his grandiose self-deception?

Coming to Patusan at a time of disorder and factional dispute, the determined and courageous Jim uses his allegiance with the chief Doramin to establish a peaceful and prosperous community. Taking the Eurasian girl Jewel as his mistress, he becomes the adored leader of the land; unlike Mr Kurtz, however, he is a beneficent deity. When a band of starving desperadoes, led by the notorious Gentleman Brown, descends upon Patusan and is quickly driven on to the defensive, Jim arranges a meeting with Brown, who seems to assess Jim's character in a flash: 'And there ran through the rough talk a vein of subtle reference to their common blood, an assumption of common experience; a sickening suggestion of common guilt, of secret knowledge that was like a bond of their minds and of their hearts.' (p. 387.) Jim finds it impossible to resist, and instead of ordering the immediate slaughter of Brown and his men, allows them safe passage back to the sea. Guided by the spiteful Portuguese Cornelius, whose position (and daughter) have been usurped by Jim, the outlaws ambush and murder a large party of natives led by Doramin's son. Jim, who had previously pledged his life for the safety of the community, walks proudly to Doramin's hut, where he is summarily shot.

It is not hard to understand the moral dilemma that Gentleman Brown thrusts upon Jim. With regard to the safety of the inhabitants of Patusan, it would no doubt have been expedient to murder Brown and his bloodthirsty followers. On the other hand, Jim could neither foresee the treachery of Cornelius, nor the circumstances leading inexorably to the ambush of the native party. Further, he is more than superficially aware that men can act basely without being themselves wicked: 'Men act badly sometimes without being much worse than others' (p. 394). Brown is irredeemably bad, thoroughly corrupt, but Jim could hardly be expected to know this; his decision to give Brown the same chance that he had himself sought cannot but be admired. It seems to me that, on balance, Jim is right to let

Brown make his escape. Moral decisions must not be judged in terms of their unforeseen consequences: had Brown and his followers simply made their exit without bloodshed, there could have been no good reason to assert that Jim had acted foolishly. Assuming Jim's choice to have been the correct one, we are left with the paradox that his jump from the *Patna* was a moral failure from which he attempted (in his own mind) to evade responsibility, while his decision with regard to Gentleman Brown was a moral triumph for which he nevertheless accepted punishment. There seems little doubt that Jim had made the most of that 'second chance' (actually it is a third chance) for which he had yearned.[12]

Marlow is, at times, sure that this is true. He tells us, for instance, that 'The time was coming when I should see him loved, trusted, admired, with a legend of strength and prowess round his name as though he had been the stuff of a hero.' (p. 175.) Perhaps the 'as though' is slightly equivocal; that Jim 'was approaching greatness as genuine as any man ever achieved' (p. 244) is certainly less equivocal; while the words 'I affirm he had achieved greatness' (p. 225) are absolutely unambiguous. Following their last meeting, Marlow is convinced that Jim 'had at last mastered his fate' (p. 324).

Perhaps Jim has 'mastered his fate', but his attitude when confronting the death that it is his responsibility to accept is far from humble. There is no doubt that the language used to describe Jim's last minutes leads one to view his death as only ambiguously redemptive; as Jim leaves his faithful servant Tamb' Itam: ' "Nothing can touch me," he said in a last flicker of superb egoism.' (p. 413.) Jim leaves Tamb' Itam and Jewel, and walks confidently up the hill to Doramin's to meet his death: 'They say that the white man sent right and left at all those faces a proud and unflinching glance. Then with his hand over his lips he fell forward, dead.' (p. 416.) Marlow's final words seem to convey to us both possible interpretations of Jim's death: that he had died in a redemptive act of self-sacrifice, and that he was the same supreme egoist to the very last:

'And that's the end. He passes away under a cloud, inscrutable at heart, forgotten, unforgiven, and excessively romantic. Not in the wildest days of his boyish visions could he have seen the alluring shape of such an extraordinary success! For it may very well be that in the short moment of his last proud and unflinching glance, he had beheld the face of that opportunity which, like an Eastern bride, had come veiled to his side.

But we can see him, an obscure conqueror of fame, tearing himself out of the arms of a jealous love at the sign, at the call of his exalted egoism. He goes away from a living woman to celebrate his pitiless wedding with a shadowy ideal of conduct. Is he satisfied—quite, now, I wonder?' (p. 416)

We seem to have two possible and apparently contradictory interpretations of Jim's fate.

But there is no need to choose between them: they are both true. In forging for himself the character of Lord Jim, Jim has successfully managed to unite what had previously been felt (by everyone except Stein) to be the incompatible demands of his fierce egoism and his social responsibilities. In 'following his dream' he remained at the level of consciousness that destroyed Mr Kurtz, but fortunately his dream was not incompatible with ordinary moral conventions, as was Kurtz's. Quite the opposite: Jim is 'one of us', his egoism is firmly grounded in accepted moral standards, his dreams of glory are not only not incompatible with the fulfilment of his moral duties, they absolutely demand it.

The everyday reality of 'hanging together' through our 'few simple notions', and the underlying reality of loneliness and absolute egoism, are often in conflict, so much so that the conflict itself should not be thought about. But Jim is fortunate in that the promptings of his 'own particular devil' are compatible with what society demands of him. He is thus able, at the end, to make a satisfactory, but not generalizable, synthesis between the entirely self-regarding demands of the naked ego and the entirely other-regarding demands of society. This is why Stein told Marlow that it might be 'very good' to be romantic; just as Part I of *Lord Jim* assesses the 'very bad' aspects of Jim's romanticism, so does Part II redress the balance (though less convincingly). Such an interpretation of the second half of *Lord Jim* helps us to account for what seems the paradoxical nature of Jim's feelings for the people of Patusan:

'he seemed to love the land and the people with a sort of fierce egoism, with a contemptuous tenderness.' (p. 248.) Jim's love and tenderness are, in the final analysis, self-regarding—but love and tenderness, even as expressions of one's essential selfishness, are not contemptible emotions.

6

Nostromo

Though longer than *Lord Jim* by only 150 pages, *Nostromo* (1904) seems on an altogether larger, almost an epic, scale; in the range of its concern for both public and private life, the events of the past and future as well as those of the present, *Nostromo* is unusual not only in Conrad's work, but perhaps in the whole of modern English literature. In it Conrad creates a land and its people, a panorama of personal history and social change, with a tangibility and profundity that makes the shadowy, idealized world of Patusan look a mere set of props at an amateur theatrical.

Nostromo is a difficult novel. Its shifts in time and point of view (though essential)[1] are not simple to unravel, though they introduce what is, after all, a problem solvable by sustained attention.[2] More perplexing, and perhaps less easily resolved, is the question of what attitude we are to take to the moral questions that the novel poses. The best way to see this is simply to ask: at the end of the novel, is the new Occidental Republic a better place in which to live than it had been in the past?[3] So complex a novel will not, of course, offer an unambiguous answer to this question, but in making a schematic contrast between two apparently contradictory answers which one might make, we may have a useful way to begin a discussion of *Nostromo*.[4]

We must begin by acknowledging that the San Tomé mine has brought a new security and affluence to the Occidental Republic. The epigraph from *The Tempest* ('so foul a sky clears not without a storm') seems to suggest—we know that Conrad chose his epigraphs with great care—that a certain progress has undoubtedly been made. It is hard to deny that the political condition in which Conrad leaves Costaguana compares favourably with that under Guzman Bento, who 'had ruled the country with the sombre imbecility of political fanaticism' (p. 137). Under Bento's reign, decent and innocent men like Don José Avellanos and Dr Monygham had been most foully tortured, hundreds of others put to death. Through the influence of the Gould Concession, which inevitably becomes a political as well as a material power, the benign Ribiera finally ascends to leadership, and, after he is deposed, the Occidental Republic shortly comes into being. At the close of the novel a reasonably tolerant government, under Don Juste Lopez, has come into power; its citizens enjoy more security, prosperity, and enlightened leadership than they could, only a generation before, have dreamed possible.

That Sulaco is prosperous there can be no doubt. The injection of foreign capital and industrial expansion has meant more jobs, and the miners at the San Tomé mine are provided with all necessary comforts and security. Surveying the events recorded in the novel, Captain Mitchell, the enthusiastic recorder of 'history', has much with which to be satisfied. Looking over the enormous plaza in the centre of Sulaco ('twice the area of Trafalgar Square') (p. 476), he points out to a visitor a famous local monument: 'Here . . . you see the bust of Don José Avellanos, "Patriot and Statesman", as the inscription says, "Minister to Courts of England and Spain, etc., etc., died in the woods of Los Hatos worn out with his lifelong struggle for Right and Justice at the dawn of the New Era." ' (p. 477.) It appears that the New Era has indeed arrived: with ever-increasing quantities of silver flowing from the San Tomé mine, it seems that Charles Gould's original premise has been justified: dedication to the national development of material interests must lead to a better way of life. In spite of the evidence that qualifies this optimistic reading of *Nostromo*, Robert Penn Warren feels that the novel is by no means a pessimistic one:

'There has been a civil war but the forces of "progress"—i.e. the San Tomé mine and the capitalistic order—have won. And we must admit that the society at the end of the book is preferable to that at the beginning.'

'History is a process fraught with risks, and the moral regeneration of society depends not upon shifts in mechanism but upon the moral regeneration of men. But nothing is to be hoped for, even in the most modest way, if men lose the vision of the time of concord, when "the light breaks on our black sky at last." '[5]

In direct contrast to Robert Penn Warren's conclusions about *Nostromo*, we have those of Albert Guerard, who calls the novel 'a pessimistic and sceptical meditation; and therefore a true one.'[6] His case—could we not predict its argument from observation of modern debate about 'underdeveloped countries'?—is that material interests have destroyed the fabric of a rich and thriving heritage, and substituted for it neither permanent stability nor a commitment to basic human values. It is Mrs Gould, with her ironic observation about the 'religion of silver and iron' (p. 71), who most poignantly senses the ways in which the quality of Costaguanan life is desecrated through the processes of material expansion. Although she originally shares her husband's belief that the San Tomé mine will become a positive, humane force in the development of Costaguana, she is nevertheless saddened by her vision of a future stripped of its native traditions. During the building of the railway that is to transform the character of life in the country she says:

> 'All this brings nearer the sort of future we desire for the country, which has waited for it in sorrow long enough, God knows. But I will confess that the other day, during my afternoon drive when I suddenly saw an Indian boy ride out of the wood with the red flag of a surveying party in his hand, I felt something of a shock. The future means change—and utter change. And yet even here there are simple and picturesque things that one would like to preserve.' (p. 120)

When she is presently answered by Charles, who remarks that no more popular feasts will be held on land owned by the Railway, we learn that 'Mrs Gould was rather sorry to think so' (p. 123). The understated tone of this simple thought gives it a resonance that lingers during the course of subsequent developments.

The destruction of a country's indigenous culture by expanding material interests may be a price worth paying, but *Nostromo* also suggests that the peace they bring is not a lasting one. After a scene in which the Goulds dream together of 'another victory gained in the conquest of peace for Sulaco' (p. 115), Conrad immediately reminds us that the reign of Guzman Bento 'had kept peace in the country for a whole fifteen years' (p. 115), and the hopes of the Goulds are put into an ironic perspective. By the close of the novel, there is the possibility that the mine will ultimately become a disruptive force in the land, exploiting the people as cruelly as had Guzman Bento. The profusion of secret societies and minor revolutionary groups that clutter the end of *Nostromo* suggest that the 'peace and prosperity' of Sulaco cannot abide. Even Antonia Avellanos and her uncle Father Corbellan are implicated in this discontent, with their plan to annex the rest of Costaguana to the Occidental Republic. Father Corbellan's dark words suggest that the industrialists of Sulaco may soon be overthrown: 'Let them beware, then, lest the people, prevented from their aspirations, should rise and claim their share of the wealth and their share of the power . . .' (p. 510.) The material interests which Charles Gould had felt to be the greatest asset of the land appear to have become, by the end of the novel, its greatest liability.

At the close, surrounded by all of the 'improvements' that have attended the material prosperity of Sulaco, Mrs Gould is aware only of the corrupting influence of the silver on the emotional and moral lives (including her own) of those people who have come into contact with it. When the dying Nostromo wishes to reveal to her the hiding-place of the lost silver, she demurs with the passionate words: 'Isn't it lost and done with? Isn't there enough treasure without it to make everybody in the world miserable?' (p. 557). A conversation between Mrs Gould and Dr Monygham may sound Conrad's final note; we have, first, Dr Monygham's appraisal of Charles Gould's hopes that material interests would lead to 'a finer justice':

> 'There is no peace and no rest in the development of material interests. They have their law, and their justice. But it is founded on expediency, and is inhuman; it is without rectitude, without the continuity and the force that can be found only in a moral principle. Mrs Gould, the time approaches when all that the Gould Concession stands for shall weigh as heavily upon the people as the barbarism, cruelty, and misrule of a few years back.' (p. 511)

This vision is extended in Mrs Gould's mind after Monygham leaves, and leads her inexorably to an insight into a future anonymous and dehumanized:

> 'It had come into her mind that for life to be large and full, it

must contain the care of the past and of the future in every passing moment of the present. Our daily work must be done to the glory of the dead, and for the good of those who come after . . .'

'There was something inherent in the necessities of successful action which carried with it the moral degradation of the idea. She saw the San Tomé mountain hanging over the Campo, over the whole land, feared, hated, wealthy; more soulless than any tyrant, more pitiless and autocratic than the worst Government; ready to crush innumerable lives in the expansion of its greatness . . .'

'With a prophetic vision she saw herself surviving alone the degradation of her young ideal of life, of love, of work—all alone in the Treasure House of the World. The profound, blind, suffering expression of a painful dream settled on her face with its closed eyes. In the indistinct voice of an unlucky sleeper, lying passive in the grip of a merciless nightmare, she stammered out aimlessly the words—"Material interest".' (pp. 520–2)

This seems not only the final vision of Mrs Gould, but also that of the narrator—for it is he who applies to it the adjective 'prophetic'.[7] Thus Guerard concludes that 'The horizon offered by the book itself seems to me, simply, Dr Monygham's dark one.'[8]

To have framed the problem in this way—which is worse: a soulless dictatorship or a soulless materialism?—is, of course, to see its obvious implication. However one reads it, *Nostromo* is a markedly pessimistic novel. Indeed, its shifts of time and place seem in themselves to disconfirm the simple view of 'progress' that Gould's liberal humanism entails. The novel's strikingly contemporary questions—what is the nature of wealth? What do we have to pay in order to gain it?—lead us only to a dispirited meditation of the apparent incommensurability of moral and material values. The undeniable benefits of materialism are not in themselves evil, but the processes which give rise to them are antipathetic to the supposed ideals on which they are based. The miners at the Campo gain a secure way of life at the expense of a vital one; are they richer, the novel asks, herded into 'villages primero—segundo—or tercero' (p. 100), dressed and housed identically, than they were as illiterate and impoverished peasants who were, nevertheless, part of a thriving, intensely human tradition? The question must be faced squarely, no attenuation of the process is imaginatively feasible: the villages are called by the only names that they genuinely generate, the clothes must be identical in order to lower cost and speed production. Where the making of money is the goal, the making of money is also the means, and the human consequences of the process enact the instrumental view of labour that capitalism entails. Is it worth it?

Having insisted on the question, Conrad characteristically gives no equally unequivocal answer. Instead, he uses that question as a way of placing his characters, as if each might be defined in terms of a notional spectrum ranging from the committed materialism of Holroyd to the sceptical rejection of it voiced by Mrs Gould late in the novel. Yet the goals of both those characters who believe that material interests have improved the way of life in Costaguana, and those who think that they have been destructive and dehumanizing, were (with few exceptions) originally the same. This is powerfully evident in an early scene between the Goulds. Charles has decided to take up the Gould Concession, despite the frantic and incessant pleas of his father that he avoid the mine at any cost. Spurred by the optimism and buoyancy of a youth spent wholly isolated from the sordid intrigues and maddening arbitrariness of Costaguanan politics, he is determined to take up the mine, and to make it work. He tells Emilia:

' "What is wanted here is law, good faith, order, security. Any one can declaim about these things, but I pin my faith to material interests. Only let the material interests once get a firm footing, and they are bound to impose the conditions on which alone they can continue to exist. That's how your money-making is justified here in the face of lawlessness and disorder. It is justified because the security which it demands must be shared with an oppressed people. A better justice will come afterwards. That's your ray of hope." His arm pressed her slight form closer to his side for a moment. "And who knows whether in that sense even the San Tomé mine may not become that little rift in the darkness which poor father despaired of ever seeing?"

She glanced up at him with admiration. He was competent; he had given a vast shape to the vagueness of her unselfish ambitions.

"Charley," she said, "you are splendidly disobedient." ' (p. 84)

113

The Goulds seem to want the same things. Ironically it is out of the consequences of a common desire for decency, justice, and security, that the future moral dissolution of their marriage is to arise.

By the end of *Nostromo* we may doubt whether 'decency', 'justice', and 'security' even mean the same things to Charles and Emilia Gould. In Costaguana—as in any state—the language of moral discrimination is shamelessly assimilated to the exigencies of political doctrine. The Goulds' parrot, with its nonsensical shrieks of 'Viva Costaguana', is implicitly an analogue to the multitude of screaming revolutionaries and loquacious politicians, with their talk of 'patriotism'. As Decoud says, the word 'patriotism' in Costaguana 'was hopelessly besmirched; it had been the cry of dark barbarism, the cloak of lawlessness, of crimes, of rapacity, of simple thieving' (p. 187). Costaguanan politics are an absurd compendium of 'pronunciamentos', declamations, and slogans: what Decoud calls 'deadly futilities' (p. 183). This point is neatly particularized when Conrad gives us the scene in which Ribiera, riding on a dying mule and besieged by a bloodthirsty crowd, is saved by Nostromo, *before* we are given the scene (which actually takes place eighteen months earlier) in which he becomes the new Chief of State; when we hear him 'pronouncing, glass in hand, his simple watchwords of honesty, peace, respect for law, political good faith abroad and at home' (p. 119), we know that the 'peace' of which he is speaking will not last.

Charles Gould, too, learns that the 'few simple notions' which had seemed to flow so easily from his premise about the expansion of material interests, are less easily derived in their Costaguanan context than the syllogism of materialism had suggested. During the course of the revolution that is ultimately to lead to the creation of the new Occidental Republic, Gould turns to Dr Monygham with the bitter remark: 'The words one knows so well have a nightmarish meaning in this country. Liberty, democracy, patriotism, government—all of them have a flavour of folly and murder.' (p. 408.) Does the novel give us reason to suppose that the process is different in other countries? Gould's incapacity to ask this question—to ask it and to answer it are the same—marks his limitations, and places him in a merely local enactment of an international tragedy.

Two views of life collide in *Nostromo*; the first sees history as the direct outcome of the ideals and actions of human beings—and thus makes it incumbent on individuals to work together towards a common good; the second sees history in predetermined patterns based either on certain socio-economic factors or on the inevitable folly, stupidity, and greed of mankind. From this collision we derive the moral typology characteristic of *Nostromo*: its tendency to create characters who are either believers or sceptics. In the dialectic between belief and scepticism—enacted in believers and sceptics—lies the basis of the prevalent tensions of *Nostromo*. To understand the novel is to understand its people and what they wish, and why they are disappointed.

Captain Mitchell would have us believe that the triumphant rise of Sulaco is a testimonial to the ideals of those who have created it. As he says (to one of the anonymous listeners with whom he is conveniently provided) on the occasion of Ribiera's famous mule ride over the mountains: 'It was history—history, sir! And that fellow of mine, Nostromo, you know, was right in it. Absolutely making history, sir.' (p. 130.) There is, trivially, truth enough in this—but only Captain Mitchell would put it so. In itself this is enough to make us uneasy. For character may enact, rather than make, history, as if men were unwitting agents compelled to realize a script complete in outline, lacking only the local detail. *Nostromo* begins with a stark anecdote which is a metaphoric analogue to the action that is to follow. A hoard of silver is reputed to have been lost on the peninsula of Azuera, 'a wild chaos of sharp rocks and stony levels cut about by vertical ravines' (p. 4). At some time in the past, two gringos and a poor peasant, with a donkey and some provisions, had set out to find the treasure, upon which a curse was popularly believed to hang. None were ever seen again. No doubt, we are told, the mozo and his donkey were mercifully allowed to die,

'. . . but the two gringos, spectral and alive, are believed to be dwelling to this day amongst the rocks, under the fatal spell of their success. Their souls cannot tear themselves away from their bodies mounting guard over the discovered treasure. They are now rich and hungry and thirsty—a strange theory of tenacious

gringo ghosts suffering in their starved and parched flesh of
defiant heretics, where a Christian would have renounced and
been released.' (p. 5)

Thus we are warned from the start that the desire for material
wealth is a lure leading to physical or spiritual death. It comes,
then, with the shock of fulfilled prophecy, when we find Martin
Decoud literally 'mounting guard' over the silver, and finally
using it as the ballast that will carry him down forever into the
depths of the sea. It comes with less of a shock—we expect it
by now—when we find both Nostromo and Charles Gould
enslaved by the silver, until the one is literally, the other
spiritually, destroyed by his fidelity to the treasure.

But this is only one of the two 'curses' that hang over, and
inexorably direct, the events of the novel. The second (which
is a particularization of the Azuera curse) lies upon the Gould
Concession itself. In his plea to his son to renounce his rights to
the San Tomé mine, Charles Gould's father can hardly put his
case too strongly: 'He groaned over the injustice, the persecu-
tion, the outrage of that mine; he occupied whole pages in the
exposition of the fatal consequences attaching to the possession
of that mine from every point of view, with every dismal inference, with words of horror at the apparently eternal character
of that curse.' (p. 57.) The neurotic tone of the letter, its
paranoid insistence on the mine as curse, gives Charles an easy
way to avoid its essential truthfulness. But if Mr Gould is a
disillusioned man, the mine has made him so. The curse is
stronger than the men who enact its fatal necessity; Charles
Gould rushes hopefully into the future, believing that the deeds
of men can redirect the aberrations of history. To him it is only
the feasibility of reopening the mine that is to be considered; as
to the wisdom of material expansion he has no doubt. From the
time that Gould re-establishes the San Tomé mine, certain
incontrovertible processes are at work—or, rather, it is these
processes that lead Gould to take up the mine in the first place.
Even a determined future needs men to act out its patterns—
patterns of which they must be largely unaware.[9]

The major 'character' of *Nostromo*, then, is not a man, but a
force; in his relation to the San Tomé mine, and to the theory
of material interests which it represents, each character defines

himself. The silver, like a moral touchstone, tests each character, defines his beliefs, insidiously searches out his illusions, reveals his qualities. When Captain Mitchell shows a visitor around Sulaco he introduces the inhabitants in terms of their relationship to the Goulds—that is, in effect, to the mine. Charles Gould is popularly known as the King of Sulaco: all of the people are thus his subjects—all are equally subjects of the mine. As Conrad was to make explicit in a letter several years before his death, it is the material interests that are at the centre of the action:

> 'I will take the liberty to point out that Nostromo has never been intended for the hero of the Tale of the Seaboard. Silver is the pivot of the moral and material events, affecting the lives of everybody in the tale. That this was my deliberate purpose there can be no doubt. I struck the first note of my intention in the unusual form which I gave to the title of the First Part, by calling it "The Silver of the Mine", and by telling the story of the enchanted treasure on Azuera, which, strictly speaking, has nothing to do with the rest of the novel.'[10]

Nostromo is a study of the way in which men view their own activity. The key term 'idealize' appears frequently in the novel, but seems somewhat loose in its applications. When it is applied to Charles Gould, it is critical; when used with reference to Dr Monygham, it is complimentary. The distinction *may* be between behaviour that is 'idealized' (distorted, out of touch with reality) and behaviour that is 'idealistic' (morally grounded in the real), but Conrad is not terminologically rigorous. (We have observed an analogous difficulty in distinguishing between principles and beliefs in 'Heart of Darkness'.) In *Nostromo*, each character's 'idealization' expresses his relationship to the dominant theme of the novel, the expansion of material interests. On the notional spectrum that has been suggested, *Nostromo*'s personae seem to fall into three distinct groups. The first of these—Holroyd, the Goulds, Don José Avellanos and his daughter Antonia, and Giorgio Viola—might be called believers, and altruists: they have confidence in the capacity of the individual to direct the future through a combination of moral principle and hard work; the second group—Nostromo, Monygham, and Decoud—are not so much unprincipled as de-principled, and are explicitly described as sceptics. As a type, the sceptic acts not out of generalized moral principle, but particular passionate impulse. To the believer, the sceptic is simply an egoist; to the sceptic, the believer is simply self-deceived.

Lying outside the two major groups are the unselfconscious and brave men, who do not idealize their behaviour, but act from a simple and unimpeachable sense of duty. They are the incarnation of Singleton (significantly, all are bachelors), and they continue to elicit Conrad's admiration. Included in the group are Don Pepé, Father Roman and Father Corbellan, Barrios, Hernandez, and Captain Mitchell. The criterion by which they are admired is once stated by Mrs Gould (as she defends her friend Don José Avellanos from Charles Gould's implied comparison of him with Holroyd): 'How can you compare them, Charles? ... He has suffered—and yet he hopes.' (p. 83.) These are the old campaigners (who have some set ethical code to which they can pay allegiance), many of them bearing the wound which, to Conrad, was a symbol of tested courage.

But Conrad had progressed significantly in artistic and intellectual understanding from the time when he romanticized the figure of Singleton; in any case, *Nostromo* takes place on the seaboard, not at sea. The simple and brave man may still have had Conrad's approval, but could no longer stand at the moral centre of his work. He was now capable of ironically assessing the limitations of the type; to take Don Pepé, for example: 'There was in that man a sort of sane, humorous shrewdness, and a vein of genuine humanity so often found in simple old soldiers of proved courage who have seen much desperate service.' (p. 99.) But the 'desperate service' chronicled in *Nostromo* is more ugly (Decoud calls it 'farcical') than inspiring. Don Pepé's faithful character may be counted upon to blow up the San Tomé mine if Gould were to be taken prisoner or killed: an instance of fidelity itself of dubious value. The enterprise to which many of these simple men—Don Pepé, Barrios, Hernandez, and Mitchell—devote themselves is not without its sordid and life-destroying aspects. Simple fidelity cannot of itself be accounted a virtue.

It is Captain Mitchell who most clearly embodies Conrad's recognition of the limitations of the simple, brave man. He is almost a parody of Singleton; he has the same seaman-like stoicism, but is equally ill-equipped to cope with the subtleties of life on land: 'The old sailor, with all his small weaknesses and absurdities, was constitutionally incapable of entertaining . . . a fear of his personal safety. It was not so much firmness of soul as the lack of a certain kind of imagination . . .' (p. 338.) His undeniable bravery when faced with the maddened Sotillo is undercut when we recognize that his purpose lies in regaining his confiscated watch. Singleton appeared a 'disgusting old brute' when he went ashore; Mitchell, while no brute, is equally incapable of dealing with the complexities and ambiguities of a life in which the code of the merchant service plays all too little a part.

Let us turn, then, to the first major group of characters, whom I have loosely termed believers or altruists, who attempt self-consciously to define, and to use as an ideal, what Don Pepé, Barrios, Hernandez, et al. do by instinct.

The prime mover of the action in Costaguana is the financier Holroyd, without whose capital Charles Gould could not have reconstituted the San Tomé mine. Holroyd is a self-made millionaire whose values are a parody of the American theory of manifest destiny. His sincere statement of this doctrine is both amusing and frightening:

> 'Time itself has got to wait on the greatest country in the whole of God's Universe. We shall be giving the word for everything: industry, trade, law, journalism, art, politics, and religion, from Cape Horn clear over to Smith's Sound, and beyond, too, if anything worth taking hold of turns up at the North Pole. And then we shall have the leisure to take in hand the outlying islands and continents of the earth. We shall run the world's business whether the world likes it or not.' (p. 77)

The progress of history is thus to be directed from a base in the United States, with a future marked 'paid', and an account rendered in dollars. Holroyd's interest in Costaguana is not originally a business venture (though it becomes an outstanding financial success), but a whim, a hobby, 'a great man's caprice' (p. 80). History is, Holroyd claims, determined by men: by himself, and by his 'man in Costaguana', Charles Gould: 'He was not running a great enterprise there; no mere railway board or industrial corporation. He was running a man!' (p. 81.)

Though controlled from abroad, Charles Gould, too, has an ideal of progress based on the expansion of material interests. There can be no doubt that he is an earnest and a good man, genuinely dedicated to his ideals of justice, security, and a better way of life for all. Gould soon learns, however, that his idealism must be tempered by the realities of political compromise; for the San Tomé mine to operate he must be willing to intrigue, to bribe, to acquiesce silently in various abuses. And it is not long before he begins to wonder whether he has not underestimated the difficulty of his undertaking:

'The Gould Concession had to fight for life with such weapons as could be found at once in the mire of corruption that was so universal as to almost lose its significance. He was prepared to stoop for his weapons. For a moment he felt as if the silver mine, which had killed his father, had decoyed him further than he meant to go; and with the roundabout logic of emotions, he felt that the worthiness of his life was bound up with success. There was no going back.' (p. 85)

The phrase 'bound up with success' demands to be visualized, and brings back to mind the figures of the two ghost-like gringos, 'under the fatal spell of their success'. Gould began his redevelopment of the mine as a moral venture ('its working must be made a serious and moral success') (p. 66), but during the course of the revolution, it seems to him as if it has brought no greater security to the land, no finer justice, no solution to what he now feels to be an unanswerable problem:

'The cruel futility of things stood unveiled in the levity and sufferings of that incorrigible people; the cruel futility of lives and of deaths thrown away in the vain endeavour to attain an enduring solution of the problem. Unlike Decoud, Charles Gould could not play lightly a part in a tragic farce. It was tragic enough for him in all conscience, but he could see no farcical element. He suffered too much under a conviction of irremediable folly. He was too severely practical and too idealistic to look upon its terrible humours with amusement, as Martin Decoud, the imaginative materialist, was able to do in the dry light of his scepticism. To him, as to all of us, the compromises with his conscience appeared uglier than ever in the light of failure. His taciturnity, assumed with a purpose, had prevented him from tampering openly with his thoughts; but the Gould Concession had insidiously corrupted his judgment . . . He had gone forth into the senseless fray as his poor uncle, whose sword hung on the wall of his study, had gone forth—in the defence of the commonest decencies of organised society. Only his weapon was the wealth of the mine, more far-reaching and subtle than an honest blade of steel fitted into a simple brass guard.

More dangerous to the wielder, too, this weapon of wealth, double-edged with the cupidity and misery of mankind, steeped in all the vices of self-indulgence as in a concoction of poisonous roots, tainting the very cause for which it is drawn, always ready to turn awkwardly in the hand. There was nothing for it now but to go on using it. But he promised himself to see it shattered into small bits before he let it be wrenched from his grasp.' (pp. 364–5)

Charles Gould's judgment has been 'corrupted' by his inability to recognize the incompatibility of financial and moral success; as Mrs Gould is bitterly to reflect late in the novel, 'There was something inherent in the necessities of successful action which carried with it the moral degradation of the idea' (p. 521). Gould's sensible assumption that he could use wealth 'as a means, not as an end' (p. 75) is, by the end of *Nostromo*, open to substantial doubt; finally, we may be more inclined to believe that the wealth has used Charles as its means.

Mrs Gould only slowly comes to recognize the subtle transformation in her husband's nature, since she, too, began with the assumption that material and moral success were not only compatible, but necessarily related. Her abandonment of this premise is partly in response to the sceptical probing of Martin Decoud, who asks (with regard to her husband): 'Mrs Gould, are you aware to what point he has idealized the existence, the worth, the meaning of the San Tomé mine? Are you aware of it?' (p. 214.) In response to the quiet moan with which the question is answered, Decoud continues with an analysis of Gould's character: '. . . he cannot act or exist without idealizing every simple feeling, desire, or achievement. He could not believe his own motives if he did not make them first a part of some fairy tale.' (pp. 214–5.) This is acute, but harsh; Gould's motives are genuine and generous, what he lacks is not exactly self-knowledge, but a certain kind of vision—not width (he has that), but clarity. He seems incapable of seeing the transformation of his moral commitments, as they become increasingly abstract, unreal, inhuman.

It later becomes clear that Decoud includes Mrs Gould too, under his heading of sentimentalists 'who will never do anything for the sake of their passionate desire, unless it comes to them clothed in the fair robes of an idea' (p. 239). At this point in the novel he is right, for Mrs Gould is just beginning to share his indictment of Charles's obsession with his mine.[11] We have only to compare two passages in order to see the similarity between Decoud's scepticism and Mrs Gould's frustrated idealism. Decoud says of Gould's attachment to the mine:

> 'Don Carlos Gould will have enough to do to save his mine, with its organisation and its people; this "Imperium in Imperio", this wealth-producing thing, to which his sentimentalism attaches a strange idea of justice. He holds to it as some men hold to the idea of love or revenge.' (pp. 244–5)

This sentiment is echoed later in the novel in the musings of Mrs Gould (though the tone may be that of the omniscient narrator; probably the two are so close as to be indistinguishable at this point):

> 'Charles Gould's fits of abstraction depicted the energetic concentration of a will haunted by a fixed idea. A man haunted by a fixed idea is insane. He is dangerous even if that idea is an idea of justice; for may he not bring the heaven down pitilessly upon a loved head?' (p. 379)

I have said that Charles and Emilia Gould began by wishing the same things, sharing the same values. The difference that emerges between them is one that is essential to the logic of *Nostromo*: whereas Gould allows his dedication to the mine to become an abstract adherence to the principles that the mine represents ('The Gould Concession was symbolic of abstract justice') (p. 402), Mrs Gould does not divorce her values from the reality that they are intended to influence. When she comes to feel that no amount of treasure will ever change men's lives for the better, indeed to believe that quite the opposite has happened, she gives up her devotion to the mine, rather than her devotion to the people. Recognizing the apparent incompatibility of material and moral values, she finally stands quite firmly for the latter. This paradoxically, and tragically, involves losing the man whom she most deeply loves, for Charles Gould is irredeemably committed to the pursuit of 'abstract justice'—which, as Mrs Gould knows from her own experience, may all too easily come down 'pitilessly upon a loved head':

'The fate of the San Tomé mine was lying heavily upon her heart. It was a long time now since she had begun to fear it. It had been an idea. She had watched it with misgivings turning into a fetish, and now the fetish had grown into a monstrous and crushing weight. It was as if the inspiration of their early years had left her heart to turn into a wall of silver-bricks, erected by the silent work of evil spirits, between her and her husband.' (pp. 221-2)

To abandon belief in progress through 'material interests', is not to give up value—quite the opposite. But decency, justice, and compassion must be informed and permeated by the spirit of love, not simply principles following logically from a material process. Her 'young ideal of life, of love, of work' (p. 522) is an emotionally grounded idealism. It is Mrs Gould to whom many of the characters of the novel—Dr Monygham, Decoud, Don José and Antonia, Giorgio Viola and his family—turn for comfort and warmth. It is she who preserves a genuine ideal of service in her hospital and charitable work. She is the only example of an idealist in *Nostromo* who recognizes the transformation of value into principle, yet is still able to reassert the impulse upon which those values were formed. Charles Gould cannot do so much: 'He seemed to dwell alone within a circumvallation of precious metal, leaving her outside with her school, her hospital, the sick mothers and the feeble old men, mere insignificant vestiges of the initial inspiration.' (p. 222.) The irony is that the rich moral reality of Mrs Gould cannot influence to any great degree the progress of Costaguanan history.[12]

Conrad's view of politics, of course, is no less sceptical than his view of materialism, because government is seen as in essence a reflection of 'material interests'. The underlying principle of politics in Costaguana, like that of materialism in general, is one of expediency. During the course of the revolution, as the Sulaco parliament prepares to capitulate to the Monteros, we find Don Juste Lopez (who significantly becomes the Chief of State of the Occidental Republic) nonsensically arguing for the 'clemency and justice, and honesty, and purity' (p. 237) of the Montero brothers. Lopez bases his faith on 'parliamentary institutions':

> 'Three silent groups of civilians in severe black waited in the main gallery, formal and helpless, a little huddled up ... These were the deputations waiting for their audience. The one from the Provincial Assembly, more restless and uneasy in its corporate expression, was overtopped by the big face of Don Juste Lopez, soft and white, with prominent eyelids and wreathed in impenetrable solemnity as if in a dense cloud. The President of the Provincial Assembly, coming bravely to save the last shred of parliamentary institutions (on the English model), averted his eyes from the Administrator of the San Tomé mine as a dignified rebuke of his little faith in that only saving principle.' (p. 406)

That Lopez's 'only saving principle' is no more saving than that of Gould is implicit in the image of his face 'wreathed in impenetrable solemnity as if in a dense cloud'.

In contrast to the unsympathetic Don Juste Lopez, we have the figure of Giorgio Viola.[13] The old man has preserved his allegiance to the ideals for which he has fought and suffered, but with his faded lithograph of Garibaldi he subtly comes to symbolize the impotence and delusion of belief in revolutionary activity as a liberating force:

> 'The spirit of self-forgetfulness, the simple devotion to a vast humanitarian idea which inspired the thought and stress of that revolutionary time, had left its mark upon Giorgio in a sort of austere contempt for all personal advantage ...
>
> This stern devotion to a cause had cast a gloom upon Giorgio's old age. It cast a gloom because the cause seemed lost. Too many kings and emperors flourished yet in the world which God had meant for the people. He was sad because of his simplicity.' (pp. 31–2)

There is a direct suggestion here that altruism (the 'spirit of self-forgetfulness'), with its dedication to 'a vast humanitarian idea' is in itself incapable of producing change. The 'vast humanitarian idea' remains unspecified, as if to suggest that *any* such idea may represent a lost cause. Not only is Giorgio, the 'Idealist of the old, humanitarian revolutions' (p. xix), portrayed with an insistence on his poignant isolation, but his standards are subjected to the same ironic scrutiny as are those of the other idealists of the novel. Conrad's first description of him is paradoxical; it begins: 'The old man, full of scorn for the populace, as your austere republican so often is . . .' (p. 16), and suggests that the old Garibaldino, too, has allowed his values to become fetishes—that he, too, cares more for his principles than for 'the people' of whom he so often speaks.

Don José Avellanos, like Giorgio Viola, has fought, suffered, and maintained his faith. He has an abiding commitment to a political structure which reinforces, rather than corrupts, the basic human values. Unlike Don Juste Lopez, he would not consider capitulating silently (or vocally) to the Monteros. His belief is not in any given political creed or institution, but in a political code permeated by an awareness of the values on which it is based, and of the lives it is designed to serve: 'The old idea of Federalism had disappeared. For his part he did not wish to revive old political doctrines. They were perishable. They died. But the doctrine of political rectitude was immortal.' (pp. 136–7.) But Don José Avellanos, too, is an old man, ill-equipped to deal with the exigencies and complexities of a modern political state. Like Singleton, he is an anachronism, a remnant of days in which man was uncorrupted by self-conscious ideals based on material considerations. The only action in which Don José consistently engages is in the taking of tea with Mrs Gould. During the course of the revolution, he breaks down completely, and is ironically entrusted to Hernandez, who takes him away on a stretcher. He does not live out the day. He is last seen by Charles Gould 'stretched out, hardly breathing, by the side of the erect Antonia, vanquished in a lifelong struggle with the powers of moral darkness, whose stagnant depths breed monstrous crimes and monstrous illusions' (p. 362). To battle with that darkness is to be defeated by it; like the 'destructive element' of *Lord Jim*, the blackness of *Nostromo* cannot be overcome, only accommodated.

Don José Avellanos's daughter, Antonia, seems yet another figure in the long line of Conrad's unconvincing romantic heroines, though she gains in vitality after the death of her father. She has inherited his patriotism, and adapted all too admirably to the prevalent Costaguanan belief in violent social change:

> 'How can we abandon, groaning under oppression, those who have been our countrymen only a few years ago, who *are* our countrymen now? . . . How can we remain blind, and deaf without pity to the cruel wrongs suffered by our brothers? There is a remedy.' (p. 509)

With her uncle, Father (now Cardinal) Corbellan, Antonia has plans to form a coalition with various secret societies based in Santa Marta, in order (as Dr Monygham sarcastically interjects) to 'Annex the rest of Costaguana to the order and prosperity of Sulaco' (p. 509). The irony is lost upon Antonia, who is incapable of grasping the ways in which Sulaco's material prosperity has adversely affected both the traditions of the people, and the lives of many of the major characters. She is quite ready to start yet another revolution (have we any doubt that it will fail?) in the vain hope that a lasting 'peace' will finally be realized. That this hope is illusory is suggested by her reply to Dr Monygham's sardonic reference to annexing all of Costaguana to the new Occidental Republic: 'I am convinced, señor doctor, . . . that this was from the first poor Martin's intention.' (p. 509.) Like Kurtz's Intended, Antonia Avellanos maintains her fidelity to a lie; but in her case, it is a dangerous faith, from which Dr Monygham disassociates himself with the single word, 'Incorrigible!' (p. 510.)

Antonia Avellanos, like all the altruistic characters of *Nostromo* (with the exception of Mrs Gould), is entangled in a paradoxical confusion of idealism and illusion. All transform their belief in social progress and a better life for 'the people' into abstract principles. Ultimately, their idealized values— whether they be of 'material interests', 'vast humanitarian ideas', 'parliamentary institutions', or patriotic 'annexations'— become divorced from the real world of suffering and deprivation which they are designed to affect. None of these characters grasps the dehumanizing effects of their idealizations; none, that is, except Mrs Gould, who is able—partly prompted by

the sceptical probings of Decoud and Dr Monygham—to reassert her human values at the expense of her 'fixed idea'.

Passing, then, from that group of characters who dedicate
their lives to some notion of social progress, and who see their
obligations in terms of their duties to society, we come to those
'sceptics' who would deny that history is a reflection of man's
ideals, but see it rather as a function of universal egoism, folly,
and illusion. All three of these characters—Nostromo, Dr
Monygham, and Martin Decoud—act not because of their
ideals, but out of what Decoud calls their 'passionate desire'.

Nostromo is certainly the least interesting and least successfully portrayed of the three. A successful, if vulgar, version of
Jim, the 'incorruptible Capataz de Cargadores' is the most
primitive form of sceptic, caring for nothing but his own
reputation. His name indicates his public personality, and
defines the nature of his aspirations. He is an indispensable
political asset, eager to be thought a hero not out of belief in
the values he supports but in order to maintain and reinforce
an idealized self-image. In the words of Martin Decoud: 'Here
was a man . . . that seemed as though he would have preferred
to die rather than deface the perfect form of his egoism. Such a
man was safe.' (p. 301.) But Nostromo's 'perfect egoism' can
remain intact only insofar as he remains indispensable. After
the lighter (in which Nostromo and Decoud are attempting to
escape) is rammed by Sotillo's ship, Nostromo recognizes that
he has been asked to take absurd risks (he manages to save the
silver, but the lighter is sunk) in an enterprise in which he is
not even superficially interested. After a long and death-like
sleep, he reawakens with a clear knowledge of the way in which
his egoism has been abused, his vanity played upon:

'The confused and intimate impressions of universal dissolution
which beset a subjective nature at any strong check to its ruling
passion had a bitterness approaching that of death itself . . . He
was as if sobered after a long bout of intoxication. His fidelity
had been taken advantage of . . . The Capataz de Cargadores,
on a revulsion of subjectiveness, exasperated almost to insanity,
beheld his all world without faith and courage. He had been
betrayed!' (pp. 417–18)

Nostromo has, of course, recognized nothing less than the truth

—that he has been exploited by people much more interested in preserving silver than in preserving him. He does not renounce his quest for reputation, but he is now self-consciously acting towards his own ends: his 'perfect egoism' is destroyed— he is corruptible.

When Nostromo returns to the Great Isabel island and finds that Decoud is certainly (though mysteriously) dead, he recognizes that the treasure is now entirely at his disposal. Having withdrawn his trust in those people who have exploited him, he decides to keep the secret of the silver to himself, and to grow rich slowly. After the formation of the Occidental Republic has occurred—largely through his famous ride to Cayta to bring back Barrios and his troops—Nostromo takes on the name Captain Fidanza (the irony could hardly be more obvious),[14] gets rich slowly, and begins reluctantly to court Linda Viola. After some time, he finds himself in love with the younger Viola sister, Giselle, but cannot free himself sufficiently from his treasure to run away with her. Like the legendary gringos, Nostromo is enslaved by his silver:

'There is something in a treasure that fastens upon a man's mind. He will pray and blaspheme and still persevere, and will curse the day he ever heard of it, and will let his last hour come upon him unawares, still believing that he missed it only by a foot. He will see it every time he closes his eyes . . . There is no getting away from a treasure that once fastens upon your mind.' (p. 460)

In a melodramatic, and much criticized, final scene, Nostromo, while making a surreptitious visit to the silver, is mistakenly shot and killed by Giorgio Viola.

Dr Monygham stands in direct opposition to Nostromo; while Nostromo has idealized his success, Dr Monygham has idealized his failure. Like Jim, he has failed to live up to his commitment to the human community (when tortured by Father Béron, one of Guzman Bento's henchmen, he betrayed a group of friends), and later sought and found redemption. But there is a crucial difference: Jim does not accept the weakness exposed by his betrayal; Dr Monygham bases his future conduct on a severe judgment upon his own guilt. Like Martin Decoud, Dr Monygham has no illusions about himself; in answer to the engineer-in-chief's assertion that life is meaningful only through 'the spiritual value which everyone discovers in his own form of activity', he says:

> 'Self-flattery. Food for that vanity which makes the world go round . . . I put no spiritual value into my desires, or my opinions, or my actions. They have not enough vastness to give me room for self-flattery.' (p. 318)

His values are framed neither in terms of some overriding ideal of social organization, nor any liberal idea of progress:

> 'Dr Monygham had made himself an ideal conception of his disgrace . . . A rule of conduct resting mainly on severe rejections is necessarily simple. Dr Monygham's view of what it behoved him to do was severe; it was an ideal view, in so much that it was the imaginative exaggeration of a correct feeling. It was also, in its force, influence, and persistency, the view of an eminently loyal nature.' (pp. 375–6)

Dr Monygham's 'ideal view' is markedly different from that of Charles Gould. Even granting that Decoud is lacking in range of understanding when he says that Gould 'cannot act or exist without idealizing every simple feeling, desire, or achievement' (pp. 214–5), it is clear that to idealize here means to distort, to make illusory. Dr Monygham's 'ideal view' is seen a essentially healthy, but like the idealization of Charles Gould, Monygham's is potentially dangerous, for it contains an 'exaggeration' of a feeling, however 'correct'. When his capacity for loyalty is directed entirely towards Mrs Gould, his fidelity is little more praiseworthy than that of Don Pepé:

> 'The doctor was loyal to the mine. It presented itself to his fifty-years' old eyes in the shape of a little woman in a soft dress with a long train, with a head attractively over-weighted by a great mass of fair hair and the delicate preciousness of her inner worth, partaking of a gem and a flower, revealed in every attitude of her person. As the dangers thickened round the San Tomé mine this illusion acquired force, permanency, and authority. It claimed him at last! This claim, exalted by a spiritual detachment from the usual sanctions of hope and reward, made Dr Monygham's thinking, acting, individuality extremely dangerous to himself and to others, all his scruples vanishing in the proud feeling that his devotion was the only thing that stood between an admirable woman and a frightful disaster.' (p. 431)

In the paragraph immediately following this description, we find Dr Monygham 'utterly indifferent to Decoud's fate', because of the obsessive nature of his loyalty to Mrs Gould. When he confronts Nostromo, who has just returned after the sinking of the lighter, he does 'not think of him humanely, as of a fellow-creature just escaped from the jaws of death' (p. 431), but as a tool to use in his scheme to save Mrs Gould.

Although Dr Monygham's 'misanthropic mistrust of mankind ... did not lift him sufficiently above common weakness' (p. 432), he is nevertheless consistently sympathetic and engaging. His voice, even when strident or bitter, has a resonance at once striking and admirable. Although he has become 'dangerous' through his fanatical devotion to Mrs Gould, Monygham has realistically appraised and accepted the weakness of his own nature, and been able to act accordingly. His heroic defiance of Sotillo is instrumental in allowing enough time for Barrios to return with his troops from Cayta; in this single act he finds a moral redemption. Conrad's final view of him is markedly sympathetic:

> 'People believed him scornful and soured. The truth of his nature consisted in his capacity for passion and in the sensitiveness of his temperament. What he lacked was the polished callousness of men of the world, the callousness from which springs an easy tolerance of one's self and others; the tolerance wide as poles asunder from true sympathy and human compassion. This want of callousness accounted for his sardonic turn of mind and his biting speeches.' (p. 520)

There is an implied comparison here between the 'capacity for passion' of Dr Monygham and the 'polished callousness' of Martin Decoud.

Yet what is at first remarkable about Decoud is his undoubted similarity to Monygham. Both are severely sceptical about human nature, scathing in their indictments of materialism, and firmly committed to intellectual clarity; further, both men, accepting that they act out of self-interest, are drawn into heroic roles in the action through idealized love for a woman. Yet while Monygham obviously elicits Conrad's approval, Decoud is most severely repudiated—or *seems* to be. The reasons for this apparent contradiction are crucial to an understanding of *Nostromo*.

The themes of the novel with which I have so far dealt—the ways in which men idealize and distort their own activity, the dangers of behaviour based on an 'exaggerated' feeling, the inadequacies of action based on an idealistic notion of social responsibility—come to a head in the character of Martin Decoud. Decoud is the most sceptical character in his assessment of the value of any form of action, and yet the most influential figure in the creation of the Occidental Republic; he is both the most detached and the most involved, both the most engaging and the most consistently disparaged, of the characters. In the paradoxes of his portrayal are embodied the major thematic conflicts of the novel.

A native Costaguanan who has settled in Paris, Decoud has come home (he is in love with Antonia Avellanos) at the outbreak of the revolution. He enters as if his sole purpose in the novel were to irritate the narrator:

'As a matter of fact, he was an idle boulevardier, in touch with some smart journalists, made free of a few newspaper offices, and welcomed in the pleasure haunts of pressmen. This life, whose dreary superficiality is covered by the glitter of universal blague, like the stupid clowning of a harlequin by the spangles of a motley costume, induced in him a Frenchified—but most un-French—cosmopolitanism, in reality a mere barren indifferentism posing as intellectual superiority . . . he was in danger of remaining a sort of nondescript dilettante all his life. He had pushed the habit of universal raillery to a point where it blinded him to the genuine impulses of his own nature.' (pp. 152–3)

Decoud has returned from Paris after arranging for a shipment of modern rifles to be sent to Costaguana, to aid in the revolution.[15] Drawn into the fray solely through his love for the patriotic Antonia, Decoud continually argues that he is himself no patriot, though in a private conversation with Mrs Gould he says 'On my word of honour, Mrs Gould, I believe I am a true *hijo del pays*, a true son of the country, whatever Father Corbellan may say' (p. 213). He becomes editor of the Ribierist paper, the *Porvenir*,[16] and subsequently has to flee for his life after Ribiera is deposed. As the outrageous Pedrito Montero swoops down upon Sulaco, Decoud (who had called Montero 'Gran Bestia' in his newspaper) arranges an escape on the silver lighter with Nostromo. Following the brilliantly conceived scene in which the lighter is rammed, Decoud is left in charge of the silver on the Great Isabel, while Nostromo returns to Sulaco to participate in the fighting in which the new Occidental Republic (an idea entirely Decoud's own) comes into existence. As the days pass and Decoud sits silently awaiting Nostromo's return, his personality begins to disintegrate:

> 'The brilliant "Son Decoud", the spoiled darling of the family, the lover of Antonia and journalist of Sulaco, was not fit to grapple with himself single-handed. Solitude from mere outward condition of existence becomes very swiftly a state of soul in which the affectations of irony and scepticism have no place. It takes possession of the mind, and drives forth the thought into the exile of utter unbelief. After three days of waiting for the sight of some human face, Decoud caught himself entertaining a doubt of his own individuality. It had merged into the world of cloud and water, of natural forces and forms of nature. In our activity alone do we find the sustaining illusion of an independent existence as against the whole scheme of things of which we form a helpless part. Decoud lost all belief in the reality of his action past and to come.' (p. 497)

Life on the island becomes a terrifying analogy for life as a whole: isolate, meaningless, demoralizing: 'His sadness was the sadness of a sceptical mind. He beheld the universe as a succession of incomprehensible images.' (p. 498.) Without the aid of any external beliefs upon which to prey, Decoud's scepticism turns inwards, until his very identity seems indistinguishable from all that is about him. After several more days, he slowly rows out to sea, puts four ingots of silver in his pockets, and shoots himself in the head:

> 'A victim of the disillusioned weariness which is the retribution meted out to intellectual audacity, the brilliant Don Martin Decoud, weighted by the bars of San Tomé silver, disappeared without a trace, swallowed up in the immense indifference of things.' (p. 501)

The tone of the last passages on Decoud is not markedly different from that of the first; it seems that *Nostromo* quite explicitly repudiates the scepticism that Decoud represents.

But this is hardly satisfactory. During the course of this

discussion, I have many times quoted Decoud's perceptive remarks about various characters. There are, in fact, times in *Nostromo* when the voice of the omniscient narrator is virtually indistinguishable from that of Decoud.[17] Conversely, there are also times when Decoud's voice is unmistakably Conradian in tone and content.[18] This has, of course, been noticed by many critics. Dr Leavis tells us that 'Decoud may be said to have had a considerable part in the writing of *Nostromo*: or one might say that *Nostromo* was written by a Decoud who wasn't a complacent dilettante, but was positively drawn towards those capable of "investing their activities with spiritual value". . .'[19] I am not so sure that Conrad approved of investing one's activities with spiritual value: *Nostromo* is (in part) an indictment of people who do just that—that Dr Leavis includes Charles Gould in a list of examples of such people seems to me to invalidate his point. In fact, if we limit a consideration of Decoud to what Decoud actually says and does, rather than to what Conrad says *about* him, we will come to a radically different conclusion about the nature of his character. Decoud not only plays a major part in the action of the novel, but speaks profoundly and feelingly about his country. In a conversation with Mrs Gould and Antonia, Decoud utters his passionate opinion about the modern state of Costaguana:

> ' "Now the whole land is like a treasure-house, and all these people are breaking into it, whilst we are cutting each other's throats. The only thing that keeps them out is mutual jealousy. But they'll come to an agreement some day . . . It has always been the same. We are a wonderful people, but it has always been our fate to be"—he did not say "robbed", but added, after a pause—"exploited!" ' (p. 174)

The tone of this, which is only one of several such speeches, should alone indicate that Decoud cannot be shrugged off as an 'idle boulevardier'. His scepticism, far from reflecting an uncompassionate nature, is based on a severe but not jaundiced appraisal of men's motives. In short, there seem to be two Decouds: the first, the detached dilettante, the idle man of the world, whom Conrad bombards with scorn, and finally dispatches into the Golfo Placido; the second, the passionate and ironic patriot who plays a major part in the action of the novel, and can be said to merit so much of the author's approval as to seem, at times, indistinguishable from Conrad himself.

In Decoud's history, we can see what we have come to recognize as a major Conradian theme: that any successful search for the unidealized reality of man's existence must lead to despair. As Robert Warren has said: 'Decoud comes to his end with no vision beyond that which skepticism can achieve by preying upon skepticism, the objective recognition of the pragmatic efficacy of faith despite the fact that faith is an "illusion".'[20] The 'objective recognition of the pragmatic efficacy of faith despite the fact that faith is an illusion' is, implicitly, the recommendation of Stein in *Lord Jim*. Finally, Decoud is condemned not by his *scepticism*, but by the fullness and clarity of his understanding, which reveals his insignificance in 'the whole scheme of things of which we form a helpless part'. His fate is, generally, that of an 'imaginative' man who tries to live without illusions. His final vision of his own tininess in an alien universe recalls Conrad's own view of the meaninglessness and chaos of the universe (in his letters to Cunninghame Graham), and is echoed by the narrator's talk of 'the crushing, paralysing sense of human littleness, which is what really defeats a man struggling with natural forces' (p. 433). In this sense, Decoud is not sceptical, he simply sees and accepts the truth about reality. Thus while Conrad uses Decoud as a vehicle for his own sceptical (and true) meditations, he also has the luxury of denying their scepticism while nevertheless insisting on their truth. Conrad's own nature—pulled between a sceptical view of human illusion in the face of a hostile universe, and an insistence on certain codes of value and behaviour—is enacted in his ambiguous relationship with his character. That is to say, Conrad is expressing, through the character of Decoud, something deep in his own nature—a pessimistic and deeply sceptical view of life—and then explicitly rejecting it on 'moral' grounds.[21] As we have seen more than once in previous works, there are more important things to a man than truth, which is incompatible with a working morality.

It should by now be clear how deeply pessimistic a book *Nostromo* is. By the end of the novel, none of the available alternatives seems very attractive. In the histories of those characters who altruistically devote themselves to the progress of civilization, we have a welter of illusion, folly, and dangerous self-deception. In those characters who reject any notion of history as a meaningful reflection of man's aspirations and values, we have either dangerous action resulting from 'passionate desire', or a self-destructive impulse which greets the knowledge of the insignificance of the human ego. This is best exemplified in contrasting speeches of Decoud and Antonia as the two argue on the balcony of the Casa Gould:

> '. . . he seized every opportunity to tell her that though she had managed to make a Blanco journalist of him, he was no patriot. First of all, the word had no sense for cultured minds, to whom the narrowness of every belief is odious; and secondly, in connection with the everlasting troubles of this unhappy country it was hopelessly besmirched; it had been the cry of dark barbarism, the cloak of lawlessness, of crimes, of rapacity, of simple thieving . . .
>
> "But we are labouring to change all that," Antonia protested. "It is exactly what we desire. It is our object. It is the great cause. And the word you despise has stood also for sacrifice, for courage, for constancy, for suffering. Papa, who—"
>
> "Ploughing the sea," interrupted Decoud, looking down.'
> (pp. 186–7)

Lying beneath this difference of opinion is the conflict which separates the sceptics from the altruists of Costaguana. Briefly, Decoud sees the truth, and therefore cannot commit himself; Antonia commits herself, and therefore cannot see the truth. The human and social tensions generated by this paradox seem to me the subject of *Nostromo*.

If we return for a moment to the altruistic characters of *Nostromo*, it is obvious that they achieve very little during the course of the revolution. In fact, Mrs Gould, Antonia, Don José and Giorgio, the most markedly sympathetic characters of the group, fail to accomplish anything worthwhile towards creating the Occidental Republic. On the other hand, those characters whom I have classified as sceptical about the social value of action actually contribute the greatest part of the heroic action of the novel. Admittedly, Gould finances the movement for secession, but that is all that he actively does. It is only through the sceptics—through the courage of Nostromo in saving the silver, and helping Barrios to return from Cayta, through the principles and ideas of Decoud, and through the finely audacious scheme of Monygham, whereby Sotillo is tricked into looking for the non-existent sunken silver—that the Occidental Republic comes into existence. Perhaps the final irony is that although the novel's sceptics are also its heroes, the outcome of their heroism (the creation of the Occidental Republic) is something that neither they, nor we, would applaud.

In Conrad's previous works, I have noted how often the theme of the 'life-lie'—the sustaining illusion in the face of an unbearable reality—has occurred. In 'Karain', 'Heart of Darkness', and Lord Jim, characters find a meaning in life through their fidelity to an illusion, in what Stein called 'following the dream'. According to Stein, a man must immerse himself in his illusions, indulge his egoistically held sense of values to the full, in order to live meaningfully (though paradoxically the process may, as in the case of Jim, be self-destructive). This process works for Jim (with the proviso that it also causes his death), but it does not work nearly so well in Nostromo. Though Conrad has some sympathy for certain of his altruistic characters —Charles Gould, Antonia and Don José Avellanos, and Giorgio—he is nevertheless finely aware that these people are self-deceivers. Unlike Jim, whose fidelity to his illusion leads him back into the human community, the altruistic characters of Nostromo are led out of it by their illusions. Furthermore, whereas Jim's fidelity allows him to act heroically for the benefit of his people, the altruistic characters of Nostromo are hardly men of action: two are women, and two old men.

The exception to these generalizations about the altruistic characters is, of course, Mrs Gould. This is largely because she abandons her concept of progress through material interest: loses her concern for 'the people', and returns to caring for people. That is, she substitutes private for public values, morality for principle. In this, she is like the two most sceptical characters of the novel, Dr Monygham and Decoud. Mrs Gould, by the end of the novel, is in fact little less sceptical than Dr Monygham himself. She has seen and accepted that man is a creature capable of vast self-deceptions, and that history is a reflection of those deceptions. I suspect that Conrad's creative and intellectual sympathy in Nostromo lies largely with the sceptics: with Dr Monygham, Decoud, and (the late convert)

Mrs Gould. On the other hand, Conrad was also aware of the positive values of idealism (in his admiration for Giorgio and Don José), and in the latent dangers of scepticism. *Nostromo* is enacted in the traditionally neutral and meaningless Conradian universe, and Conrad's essential admiration for Decoud's insight (Decoud notices this about the universe too) is undercut by his feeling that one really cannot afford such insights. Consequently, Conrad has it both ways: writes his novel from Decoud's point of view, and yet repudiates Decoud. This is, no doubt, a useful compromise, and accounts for much of the novel's dramatic tension (and perhaps, too, for the 'hollow reverberation' which F. R. Leavis feels in *Nostromo*).[22] But it is a compromise behind which lurk the possibilities of an artistic self-betrayal. The apparent distaste with which Conrad viewed the 'Decoud' in himself was not strong enough, in *Nostromo*, to quench his scepticism, but it may cause us to see, in this novel, the seeds of Conrad's later decline. In the novels from *Under Western Eyes* until his death, Conrad repeatedly turned away from scepticism and the clarity of egoism, towards an increasingly severe affirmation of ethical standards and social responsibility. That is, Antonia finally wins her argument with Decoud;[23] but who could deny, after reading *Nostromo*, that without the ironical counterbalance of Decoud's scepticism, Antonia's values and aspirations are naïve and uninteresting?

7
The Secret Agent

That the furtive intrigues of the nameless Comrades who slither through the final pages of *Nostromo* mark the first step in a sustained consideration of anarchies, should be clear from the nature of Conrad's next two short stories.[1] Written in 1906, both are dominated by a mood of lofty contempt for the triviality and insolence of anarchism and anarchists. In 'The Anarchist', a simple French peasant is arrested for shouting anarchist slogans while drunk. At his trial, he is defended by an ambitious socialist lawyer, who succeeds in winning him a maximum sentence. Unable to find work upon his release, he is coerced into joining an extremist group, and finally transported. Through the murder of two of his 'comrades' he is able to escape to an obscure cattle island, where he finds work as a mechanic, and is ironically nicknamed 'Anarchisto de Barcelona'. Apparently the major cause of anarchism is drunkenness, the major effects exile and anonymity.

In the more impressive of the two stories, 'The Informer: An Ironic Tale', an unnamed narrator who is a collector of Chinese bronzes and porcelain is sent a curious specimen by a friend who is also a collector—'of acquaintances'. This specimen is Mr X, 'the mysterious unknown Number One of desperate conspiracies suspected and unsuspected, matured or baffled' (p. 74). After the narrator has shown Mr X (who is also a student of Chinoiserie) through his collection, they dine together. During the course of a leisurely and elegant meal (Mr X is particularly fond of '*bombe glacée*'), the anarchist tells a story of intrigue and betrayal set in the narrator's own city of London. It seems that a double agent, named Sevrin, has infiltrated the local anarchist cell to such good effect that all of its plans inevitably end in failure. Mr X, who has come from Brussels to sort out the situation, tricks Sevrin into revealing himself by staging a bogus police raid on the premises of the society. Sevrin, after admitting that he had betrayed his fellow revolutionaries 'through conviction', poisons himself. The story, while ordinary enough, gains some impact through the device of assuming the values of anarchism to be the norm, and the 'betrayal' of the informer to be an aberration from accepted behaviour. Although Conrad's anarchists are a shadowy and unconvincing lot, Sevrin is not made into a hero—he is as unconvincing as are the rest of the characters.

Except, perhaps, for Mr X himself, whose relationship with the narrator provides the most interesting aspect of 'The Informer'. The two men remain nameless so as to stand in direct contrast with each other as types: the narrator is 'a quiet and peaceable product of civilisation' (p. 76); Mr X, the world's foremost anarchist. And yet the two are strikingly similar in their habits and tastes. There is a suggestion (which is never adequately developed) that Mr X represents a latent aspect of the narrator's self, a potential outlaw-double. As Mr X tells his anarchist anecdote, his listener momentarily glimpses that abyss which Marlow, too, discovered in his encounter with his potential self, Mr Kurtz: 'I suppose I am impressionable and imaginative. I had a disturbing vision of darkness, full of lean jaws and wild eyes, amongst the hundred electric lights of the place. But somehow this vision made me angry, too.' (p. 77.) Thus the characteristic Conradian themes of the dangers of imagination, and the abyss lurking at the core of human experience, forever threatening personal and social stability, are latent here. But the narrator never understands that his similarities with Mr X might go deeper than their superficially shared tastes. The anarchist, however, is not so unimaginative; it seems (as the collector of acquaintances later tells his friend) that Mr X 'likes to have his little joke sometimes' (p. 102). The narrator is not amused, and the story ends with his words: 'I have been utterly unable to discover where in all this the joke comes in.' (p. 102.) Although 'The Informer' has no pretensions as a serious study of anarchism, there is considerable delicacy in its treatment of the relationship between the two human types that stand at its centre.

A second noteworthy aspect of the story lies in the several ways in which it presages those two more important works, *The Secret Agent* (1907) and *Under Western Eyes* (1911), in both of which an anarchist sect is infiltrated by a secret agent, who is subsequently killed or tortured. *The Secret Agent* also imports one of its characters from the short story, which introduces the Professor, a fervent terrorist who 'was engaged in perfecting some new detonators': 'His was the true spirit of an extreme revolutionist. Explosives were his faith, his hope, his weapon, and his shield.'[2] (p. 88.) *Under Western Eyes* draws from 'The Informer' not a character, but a point of view (the use of an elderly and naïvely civilized narrator) and a structural device (the diary through which the author, though still committed to his narrator, is able to reveal the double agent's thoughts). Finally, both of the later novels echo a remark which the narrator of 'The Informer' makes to himself by way of consolation: 'The idea of anarchy ruling among anarchists was comforting, too. It could not possibly make for efficiency.' (p. 80.)

But *The Secret Agent* is something more than the next stage in an intellectual consideration of anarchism, for Conrad was later to imply that the connection between the ending of *Nostromo* and the inception of *The Secret Agent* was also imaginatively necessary. In the Author's Note to *The Secret Agent*, Conrad recollects his attempt, following the completion of *Nostromo* in 1904, to find another subject for a novel. Ideas began slowly to collect themselves—first, in the implications of an anecdote related by Ford Madox Ford; second, in the possibilities of an irate phrase uttered by the Secretary of State, Sir William Harcourt.[3] A plot began gradually to crystallize:

'It was at first for me a mental change, disturbing a quieted-down imagination, in which strange forms, sharp in outline but imperfectly apprehended, appeared and claimed attention as crystals will do by their bizarre and unexpected shapes. One fell to musing before the phenomenon—even of the past: of South America, a continent of crude sunshine and brutal revolutions, of the sea, the vast expanse of salt waters, the mirror of heaven's frowns and smiles, the reflector of the world's light. Then the vision of an enormous town presented itself, of a monstrous town more populous than some continents and in its man-made might as if indifferent to heaven's frowns and smiles; a cruel devourer of the world's light. There was room enough there to place any story, depth enough there for any passion, variety enough there for any setting, darkness enough to bury five millions of lives.' (pp. xi–xii)

Thematically, then, *The Secret Agent* may be said to begin somewhat after *Nostromo* ends: with an established and peaceful society which is ominously threatened from within. If *Nostromo* is a critique of the self-deceptions and misguided idealism of people striving to create, then *The Secret Agent* is an indictment of people attempting to destroy.

Yet it seems at first as if the scepticism of Conrad's anarchists is a logical extension of the dominant scepticism with which I believe *Nostromo* to end. Thus we have the words of Michaelis, *The Secret Agent*'s 'ticket-of-leave apostle':

'All idealisation makes life poorer. To beautify it is to take away its character of complexity—it is to destroy it. Leave that to the moralists, my boy. History is made by men, but they do not make it in their heads. The ideas that are born in their consciousness play an insignificant part in the march of events. History is dominated and determined by the tool and the production—by the force of economic conditions. Capitalism has made socialism, and the laws made by the capitalism for the protection of property are responsible for anarchism. No one can tell what form the social organisation may take in the future. Then why indulge in prophetic phantasies? At least they can only interpret the mind of the prophet, and they can have no objective value. Leave that pastime to the moralists, my boy.' (p. 41)

This looks very much like an abstract of the implicit argument of *Nostromo*—but it is a view from which Conrad, throughout the entire course of *The Secret Agent*, disassociates himself. The sceptical musings which prompted *Nostromo* are themselves subjected, in *The Secret Agent*, to a profoundly sceptical renunciation. If *Nostromo* found capitalism destructive of cultural richness and the integrity of individual human lives, *The Secret Agent* nevertheless suggests that the process is not only irreversible, but ought not to be regretted. In short, Conrad has no sympathy whatsoever with his anarchists.

It is because of this lack of sympathy—emotional or intellectual—that *The Secret Agent* seems to stand apart from the books that precede it. Its virtues—its economy, control of time, precision of tone—demand a reading unlike that usually accorded to Conrad's other works. But because Conrad had no sense of the sincerity or value of revolutionary activity, *The Secret Agent* ought to be regarded as no more than a memorable tour de force. It has none of the tensions that make *Lord Jim* or *Nostromo* so compelling—it fails to suggest either the attractiveness, the clarity, or the necessity, of a vision based on the honesty of egoism. According to J. I. M. Stewart:

> '*The Secret Agent* has the speed and directness of a very good thriller largely because it is not bedevilled by doubt; Marlow is in abeyance; there is nothing equivocal in the book's moral stance. Winnie Verloc, Winnie's mother, and Winnie's brother are several types of that humbleness, innocence, helplessness which must perpetually suffer in a world in which a mere mean and obtuse egoism, as in Mr Verloc, or various corruptions of political feeling, as in a majority of the other characters, operate in disregard of those moral imperatives which alone give dignity to human life.'[4]

It is because the *only* egoism in *The Secret Agent* is 'mean and obtuse'—because none of its characters has the audacity of Kurtz, the romantic dreams of Jim, or the astonishing clarity of Decoud—that the work achieves its special status as probably the most perfectly sustained yet also the thinnest of Conrad's major novels. It creates a group of unworthy and contemptible characters—and then brilliantly castigates them for their unworthiness and contemptibility. This is not a negligible achievement, but not, surely, a great one.

Michaelis is one of a group of four anarchists who meet regularly at the home of Adolf Verloc, proprietor of a modest pornography shop in Soho, the famous agent Delta of a foreign power (probably Russia), and a secret informer for Chief Inspector Heat of the London police. Verloc has embraced anarchism because he is too lazy to work:

> 'He was too lazy even for a mere demagogue, for a workman orator, for a leader of labour. It was too much trouble. He required a more perfect form of ease; or it might have been that he was a victim of the philosophical unbelief in the effectiveness of every human effort. Such a form of indolence requires, implies, a certain amount of intelligence. Mr Verloc was not devoid of intelligence—and at the notion of a menaced social order he would perhaps have winked to himself if there had not been an effort to make in that sign of scepticism.' (p. 12)

The phrase 'a victim of the philosophical unbelief in the

effectiveness of every human effort' reminds us that only nine years before the publication of *The Secret Agent*, Conrad had specifically so described himself to Cunninghame Graham. Throughout the course of the next nine years, Conrad was to use his lurking suspicion that life was ultimately meaningless as a source of tension in his stories and novels. *Nostromo* derives a great measure of its impact from the 'philosophical unbelief' of those two generally admirable men, Monygham and Decoud. But Verloc is never considered seriously: his beliefs are mocked as unbeliefs, his 'scepticism' is that of a man simply slothful and inadequate. He is incapable of transforming his egoism into anything valuable either to himself or to his society—he has neither the clarity of Decoud nor the fearless commitment of Monygham.

I have said that while the fate of Decoud seems to enact Conrad's rejection of scepticism and anti-social egoism, the words of Decoud represent Conrad's own darkly pessimistic side. *The Secret Agent* has no such character: the lurking identification between Conrad and Decoud (or, for that matter, the identification of Marlow and Kurtz, or Marlow and Jim) is totally absent from the author's relationship with Verloc, or any of the other anarchists. That is, in *The Secret Agent*, Conrad sides himself completely with man's legal and moral obligations, and is unable to accept in anarchism a possibly valuable extension of his vision of personal autonomy.

Verloc's cohorts are, in fact, a laughable group of misfits. Kurl Yundt, 'the terrorist', 'was old and bald, with a narrow, snow-white wisp of a goatee hanging limply from his chin' (p. 42). This pathetic old creature is wont to speak in blood-curdling terms; he has a dream

'of a band of men absolute in their resolve to discard all scruples in the choice of means, strong enough to give themselves frankly the name of destroyers, and free from the taint of that resigned pessimism which rots the world. No pity for anything on earth, including themselves, and death enlisted for good and all in the service of humanity—that's what I would have liked to see.' (p. 42)

These words are not without power, but they are undercut and devalued when the epithet 'senile sensualist' is attached to their speaker. The same is true of Michaelis, whose beatific dreams of a just socialistic future are conjoined with the physical absurdity of their originator:

> 'Michaelis, the ticket-of-leave apostle, was speaking in an even voice, a voice that wheezed as if deadened and oppressed by the layer of fat on his chest. He had come out of a highly hygienic prison round like a tub, with an enormous stomach and distended cheeks of a pale, semi-transparent complexion, as though for fifteen years the servants of an outraged society had made a point of stuffing him with fattening foods in a damp and lightless cellar. (p. 41)

Why sheer physical grossness, or senility, should militate against the value of what a man has to say, I am not sure. There can be no doubt, though, that Conrad here used his characters' physical condition as an outward sign of an inward lack of fitness. The fourth member of the group, Tom Ossipon, is a former medical student who has been attracted to anarchism, like Verloc, because it seems to offer a perfect form of idleness. He attends the meetings at Verloc's establishment partly because he is attracted by Winnie Verloc, and partly because he claims to be scientifically interested in her half-wit brother, whom he has labelled 'the degenerate'.

A senile old man, two fat men incapable of work, and a failed medical student—these are Conrad's anarchists. They have one thing in common: being incapable of work, they are supported by women: Michaelis has become the spoiled darling of an eccentric and wealthy aristocratic *dame*; Yundt is looked after by a woman who inexplicably loves him; Ossipon lives by sponging off a series of women only too happy to pay for association with a handsome man; Verloc is largely supported by his wife, who runs the shop while he is engaged in his anarchist activities. To be thus dependent must have seemed to Conrad the ultimate sign of depravity and unmanliness.

Although the anarchists' major antagonists—Inspector Heat, his Assistant Commissioner, and Sir Ethelred, the Secretary of State—are morally somewhat preferable to Verloc and his cronies, they are nevertheless not a particularly attractive group. Inspector Heat is a typically dedicated policeman, interested not in justice, but in arrests; when Stevie is blown up, Heat's only reaction is that it provides an opportunity to link

Michaelis with the crime. Inspector Heat detests anarchists, because he cannot understand them:

'. . . he could understand the mind of a burglar, because, as a matter of fact, the mind and the instincts of a burglar are of the same kind as the mind and the instincts of a police officer. Both recognise the same conventions, and have a working knowledge of each other's methods . . . Products of the same machine, one classed as useful and the other as noxious, they take the machine for granted in different ways, but with a seriousness essentially the same.' (p. 92)

The anarchists' rejection of the machine and all its workings seems sheer lunacy to Heat. His answer to how to deal with the problem is straightforward enough: terrorists 'ought to be shot at sight like mad dogs' (p. 95).

Heat is a pragmatic and unimaginative man, a perfect police officer: the Fussy Joe of *The Secret Agent*. But his superior, the Assistant Commissioner of Police, recognizes that whereas Heat would like simply to round up all the possible suspects and dump them in gaol, his job may be to establish their innocence, in order to deal with the foreign powers behind them. The problem is complicated by the fact that Heat relies on Verloc as an informer, while the Assistant Commissioner cannot arrest Michaelis because the lady patroness of Michaelis is his wife's particular friend. We thus have a crime in which two major suspects—Verloc and Michaelis—cannot reasonably be arrested, while a third, the Professor, can never be arrested without blowing himself (and anyone in the vicinity) to bits.

Sir Ethelred, the pompous Secretary of State, is appalled by the bombing outrage largely because he has previously been assured (by Heat) that it was inconceivable that anything of the sort might happen. His vanity is wounded; besides, he is too busy with his own 'revolution' (nationalizing the fisheries) to concern himself with the details of such a sordid affair. He simply wants the problem solved. But the final solution has little to do with enforcement of the law. Once Heat has informed Winnie Verloc that someone has been blown up (Heat thinks it is Verloc, Winnie knows it to be her beloved brother Stevie), the police are not needed to see that punishment is meted out. Verloc's personal life is a tangle of misunderstanding and dishonesty, in which each member of his household seems inevitably in ignorance of the real meaning of the others' actions: Verloc thinks that 'he is loved for himself'; Winnie thinks that Verloc loves Stevie 'for himself'; Winnie feels that her mother (who has gallantly moved out of Verloc's in order to protect Stevie's future) has acted callously. Inevitably, these mangled personal relationships lead to a bitter and absurd conclusion. Verloc attempts to console Winnie on the death of her brother by reminding her how lucky she is that it was not he; obsessed by the notion that Verloc has intentionally murdered Stevie, and appalled by his insensitive sexual overtures to her while she is in a state of shock, she thrusts a carving knife into his chest, and he expires with the single word 'Don't'.

But the misunderstandings have hardly begun. Tom Ossipon, who believes that it was Verloc who was blown to bits, comes round to the Verlocs' to have a go at Winnie, and through her at Verloc's money. Mistaking his interest for genuine sympathy at the death of her brother, the terrified Winnie, pictures of the gallows hideously present in her mind, clings to him hysterically. Upon finding that she has just murdered Verloc, however, Ossipon forsakes all claims on the money, and callously dispatches her on an evening boat-train. He reads an account of her suicide the next morning, and the novel closes with him wandering obsessively through the murky London streets.

The Secret Agent is unusual in Conrad's work not by virtue of its subject or location, but in its tone. Conrad stated his feelings explicitly in his Author's Note; when Ford told him the original story on which the novel is based: 'I remember, however, remarking on the criminal futility of the whole thing, doctrine, action, mentality; and on the contemptible aspect of the half-crazy pose as of a brazen cheat exploiting the poignant miseries and passionate credulities of a mankind always so tragically eager for self-destruction.' (p. ix.) His attitude towards the events chronicled in *The Secret Agent* could hardly, therefore, be anything other than ironic, a method that 'was formulated with deliberation and in the earnest belief that ironic treatment alone would enable me to say all I felt I would have to say in scorn as well as in pity' (p. xiii). There is plenty of scorn in *The Secret Agent*, but surely little pity—and it may be that the two are scarcely compatible. The effect of Conrad's irony (which is brilliantly sustained) seems to militate against whatever pity one might humanly expect to feel, given the situation. Aristotle tells us that pity is caused by the observation of undeserved misfortune, but the personages who meet the misfortune are, in his understanding, necessarily of an 'intermediate' type—not pre-eminently good, but fundamentally so, and certainly not contemptible.

Though there may be a tragic situation in *The Secret Agent*, there is certainly no tragedy. The novel, as most critics have rightly pointed out, is in effect comic. In Aristotelian terms, we see a bad man moving from a happy situation to a miserable one. Such a spectacle may appropriately occasion scorn, never pity. Even the deaths of the three members of the Verloc household could not be called pitiable. Stevie's death takes place off-stage, and in describing Winnie's horrified reaction to it Conrad indulges himself with some of the novel's most grotesquely amusing writing:

'A park! That's where the boy was killed. A park—smashed branches, torn leaves, gravel, bits of brotherly flesh and bone, all spouting up together in the manner of a firework. She remembered now what she had heard, and she remembered it pictorially. They had to gather him up with the shovel. Trembling all over with irrepressible shudders, she saw before her the very implement with its ghastly load scraped up from the ground. Mrs Verloc closed her eyes desperately, throwing upon that vision the night of her eyelids, where after a rainlike fall of mangled limbs the decapitated head of Stevie lingered suspended alone, and fading out slowly like the last star of a pyrotechnic display.' (p. 260)

Verloc's death is a similarly absurd and macabre business, while that of Winnie herself (which is potentially the most pathetic) is anonymously rendered through the lurid prose of a newspaper report. The characters are portrayed rather as the friend of the narrator of 'The Informer' regards his acquaintances—as interesting human types. Like a bemused collector Conrad holds each character before our eyes, pinched between his fingers, prodding and poking it to discover its weirdly amusing grimaces. Verloc and his anarchist colleagues are specimens of a particularly odious type; Winnie and Stevie, while basically sympathetic, are nevertheless thoroughly stifled by misfortune and misunderstanding. The vision is almost overwhelmingly ugly.

For it is not only Conrad's anarchists who are unattractive, but his law enforcers as well. Society is hideous: the smoke-filled streets of London, with their damp, fish-like people, are a murky human aquarium of squalor and misery, unrelieved by more than flashes of decency or compassion. Anarchism is unacceptable, but society is hardly worth preserving; egoism is bad, but altruism is ultimately only disguised self-interest; crime cannot be condoned, but the law is itself corrupt. Life, as Winnie Verloc muses, 'doesn't stand much looking into.'

Conrad refers to Winnie's desire 'not to know too much' (p. 169) as 'tragic' (p. xiii) because a full vision of the human predicament will indicate only too clearly how detestable is man's fate. *The Secret Agent* is a devastating chronicle of failure of imagination, of the inability of people to understand each other's needs or desires, of the sordid and hopeless lives of 'five millions of people'. There is a terrible paradox latent in Winnie's notion that 'life doesn't stand much looking into': if one fails to look into things, then misunderstanding and illusion inevitably lead to disaster; on the other hand, if one does look into things, then the revealed reality may drive one to despair. *The Secret Agent* is Conrad's bleakest novel because in it the possibility of maintaining one's 'illusions' in the face of an unendurable reality is negligible. Verloc's belief that he was loved for himself, or Winnie's confidence in his love of Stevie, neither of these 'illusions' is a sufficient protection—rather, they cause the misunderstanding which leads to the three deaths.

In Conrad's previous books, imagination led men like Marlow, Decoud, and Dr Monygham, to recognize the hideous meaninglessness of man's life, to view the abyss yawning beneath conventional notions of fidelity and honour. Such an insight, while potentially destructive, at least had the virtue of clarity, and even offered the possibility of socially useful behaviour. All of this is lost in *The Secret Agent*. One might have expected, given what we have seen of Conrad's temperament and native pessimism, that he would have had a certain sympathy for his anarchists, a sympathy flowing out of the same well of disbelief as that from which he deeply sympathized with Decoud. Certainly the society which the anarchists had dedicated themselves to destroying is a distasteful one. Why then, should Conrad so strongly have opposed its overthrow? There is no good answer; finally, *The Secret Agent* is an expression not of an ideology, but of a prejudice.

Writing to Galsworthy, who had apparently questioned Conrad's 'treatment' of his characters, Conrad replied:

> 'After all, you must not take it too seriously. The whole thing is superficial and it is but a tale. I had no idea to consider Anarchism politically, or to treat it seriously in its philosophical aspect; as a manifestation of human nature in its discontent and imbecility. The general reflections whether right or wrong are not meant as bolts ... They are, if anything, mere digs at the people in the tale. As to attacking Anarchism as a form of humanitarian enthusiasm or intellectual despair or social atheism, that—if it were worth doing—would be the work for a more vigorous hand and for a mind more robust, and perhaps more honest than mine.'[5]

Although this has the characteristically self-effacing tone of many of Conrad's letters in reply to criticism, it is nevertheless a fair résumé of his attitude to his characters as revealed in the novel. Robustness and honesty are exactly what are lacking in *The Secret Agent*: the robustness and honesty required to accept, as Conrad had often previously accepted, the metaphysical and social rationale for anarchism, and the powerful attraction of anti-social thinking and acting. Without such honesty, Conrad could never have found the Decoud in himself. But Conrad repudiated this Decoud—a step that came, as I remarked in talking about *Nostromo*, perilously close to a form of self-betrayal. That betrayal is evident in *The Secret Agent*, in which Conrad's conventional values of honour, fidelity, and hard work, as the keys to social stability, totally overwhelm his deep-seated (and deeply mistrusted) sense that, after all, man is ultimately alone in a hostile universe, and social order is based on arbitrary rules.

But what of these values—of honour, fidelity, and hard work —without which society cannot survive? What role do they play in the world of *The Secret Agent*? What social goals, what vision of a better future, we may well ask, make man's suffering and striving worthwhile? We are offered nothing but the murky purposelessness of London life. In *Nostromo*, the sufferings of Don José Avellanos, even those of Charles Gould, may be justified by the intensity and humanity of their vision. But the proponents of social equilibrium and conventional morality in *The Secret Agent* have no vision save their commitment to the law—a commitment compounded of short-sightedness, vanity, and ambition.

Only poor Stevie, 'the degenerate', has a genuine vision: 'It was a bad world. Bad! Bad! . . . Bad world for poor people.' (p. 171.) His childlike compassion and simple desire to see people happy and well cared for may mark Stevie as the only genuine revolutionary in *The Secret Agent*. But he is the 'degenerate', rendered impotent by his simplicity, smothered by his sister's love. Like his habit of drawing endless series of concentric circles, his desire for a better world is 'a mad art attempting the inconceivable' (p. 45).

Ultimately *The Secret Agent* has its imaginative roots not so much in its connection with *Nostromo* as in its clear associations with *The Nigger of the 'Narcissus'*.[6] It is worth remarking that in Conrad's description of his first thoughts about the new novel,[7] he returned to a dichotomy from *The Nigger*: the degradation of life on land as compared with life at sea. This distinction was not a very adequate one in the earlier work; it is even less adequate in the later. Conrad's attitude to his anarchists is close in tone and content to his previous attitude to Donkin—the only one of the characters from the *Narcissus* who would have felt at home in Conrad's London. One is left with the curious feeling that life aboard ship is richer and more various (even in human types) than life on land.

A second connection between *The Secret Agent* and Conrad's early work lies in the redeployment of the withering ironic tone of 'An Outpost of Progress'.[8] But such irony has markedly diminishing returns: when it works too well it undercuts what it seeks to establish. Thus Kayerts and Carlier—and most of the characters of *The Secret Agent*—are finally unworthy even of the sustained scorn to which they are subjected. The successful control and ironic thrust of *The Secret Agent* is purchased at the cost of a certain fundamental seriousness. It may be objected that this statement seems to value one kind of art above another: to implicitly suggest that a novel that seriously engages itself with moral complexities is attempting more than a novel (however brilliant) which does not do so. But I see no reason to shirk this suggestion—it is, after all, one that Conrad explicitly supported.[9]

The Secret Agent is thought by some critics (particularly F. R. Leavis)[10] to be one of Conrad's very greatest novels. Its virtues are certainly considerable. It has a singleness of mood and purpose, a tightness and economy, which no doubt mark it as a technical masterpiece. But in comparison with certain of Conrad's other works one feels a basic thinness about the novel, as if its technical neatness and unity of design are produced at the cost of complexity of thought and emotion, of the balanced points of view and tensions upon which so many of his greatest works depend. Perhaps this feeling may lie behind Conrad's own doubts about the novel. In his next novel (*Under Western Eyes*) he returns to the subject of the revolutionary disruption of society, and does so in a way both more complex and more honest than in *The Secret Agent*.

8

Under Western Eyes

After finishing *The Secret Agent*, Conrad began work on *Chance*, but soon put it aside to work on a short story entitled 'Razumov'.[1] Writing to Galsworthy early in 1908, he announced the commencement of his new work, in which he hoped to 'capture the very soul of things Russian,—Cosas de Russia':

> 'Listen to the theme. The Student Razumov (a natural son of Prince K.) gives up secretly to the police his fellow student, Haldin, who seeks refuge in his rooms after committing a political crime (supposed to be the murder of de Flehve). First movement in St Petersburg. (Haldin is hanged of course.)
>
> 2nd in Genève. The student Razumov meeting abroad the mother and sister of Haldin falls in love with that last, marries her and, after a time, confesses to her the part he played in the arrest of her brother.
>
> The psychological developments leading to Razumov's betrayal of Haldin, to his confession of the fact to his wife and to the death of these people (brought about mainly by the resemblance of their child to the late Haldin), form the real subject of the story.'[2]

This melodramatic plot was fortunately altered during the composition of the last part of the novel.[3]

The phrase 'Cosas de Russia' immediately reminds us of Costaguana, from which *Under Western Eyes* (1911) draws, as a theme, its study of a national character. More importantly, *Under Western Eyes* continues the exploration of anarchism and its futile political consequences that was so important in *The Secret Agent*. But above all, its affinities are with *Lord Jim*— another novel that began as a short story, and was later composed in two distinct parts, the first a chronicle of guilt, and the second (set in a different place) of atonement. *Under Western Eyes* is once again the story of an average man who commits some fundamental act of cowardice and betrayal, and whose efforts to achieve some redemptive action are chronicled by a narrator who is peripherally involved in the drama. Unlike Marlow, however, the nameless old teacher of languages never

attains an intimate relationship with the novel's protagonist—
partly because circumstances make this impossible, but more
importantly because, to the 'Western eyes' that he represents,
Razumov is not 'one of us' but 'one of them'. He frequently
reiterates his belief that no Westerner can fathom the perverse
mystery of Russian character: 'this is a Russian story for
Western ears, which, as I have observed already, are not
attuned to certain tones of cynicism and cruelty, of moral
negation, and even of moral distress already silenced at our
end of Europe.' (pp. 163–4.) One may be inclined to ask (in the
last words that Razumov addresses to the old teacher): 'How
did this old man come here?' (p. 355).

Conrad would go no further in his defence of his narrator
than his words in the Author's Note: 'He was useful to me and
therefore I think that he must be useful to the reader both in
the way of comment and by the part he plays in the development of the story.' (pp. viii–ix.) The problem is one of novelistic
perspective; the narrator, by distancing us, helps us to get close.
Razumov (seen through these Western eyes) is personally more
sympathetic than his Dostoyevskian prototype, Raskolnikov,
whose unmediated intensity seems more than, even other than,
human. But a useful narrator need not also be a trustworthy
one: the obtuse tone of many of his remarks reminds us that he
is distinguishable from his author, whose last novel had been a
tale of the cynicism, cruelty, moral negation, and moral distress,
of 'our end of Europe'.

Conrad did, however, share with his narrator the opinion
that all Russians are 'under a curse' (p. 194).[4] This being so,
we must read *Under Western Eyes* with particular care. We have
proceeded thus far under the assumption that the themes and
situations of Conrad's previous works can be abstracted into
statements about man in general, about the relationship between a man's essential isolation and his role in a given society.
It is, of course, a defining criterion of great works of literature
that they are at once uniquely particular and yet somehow
universal. Thus, while Costaguana is an intricately detailed and
particular country, it becomes not merely any country in which
certain economic and social conditions pertain, but finally, any
country. What is troubling about *Under Western Eyes* is that it
seems a study in national psychopathology, of the madness of a

people that are not resonant to us as human beings—only as Russians. The old teacher tells us that 'It is unthinkable that any young Englishman should find himself in Razumov's position' (p. 25), a statement which is, trivially, true enough, but disturbing in tone and implication. Does it not render Razumov an anomaly, a specimen?

It was perhaps with this question in his mind that Conrad set about writing the Author's Note to *Under Western Eyes*. Although he insists on the particularity of his novelistic situation (the novel is an attempt to render 'the psychology of Russia itself') (p. vii), he is at pains to emphasize the *general* interest of his story. He insists on the 'general truth' (p. vii) of the action, and the 'general knowledge' (p. viii) on which that action is based. Thus, while the narrator seems certain that there are no points of contact between Russians and Westerners, Conrad assures us that there are. After all, what was unusual about Russians in 1910 was not that they were peculiarly mad people, but that they lived under a kind of political tyranny that was unknown in Western Europe.

Conrad's lengthiest statement about Russia is contained in the 1905 essay 'Autocracy and War',[5] ostensibly a reflection on the progress of the Russo-Japanese war, but actually as a means by which Conrad could make a startlingly vehement and comprehensive attack on Russia:

'. . . a yawning chasm open between East and West; a bottomless abyss that has swallowed up every hope of mercy, every aspiration towards personal dignity, towards freedom, towards knowledge, every ennobling desire of the heart, every redeeming whisper of conscience.' (p. 100)

The words 'chasm' and 'abyss' suggest the depth of Conrad's loathing, for they are associated with imagery otherwise reserved, as I have said, for ultimate tragic apprehensions. Corrupt in its traditions and values, Russia is seen as having a past incapable of generating new relevances; it appears that no alleviation of this tragic situation is imaginable:

'It is impossible to initiate a rational scheme of reform upon a phase of blind absolutism; and in Russia there has never been anything else to which the faintest tradition could, after ages of error, go back as a parting of the ways.' (p. 96)

'But under the shadow of Russian autocracy nothing could grow. Russian autocracy succeeded to nothing; it had no historical past, and it cannot hope for a historical future. It can only end.' (p. 97)

Given such sentiments, the creative conflict out of which *Under Western Eyes* emerged was one that would tax Conrad's powers. He had himself experienced the awful workings of Russian autocracy during his childhood exile with his parents, and the resultant feelings of hatred and incomprehension may eventually have found their way into the mouth of his narrator. By this compromise, Conrad sought to obtain that authorial 'detachment' of which he speaks in his Author's Note. His initial description of Razumov is carefully designed to emphasize his hero's human (rather than Russian) dimensions:

'Razumov is treated sympathetically. Why should he not be? He is an ordinary young man, with a healthy capacity for work and sane ambitions. He has an average conscience. If he is slightly abnormal it is only in his sensitiveness to his position. Being nobody's child he feels rather more keenly than another would that he is a Russian—or he is nothing.' (p. ix)

Thus Razumov is exceptional only in his isolated 'position'.

For Razumov is more entirely alone than any other character in all of Conrad's fiction:

'. . . no home influences had shaped his opinions or his feelings. He was as lonely in the world as a man swimming in the deep sea. The word Razumov was the mere label of a solitary individuality. There were no Razumovs belonging to him anywhere. His closest parentage was defined in the statement that he was a Russian.' (pp. 10–11)

The bastard son of the famous Prince K—, Razumov wants only to establish himself through his work, and particularly through the writing of a prize essay: 'Distinction would convert the label Razumov into an honoured name.' (pp. 13–14.) The lack of identity suggested by the word 'label' reminds us that we have in Razumov a man who is quite specifically suited to become the focus of the tension between social obligation (finding a 'name' is seen in terms of social recognition, for instance) and personal isolation. His attempt to use this isolation as a ground out of which his prestige can flower is, however, inevitably interrupted by the intrusion of Victor Haldin. Ironically, it is exactly Razumov's isolation that attracts Haldin to him: 'It occurred to me that you—you have no one belonging to you—no ties, no one to suffer for it if this came out by some means.' (p. 19.) Haldin's presumption upon Razumov is entirely unsolicited, and places him in what is to become an intolerable situation. In response to Haldin's plea that he go to fetch the peasant Ziemianitch, he can feel nothing but the incipient threat to his own self-interest: 'Razumov, of course, felt the safety of his lonely existence to be permanently endangered.' (p. 21.) His response is motivated only by the desire that he himself be minimally implicated, and so it inevitably occurs to Razumov (after finding Ziemianitch hopelessly drunk) that he will be safer if he turns Haldin in than if he aids in his escape.

This motive quickly begins to transform itself into an apparent political rationale:

> ' "Haldin means disruption", he thought to himself, beginning to walk again. "What is he with his indignation, with his talk of bondage—with his talk of God's justice? All that means disruption. Better that thousands should suffer than that a people should become a disintegrated mass, helpless like dust in the wind. Obscurantism is better than the light of incendiary torches." '
> (p. 34)

Man cannot be free, life cannot cohere, without a structure that binds like with like. Haldin, who 'means disruption', is a threat to this structure and therefore a threat to the metaphysical safety of every man. Thus Haldin's appeal to Razumov as a 'brother'—an appeal designed to cut sharply through his self-imposed isolation—only causes Razumov to think of his greater obligation to that society which Haldin threatens with disintegration. 'Have I not got forty million brothers?' (p. 35.) It must therefore follow that his obligation to this great family, the Russian people, transcends his obligation to any one member of it: 'That's patriotism.' (p. 36.) From this it becomes inevitable that Razumov must turn Haldin in to the police:

'Betray. A great word. What is betrayal? They talk of a man betraying his country, his friends, his sweetheart. There must be a moral bond first. All a man can betray is his conscience. And how is my conscience engaged here; by what bond of common faith, of common conviction, am I obliged to let that fanatical idiot drag me down with him? On the contrary—every obligation of true courage is the other way.' (pp. 37-8)

Having decided to abandon Haldin, Razumov gets, not re-assurance, but a glimpse of that abyss which threatens so many of Conrad's heroes at times of fundamental loneliness and terror:

'Razumov longed desperately for a word of advice, for moral support. Who knows what true loneliness is—not the conventional word, but the naked terror? To the lonely themselves it wears a mask. The most miserable outcast hugs some memory or some illusion. Now and then a fatal conjunction of events may lift the veil for an instant. For an instant only. No human being could bear a steady view of moral solitude without going mad.' (p. 39)

Unable to bear this knowledge of his own immutable isolation— the same knowledge that drove Decoud into suicide—Razumov seeks solace in the advice of his father, and the betrayal of Haldin is set irrevocably on its way.

But instead of finding himself free to return to his work after Haldin's capture, Razumov is not only harassed by repeated official inquiries into his relations with Haldin, but brutally deprived of peace by his own conflicts:

'Was it possible that he no longer belonged to himself? But why not keep on as before? Study. Advance. Work hard as if nothing had happened . . .' (p. 301)

But something has happened; instead of finding, as he had expected, that the values through which he has acted have been reinforced by his behaviour, Razumov instead finds that:

'. . . everything abandoned him—hope, courage, belief in himself, trust in men. His heart had, as it were, suddenly emptied itself. It was no use struggling on. Rest, work, solitude, and the frankness of intercourse with his kind were alike forbidden to him. Everything was gone.' (p. 303)

Sick and guilty, but without any sustaining logical reason for being so, Razumov is interned upon the 'rack' (p. 65) of his conflict. This image recurs during the course of his first interview with Councillor Mikulin:

> 'At that moment Razumov beheld his own brain suffering on the rack—a long, pale figure drawn asunder horizontally with terrific force in the darkness of a vault, whose face he failed to see. It was as though he had dreamed for an infinitesimal fraction of time of some dark print of the Inquisition . . .' (p. 88)

The oddity of the construction here (it appears that Razumov's brain is a 'long, pale figure' with a shielded face) imperfectly suggests two dimensions to this image of conflict (being pulled in two directions): first, that between competing rational forces —the 'brain' on the rack; second, that between 'brain' and 'figure'—perhaps the strain between the rational faculty and the needs of the whole man. The twisted anatomy of the image may reflect Razumov's own confusion, and directs us to a consideration of the nature of the demands imposed on Razumov.

We have, first of all, the conflict between what Haldin asks of Razumov, and what the state demands of him—between revolution and patriotism. This is a conflict of the 'brain', between two ideologies, each logically coherent, yet mutually irreconcilable, which find their expression in Razumov's abbreviated statement of belief:

> 'History not Theory.
> Patriotism not Internationalism.
> Evolution not Revolution.
> Direction not Destruction.
> Unity not Disruption.' (p. 66)

It is part of the point here that each of these ideologies has its sustaining intellectual and moral justification—a point that is brilliantly made with characteristic off-handedness: at one point the old teacher mentions 'M. de P—'s murder (or execution)' (p. 306) and in so doing neatly encapsulates the different descriptions one may offer of the same event, depending on one's ideological bias. Razumov's adherence to the left-hand side of his ideological shopping list places him distinctly on the side of General T—, and, for that matter, of the murdered tyrant, de P—. In the context of pre-revolutionary Russia, this is what 'patriotism' means. In betraying Haldin, Razumov supports a status quo which, whatever its putative intellectual basis, has no moral one. The old General proclaims a code behind the attractive rhetoric of which an autocratic regime wields its ugly power. His words are a painful echo of those of Razumov himself, but they are hideously empty in the context of his deeds:

> 'My existence has been built of fidelity. It's a feeling. To defend it I am ready to lay down my life—and even my honour—if that were needed. But pray tell me what honour can there be as against rebels—against people that deny God Himself—perfect unbelievers! Brutes.' (p. 51)

But what is one being faithful to? It seems wholly unsatisfactory to answer, as have some critics,[6] that Conrad would have identified himself, as did Razumov, with the values posited in the left-hand column above. Such a formulaic response to a complicated moral situation (Razumov writes his list in a 'childish' hand) fails to recognize the complex configuration of duties and decisions that are entailed by the dilemma in which Razumov is involved. He is trapped in an impossible position, torn between the pleasing rhetoric of Haldin (which justifies not only the murder of de P—, but also of many innocent victims) and the attractive political ideology of General T— (which provides the working rationale of autocracy). Having chosen not to send Haldin away as soon as his request was clear (which, on balance, would probably have been best), Razumov must make a political choice. Strictly speaking, his 'isolation' ends the moment Haldin enters his room, for any choice in response to Haldin's request is a political choice. The *logic* by which he betrays Haldin is undeniable, based as it is on an ideal of public responsibility: 'and the life goes on as before with its mysterious and secret sides quite out of sight, as they should be. Life is a public thing.' (p. 54.) 'Life is a public thing' means to him that his essential obligations are ultimately political.

But if this is true, why is Razumov tormented by his decision to turn Haldin in to the police? Unlike Jim, he has not contravened the law; he has obeyed it. Although he has been prompted by fear and self-concern, his rejection of Haldin's utopianism is genuine.[7] The situation in which he is placed is itself morally ambiguous, but complicated by the fact that it is not reducible to an intellectual model of the kind that Razumov creates. It is a situation in which neither of the possible decisions is satisfactory. The 'brain' doesn't appear to offer a solution. The rack tightens.

But there is still the image of the faceless figure, which Razumov sees as in a nightmare, with the same internal eye with which he envisaged Haldin's phantom in the snow. Life, it appears, is not wholly a 'public' thing. His decision may have been valid as a public gesture, but is invalidated by his own revulsion from it. After all, his initial impulse had been to help Haldin to escape; the decision to betray him came only after trying to aid him and failing. The moral error lies not in turning Haldin in to the police (Prince K— would have done so unhesitantly, without being guilty of betrayal), but in turning him in *after* having won his trust by a promise of aid. Razumov makes this fatal mistake because he is insufficiently aware of his real motives:

> 'For a train of thought is never false. The falsehood lies deep in the necessities of existence, in secret fears and half-formed ambitions, in the secret confidence combined with a secret mistrust of ourselves in the love of hope and the dread of uncertain days.' (pp. 33–4)

Although the general drift of this passage is clear enough (Razumov is guilty not because of an error of the 'brain', but because of the depths of unknown motives and terrors which force him into actions which may only *appear* to be rational), it is not very clear. It seems to suggest that Razumov's error could not have been avoided (it appears to have sprung directly from 'the necessities of existence'), and one wonders whether any man in his situation could have acted other than as Razumov did. It is impossible to answer this question with any confidence, but I suspect that Conrad would have thought not: his insistence on the determinative effects of Razumov's 'aloneness' suggests that Razumov is very much at the centre of a general human drama. Certainly, the narrator doubts whether Razumov's action (like Jim's jump) could properly be described as a choice: 'Indeed, it could hardly be called a decision. He had simply discovered what he had meant to do all along.' (p. 39.)

When he returns to his room after ostensibly having informed Ziemianitch of his assignation with Haldin, Razumov must delay Haldin long enough for the police to act. In confronting Haldin for this final time, Razumov passionately tries to make his unwanted visitor understand his feelings and actions. His speech is an elaborate rationalization of his act of betrayal, though Haldin does not know this. There is no mention in it of political allegiance to those 'forty million brothers' who had seemed so important a cause in justifying his betrayal. Instead Razumov attempts to use his aloneness as an explanation for his reactions:

'You are a son, a brother, a nephew, a cousin—I don't know what—to no end of people. I am just a man. Here I stand before you. A man with a mind. Did it ever occur to you how a man who had never heard a word of warm affection or praise in his life would think on matters on which you would think first with or against your class, your domestic tradition—your fireside prejudices? . . . Did you ever consider how a man like that would feel? I have no domestic tradition.' (p. 61)

This lack of a 'domestic tradition'—with its associated virtues of 'warm affection' and 'praise', in short with its primary virtue of *love*—is what really isolates Razumov and causes his tragedy. It is only through finding—or, more properly, creating—some such context that he will be redeemed. His crime has not been a betrayal of public duty, but of that humanity enacted in our capacity to love.

Speaking of 'the moral discovery which should be the object of every tale' (p. 67), the old teacher of languages attempts to understand Razumov's behaviour in terms of Russian 'cynicism'. We do not have to accept his explanation (Natalia Haldin is, after all, no cynic) to accept his premise: the real subject of Razumov's story is his discovery of his moral failure, and his attempts to atone for it. Razumov, like so many of Conrad's heroes, must learn 'How to be'.

The underlying irony of the first part of *Under Western Eyes* is that Razumov's action, which was intended to simplify his future, instead complicates it immensely. The active interest in his affairs displayed by the Russian police isolates him far more brutally than he could previously have dreamed. There is no escape; when he attempts summarily to walk out of an interview with Councillor Mikulin by insisting on his right 'to retire', he is immediately halted by the terrible question 'Where to?' (p. 99) with which the first part of the novel ends.

The reader is not informed of Razumov's status as a secret agent until Part Four (at page 307), because Parts Two and Three, which take place wholly in Geneva, begin six months before Haldin's murder of de P——, and move slowly towards the entrance of a Razumov who has apparently come to join a group of exiled Russian revolutionaries led by Peter Ivanovitch.[8] The Geneva episodes lack the artistic and psychic tension of the Russian section of the novel. This may indicate some loss of control on Conrad's part, but is necessary to increase sympathy for Razumov by withholding the information that he is a spy. The reader, of course, knows that Razumov has betrayed Haldin—the absence of which knowledge on the part of all the other characters provides the dominant irony of the plot. By providing the reader with one crucial piece of information, but not with the other, Conrad can both ironically perspective Razumov's welcome in Geneva, and at the same time undercut the reader's self-congratulation at knowing more than the 'gullible' revolutionaries—thus making their gullibility more credible, and implicating the reader in the misunderstandings on which the plot is based. This withholding of crucial information affects to a major degree our understanding of Razumov's motives for having come to Geneva: when he says to Peter Ivanovitch that he has been driven to Geneva by an 'irresistible force', Razumov is referring to Councillor Mikulin—but the reader, not knowing this, is likely to think of an internal force, perhaps a need to destroy himself by facing the relatives and associates of the man he has betrayed. Thus one level of irony is underlain by another: the reader, in his ignorance, may be more able to understand Razumov's deepest motives than is Razumov himself. After all, Razumov's final redemption is to involve confronting Haldin's sister, and then the anarchist group, with his fatal secret—a conclusion that the reader can recognize as psychically necessary because of the structure of the narrative.

Unlike the almost wholly laughable group of 'anarchists' assembled under the paunchy wing of Verloc, the Geneva revolutionary group has a certain variety and depth. Like Verloc, its leader, Peter Ivanovitch, is fat, and supported by a woman. We need to know little more; although he is on stage quite a lot, he counts for little in the course of events, being merely one of 'the apes of a sinister jungle' (p. ix). Most of the people with whom he is associated (Nikita, Julius Lasparra and his frowzy daughters, Madame de S——) are little improvement on Michaelis and Ossipon, but in Sophia Antonovna Conrad at last finds a revolutionary with some stature and dignity. Although he thinks her 'wrong-headed' (p. ix), Sophia is nevertheless an old soldier of revolutionism, and her words have the authority and strength that Conrad always accords to her type.[9]

'And what is death? At any rate, not a shameful thing like some kinds of life ... The subservient, submissive life. Life? No! Vegetation on the filthy heap of iniquity which the world is. Life, Razumov, not to be vile must be a revolt—a pitiless protest—all the time.' (p. 260)

Though Conrad affords this degree of imaginative sympathy to Sophia Antonovna he had no more respect for her beliefs than for those of General T——. This is quite clear from the Author's Note:

'The ferocity and imbecility of an autocratic rule rejecting all legality and in fact basing itself upon complete moral anarchism provokes the no less imbecile and atrocious answer of a purely Utopian revolutionism encompassing destruction by the first means to hand, in the strange conviction that a fundamental change of hearts must follow the downfall of any given human institutions. These people are unable to see that all they can effect is merely a change of names. The oppressors and the oppressed are all Russians together; and the world is brought once more face to face with the truth of the saying that the tiger cannot change his stripes nor the leopard his spots.' (p. x)

No doubt Sophia Antonovna and Councillor Mikulin are

attractive characters when contrasted with Peter Ivanovitch or General T—, but they are nevertheless fatally embroiled in an impossible political conflict. Mikulin's question to Razumov —'Where to?'—simply does not admit of *any* answer couched in political terms. The predominant tension in *Under Western Eyes*, unlike that of *The Secret Agent*, is not between anarchism and fidelity, but between any form of political loyalty and the demands of private morality. We must thus ask how, if the novel is (as Jocelyn Baines suggests) about 'the ultimate futility of all political action',[10] a man is to uphold his obligations to his fellows? By the end of the first part of *Under Western Eyes* it is abundantly clear that the choice between patriotism and anarchism (at least in a Russian context) is either false or tragic.

The choice may be false, because it could be avoided: Tekla and Natalia Haldin refuse to be defined by allegiance to any political creed. It is through his association with these two women that Razumov finally achieves redemption, and escapes from his 'rack'. Marlow had reacted against the illusions of women in 'Heart of Darkness' by calling them 'out of it'; in *Under Western Eyes*, 'out of it' is the only place (in Stein's sense) 'to be'.

Tekla is instrumental in providing the necessary confidence and human connection necessary to Razumov's later decision to confess. Drawn by her avowed hatred of Peter Ivanovitch ('Great men are horrible') (p. 232), he sees in Tekla's 'disillusionment' and isolation a reflection of his own predicament. During the course of their conversation, he remarks that it is odd that he doesn't even know her name. She responds:

' "Is it strange? No one is told my name. No one cares. No one talks to me, no one writes to me. My parents don't even know if I'm alive. I have no use for a name, and I have almost forgotten it myself."

Razumov murmured gravely, "Yes, but still . . ."

She went on much slower, with indifference—

"You may call me Tekla, then. My poor Andrei called me so. He lived in wretchedness and suffering, and died in misery. That is the lot of all us Russians, nameless Russians. There is nothing else for us, and no hope anywhere, unless . . ."

"Unless what?"

"Unless all these people with names are done away with," she finished, blinking and pursing up her lips.

"It will be easier to call you Tekla, as you direct me," said Razumov, "if you consent to call me Kirylo, when we are talking like this—quietly—only you and me." ' (pp. 235–6)

Although Razumov identifies Tekla as a 'revolutionist', and she is drawn to him for his strength ('You kill the monsters') (p. 236), the pact that is tacitly formed here transcends political boundaries. Paradoxically, Tekla's passionate plea that 'all these people with names' must be 'done away with' is balanced in this passage by the fact that in it both she and Razumov establish personal identity. The 'label' Razumov becomes 'an honoured name', Kirylo, which Tekla must call him only when they are conversing together in *private*. For the first time Razumov's notion that 'Life is a public thing' is directly challenged, as he makes a tentative step towards establishing a personal relationship based on those values of 'domestic tradition' for which he had so envied Victor Haldin. As for the 'people with names', the 'great men' whom Tekla so detests, they are the men defined by public role, the political men on both sides of the ideological spectrum: the Peter Ivanovitches, and the government figures (who, by a wonderful ironic touch, are too august to be named) de P—, General T—, and Prince K—.

While the scene just quoted is so quietly understated as to seem unremarkable, the confession scene with Natalia Haldin is the novel's most intense, indeed even melodramatic, moment. It has been preceded by scenes of increasing warmth and frequency between Razumov and Natalia, most of which are reported second (and sometimes third)[11] hand by the narrator. We may have some reason to doubt whether this intimacy is psychologically very likely. Though there is no doubt that Natalia has every reason to be attracted by the man so esteemed by her brother, our belief in Razumov's attraction to her must be taken on trust, as it is substantiated largely by the narrator's descriptions of her graces. One might account for this incongruity by positing some internal force that drives Razumov to confront his own guilt; certainly the obsessive, Dostoyevskian power of the scene might bear this out. Just as Sonya is an emblem of goodness to Raskolnikov, so is Natalia Haldin to Razumov.

Razumov is ultimately drawn by the magnetism of Natalia's goodness to the moment when he must confess, the moment when, 'tottering suddenly on the very edge of the precipice' (p. 349), a man admits what is darkest in him. Such an admission can only be efficacious, Razumov feels, in the presence of one who has 'no guile, no deception, no falsehood, no suspicion' (p. 349). Even so, he needs to be reassured that she believes in 'the efficacy of remorse' (p. 352), and her words confirm the depth of her faith:

> 'Listen Kirylo Sidorovitch. I believe that the future will be merciful to us all. Revolutionist and reactionary, victim and executioner, betrayer and betrayed, they shall all be pitied together when the light breaks on our black sky at last. Pitied and forgotten; for without that there can be no union and no love.'
> (p. 353)

Strengthened by this transcendent statement of faith, Razumov slowly reveals himself to Natalia as the man responsible for the death of her brother. Offering no excuse but his terrible, inhuman, isolation, he runs out into the rain, returning to his room to announce 'I am washed clean' (p. 357) to his landlord. Only two things remain: first, to record his full confession in his diary; second, to share that confession with the revolutionists, in one final action extricating himself from his involvement both with them and with Mikulin. His short and tormented life of allegiance to political causes is over.

Razumov's diary provides the best statement of his final position. It is both a confession and a record of initiation into what the old teacher calls 'another profounder knowledge' (p. 357). Beginning with the astonishingly unlikely revelation that he was originally prompted by a desire to 'steal the soul' of Haldin's sister, Razumov acknowledges his gradual recognition of Natalia's trustful and loving nature: 'I've never known any kind of love. There is something in the mere word . . .' (p. 360.)

> 'It was as if your pure brow bore a light which fell on me, searched my heart and saved me from ignominy, from ultimate undoing. And it saved you too. Pardon my presumption. But

there was that in your glances which seemed to tell me that you . . .
Your light! your truth! I felt that I must tell you that I had
ended by loving you. And to tell you that I must first confess.
Confess, go out—and perish.' (p. 361)

The result of this confession is, as Natalia had assured him it
would be, efficacious. Though he continues to regret what he
has done, he is released from the rack of his conflict. Razumov
realizes at the end that his position, torn between conflicting
versions of social responsibility, has to be transcended by a
vision of autonomous human responsibility. The values of
fidelity and faith are not public ones, but essentially flow out
of the autonomy of the individual. The spirit of love, which
informs no political view of the human condition, has at last
allowed him his freedom as a realized human being:

'I suffer horribly, but I am not in despair. There is only one more
thing to do for me. After that—if they let me—I shall go away and
bury myself in obscure misery. In giving Victor Haldin up, it was
myself, after all, whom I have betrayed most basely.' (p. 361)

This from a man who had previously declared that 'all a man
can betray is his conscience'; thus the bonds of solidarity that
unite men are ultimately seen, in *Under Western Eyes*, not as the
arbitrary moral codes of a given society, but the transcendent
imperatives of faith. In allowing Victor Haldin to go free
Razumov would not have been condoning the man's action,
but simply behaving humanely to a fellow creature.

Razumov's conclusion—the very last words of his diary—is
particularly interesting:

'Only don't be deceived, Natalia Victorovna, I am not con-
verted. Have I then the soul of a slave? No! I am independent—
and therefore perdition is my lot.' (pp. 361–2)

He reiterates the claim of newfound 'independence' in his last
words to the anarchists (to whom he has gone at midnight to
confess):

'Today, of all days since I came amongst you, I was made safe,
and today I made myself free from falsehood, from remorse—
independent of every single human being on this earth.' (p. 368)

But before he can leave, he is pinned unresisting to the wall, while Nikita brutally bursts his eardrums.

At this point it should be clear that Razumov has utterly renounced any way of being that involves an 'institutional' response to his responsibilities as a person. The 'profounder knowledge' that he has gained has involved a transition from one kind of social alienation to another: from the 'solitary' existence of his days as a student to the 'independent' existence that he attains at the end of the novel. After the agony of his involvement with Haldin, and the resultant term of hypocrisy, conflict, and despair, Razumov has finally transcended politics, stepped right out of any form of 'patriotism'—and, in so doing, established both an independent existence (the shift from a 'label' to a 'name') and a community of devoted friends. He has, through his suffering and remorse, created that 'domestic tradition' that he had lacked. When Tekla follows him to the hospital following the tram accident caused by his deafness— itself beginning to have some symbolic value—she announces that she is his 'relative'.

It has been a bitterly won victory, but it is perhaps supported and expanded by Natalia Haldin's final vision:

> 'I must own to you that I shall never give up looking forward to the day when all discord shall be silenced. Try to imagine its dawn! The tempest of blows and of execrations is over; all is still: the new sun is rising, and the weary men united at last, taking count in their conscience of the ended contest, feel saddened by their victory, because so many ideas have perished for the triumph of one, so many beliefs have abandoned them without support. They feel alone on the earth and gather close together. Yes, there must be many bitter hours! But at last the anguish of hearts shall be extinguished in love.' (pp. 376-7)

But just as the promised 'clear sky never dawns without a storm' over Costaguana, so too the 'advent of loving concord' (p. 377) to which Natalia looks forward will be a long time in coming.[12] We may wonder if it is to come at all: just as it was impossible firmly to decide whether Costaguana had moved closer to the promised day, so too are we doubtful that the era promised by Natalia's final words will ever dawn. Her vision is ultimately a transcendent one, laden with imagery of the Last

Judgment, and it offers scant hope for the foreseeable future. In the meantime, man is doomed to the achieved tragic insight of his 'independence', and woman to a life of dedicated service.

Razumov is accompanied back to Southern Russia by the devoted Tekla. The last words about him are appropriately left to Sophia Antonovna, whose vision of life as 'a pitiless protest' most adequately accounts for Razumov's history:

> 'There are evil moments in every life. A false idea enters one's brain, and then fear is born—fear of oneself, fear for oneself. Or else a false courage—who knows? Well, call it what you like; but tell me, how many of them would deliver themselves up deliberately to perdition (as he himself says in that book) rather than go on living, secretly debased in their own eyes? How many? . . . And please mark this—he was safe when he did it. It was just when he believed himself safe and more—infinitely more—when the possibility of being loved by that admirable girl first dawned upon him, that he discovered that his bitterest railings, the worst wickedness, the devil work of his hate and pride, could never cover up the ignominy of the existence before him. There's character in such a discovery.' (pp. 379–80)

Finally it is one's own 'eyes' that are important, be they Eastern or Western—the 'character' of the individual man is ultimately the theatre in which the basic human struggles are played out. *Under Western Eyes* is unique in Conrad's work in that it seems so strongly to place itself on the side of autonomous man, but that may well be because in the context of Russian life there is no other viable choice. There is no choice between General T— and Peter Ivanovitch—and the failure of this particular society to offer a viable alternative, an order based on something worth being faithful to, results in tragic dilemmas like that of Razumov. It may be, as Albert Guerard says, that Razumov's final triumph is 'a genuine one',[13] but it is pitiful that it need have happened at all.

One is left with a feeling of bitter pessimism; Natalia Haldin's transcendent vision of 'loving concord' is little solace, and Sophia Antonovna's striking analysis of Razumov's 'character' is finally undercut by her last words. Responding to the old teacher of languages' lack of enthusiasm for Peter Ivanovitch's marriage to a peasant girl, she announces to him:

'Peter Ivanovitch is an inspired man' (p. 382). Such a sentiment doesn't offer us much hope.

Impressive as *Under Western Eyes* is, we are left with some doubt whether it is finally appropriate to read it as a statement about the human condition—as one might read *Lord Jim*, for instance.[14] Its final vision of personal tragedy, devotion, and love, is tempered by its failure to see *any* possible amelioration of the political ills that it so powerfully documents. Natalia's vision of loving concord is all very well, but it appears to take the place of any more fundamental concern with political reality. Are we to believe that opposition to the tyrannical regime of the de P—s is unjustified? Sophia Antonovna is in many ways an attractive character, but the novel's last line leaves us with a memory of her as a gullible and 'wrong-headed' woman. It appears that, *in Russia*, the General T—s and de P—s are an inevitability. Conrad's refusal to accept that a change of institutions might effect a change of hearts is perhaps understandable when one looks at the horrors committed in the name of Freedom, but this ought not to mean that opposition to an autocratic regime is profitless. Natalia Haldin's final answer—a life of dedicated service amongst the sick and poor—in effect serves the purposes of the very government that has created that sickness and poverty. The refusal to engage oneself in politics, in this sense, is itself a political stance (as Councillor Mikulin points out) in that it supports the status quo. A transcendent faith in the future does not mitigate social evil. It is with that evil, and with the shell of a defeated but victorious Razumov, that we are left at the end of the novel.

Though *Under Western Eyes* is limited by its Russianness in the ways that I have suggested, it may be that it is also served by it. There seems a distinct movement discernible from *Nostromo*, with its sceptical renunciation of the ideal of 'progress', through *The Secret Agent*'s bleak incapacity to see anything but mischance or misunderstanding in human affairs, to the almost overwhelming hopelessness of life in Czarist Russia—which comes almost to stand as a metaphor for an increasingly dark vision of human social life as seen in general. *Under Western Eyes* is Conrad's last sustained version of man's social and political life—as if, having said *that*, nothing more could be said. The dramas of his later novels are no longer those on the largest scale, but rather of individuals struggling for some kind of fulfilment or tranquillity in a universe increasingly inhospitable to its human inhabitants. And hand in hand with this movement comes the emergence of that creed which E. M. Forster sought, but which we have failed to find, in the greatest of Conrad's works.

9

Conclusion: *Chance, Victory, The Shadow Line*

Chance (1913) and *Victory* (1915) are generally agreed to be transitional works, sharing many of the characteristics and virtues of Conrad's earlier novels, yet beginning also to reveal those defects that mar the later works. In both novels we can see the tensions of which I have been speaking at work, but in both these tensions are modified and resolved in important, and novelistically unprofitable, ways.

Chance seemed to Conrad one of his most successful novels; writing to his agent, J. B. Pinker, some time after its completion, he maintained:

> 'It's the biggest piece of work I've done since *Lord Jim*. As to what *it is* I am very confident. As to what will happen to it when launched—I am much less confident. And it's a pity. One doesn't do a trick like that twice.'[1]

His faith in the work was justified by its sales.[2] This popular success was particularly gratifying to Conrad:

> 'This gave me a considerable amount of pleasure, because what I always feared most was drifting unconsciously into the position of a writer for a limited coterie; a position which would have been odious to me as throwing a doubt on the soundness of my belief in the solidarity of all mankind in simple ideas and in sincere emotion.'[3]

The whole of the Author's Note continues to betray an underlying unease, as if Conrad were aware of the need to defend his work against some barely apprehended attack:

> 'I cannot say that any particular moral complexion has been put on this novel but I do not think that anybody has detected in it an evil intention. And it is only for their intentions that men can be held responsible.' (p. x)

The final sentence is either unclear, or simply false; it suggests the slackness of thinking, and of writing, that all too frequently infect *Chance* itself.

Once again Marlow is employed as a narrator, but he has the creaky feel of someone brought out of retirement to do a command performance: all the motions are familiar, but none work. He enters *Chance* as a vaguely weary man of the world, who has (by an incredibly circuitous route) come across a story sufficiently interesting to elicit a series of digressions, comments and philosophical disquisitions against which the action may (presumably) be better understood. His view of the universe is characteristically Conradian—almost formulaicly so:

> 'It was one of those dewy, clear, starry nights, oppressing our spirit, crushing our pride, by the brilliant evidence of the awful loneliness, of the hopeless obscure insignificance of our globe lost in the splendid revelation of a glittering, soulless universe.' (p. 50)

In this traditional setting wander the lonely protagonists of what appears to be another of Conrad's dramas of conflicting obligations and values. His principal characters are profoundly isolated: Flora de Barral, alone and pathetically dependent after her father's ruin, is saved from total despair only because she is incapable of understanding what has happened to her:

> 'Could one conceive of her more mature, while still as ignorant as she was, one must conclude that she would have become an idiot on the spot . . .' (p. 117)

Captain Anthony, on the other hand, has chosen his loneliness with his profession: 'his life had been a life of solitude and silence—and desire.' (p. 328.) The theme of 'solitude and silence', of Kurtz and Decoud, is familiar and promising, but previous attempts to handle 'desire' have all too often been disastrous. And it is *through* desire that Anthony and Flora attempt to transcend their 'moral loneliness'.

There are thus obvious parallels between *Chance* and *Under Western Eyes*, in which Razumov can only escape his terrible initial isolation through the experience of love. But 'love' in *Under Western Eyes* is not simply sexual love, but those 'domestic' values of human relatedness that allow a community of feeling and value in the face of the vast social and moral failures of Russia. Razumov's betrayal of Haldin is also a betrayal of his capacity actively to participate in this privately extended human community; Anthony's failure (to consummate his marriage) is, in contrast, less weighty. Marlow seeks to give this painful event an extended (but not altogether convincing) significance:

> 'Pairing off is the fate of mankind. And if two beings thrown together, mutually attracted, resist the necessity, fail in understanding and voluntarily stop short of the—the embrace, in the noblest meaning of the word, then they are committing a sin against life, the call of which is simple. Perhaps sacred. And the punishment of it is an invasion of complexity, a tormenting, forcibly tortuous involution of feelings, the deepest form of suffering from which indeed something significant may come at last, which may be criminal or heroic, may be madness or wisdom—or even a straight if despairing decision.' (pp. 427–8)

This seems to me impossible to take seriously; further, it introduces a language ('sin', 'sacred') in which one can see the seeds of a growing sentimentality.[4] But one can also see its connection with the terrifying tangle of misunderstandings out of which arose the events of *The Secret Agent*. Once again, human ignorance and egoism cause misunderstanding, while at the same time knowledge is of dubious value:

> 'I think that to understand everything is not good for the intellect. A well-stocked intelligence weakens the impulse to action; an overstocked one leads gently to idiocy.' (p. 62)

This echo of a theme from (most notably) *Nostromo* is merely stated in *Chance*, but never embodied in the action. Even if there were the possibility of 'understanding everything', the theme of the corrosive effects of knowledge is an empty one in *Chance*: the failure of understanding between Anthony and Flora is caused by too little knowledge, not too much. The only 'wide understanding' open to us is Marlow's, and even that is only intermittently satisfying.

The most important, and least satisfying, of Marlow's notions—I don't think it necessary to say 'ideas'—is that of 'chance'; a typical statement purports to explain why de Barral should have hired and maintained a vicious governess:

> 'And if you ask me how, wherefore, for what reason? I will answer you: Why, by chance! By the merest chance, as things do happen, lucky and unlucky, terrible or tender, important or unimportant; and even things which are neither, things so

completely neutral in character that you would wonder why they do happen at all if you didn't know that they, too, carry in their insignificance the seeds of further incalculable chances.' (pp. 99–100)

But this is simply nonsense; de Barral may have hired the governess through chance, but it is his thoughtless egoism and inadequate judgment that allow her to stay in her position. Certainly the notion of the 'accidental' nature of things—like the idea that 'all we are responsible for is our intentions'—cuts the very ground from under any concept of human responsibility. The assertion that Flora and Anthony have committed a 'sin against life' makes no sense whatever if that sin is caused by 'chance'.[5]

The problem that separates the two lovers seems to be caused not only by 'chance', but also by themselves, because the isolation in which each of them is enmeshed allows no grasp of a standard against which their behaviour could be measured:

'He had broken away from his surroundings; she stood outside the pale. One aspect of conventions which people who declaim against them lose sight of is that conventions make both joy and suffering easier to bear in a becoming manner. But those two were outside all conventions. They were as untrammelled in a sense as the first man and the first woman. The trouble was that I could not imagine anything about Flora de Barral and the brother of Mrs Fyne. Or if you like, I could imagine *anything*, which comes practically to the same thing.' (p. 210)

Anthony is, however, no Kurtz, though the language here reminds us of that of 'Heart of Darkness'; he is an average, inarticulate man of slow imagination and strong desire, and his love for Flora is an amalgam of real passion and dangerously sentimentalized pity. Marlow tells us that:

'If Anthony's love had been as egoistic as love generally is, it would have been greater than the egoism of his vanity—or of his generosity, if you like—and all this could not have happened. He would not have hit upon that renunciation at which one does not know whether to grin or shudder. It is true too that then his love would not have fastened itself upon the unhappy daughter of de Barral. But it was a love born of that rare pity which is not akin to contempt because rooted in an overwhelmingly strong capacity for tenderness—the tenderness of the fiery predatory kind—the tenderness of silent, solitary men, the voluntary, passionate outcasts of their kind. At the same time I am forced to think that his vanity must have been enormous.' (p. 331)

Guerard rightly points out the ambivalence of this attitude,[6] with its conflict between a critical assessment of Anthony and a sentimentalized picture of him as a 'passionate outcast'. Ultimately, it is the sentimentalized picture that wins, for the final triumphant embrace that marks his victory is unequivocally endorsed; what Edward Crankshaw calls 'the spiritual rescue of Flora de Barral from the forces of darkness'[7] is unambiguously achieved.

Flora is granted not a lifetime of happiness, but only the six years to the time when Anthony is accidentally drowned. It is not clear what to make of this ending: whether it is simply a gratuitous piece of bad luck, or whether it is meaningfully connected to a metaphysical apprehension about the intransigence of things—indeed, the novel does not allow us clearly to distinguish the two. The contrast with Conrad's earlier novels should be clear. Whereas the loneliness from which Flora and Anthony suffer is something that had previously been seen as having potentially positive functions (in the self-knowledge and self-judgment of Kurtz, the value-generating autonomy of Jim, the clarity of Decoud, the achieved 'freedom' of Razumov), here human loneliness is not so much an ambiguous metaphysical condition as a state to *get over*. Crankshaw's reasonable belief that the theme is the 'spiritual rescue' of Flora from 'the forces of darkness' reminds us that such forces, in Conrad's previous novels, might be accommodated in one way or another, but could never *by definition* be escaped from. In earlier novels to escape from the darkness would have meant: ceasing to be human. Although Flora's good fortune is later undercut by bad, the theme of the capricious workings of 'chance' has little of the moral drama that had characterized most of Conrad's earlier work.

Victory has distinct thematic similarities to *Chance*, being once again the story of a love affair in which a much-abused woman is rescued by a solitary man. But Axel Heyst, unlike Captain

Anthony, is a complicated and self-aware figure, whose isolation is not merely a corollary of his chosen profession, but an articulate decision taken in the light of an implicitly Schopenhauerian understanding of the universe. With the possible exception of Razumov, Heyst is more firmly at the centre of the novel than is any other of Conrad's heroes. Indeed, *Victory* is quite explicitly a dramatized test of Heyst's attitude to his own existence.

Heyst is a thoroughgoing sceptic, who believes that 'all action is bound to be harmful' (p. 54); unlike Decoud, whom he resembles in this, he is equally sceptical about intelligence: 'Thought, action—so many snares! If you begin to think you will be unhappy.' (p. 193.) Attempting to become a sort of Singleton-with-an-education, Heyst wanders, or lives on his island, as an enactment of a profound philosophical isolation from the affairs of human beings:

> 'Heyst was not conscious of either friends or enemies. It was the very essence of his life to be a solitary achievement, accomplished not by hermit-like withdrawal with its silence and immobility, but by a system of restless wandering, by the detachment of an impermanent dweller among changing scenes.' (p. 90)

His description of himself to Lena emphasizes the extent to which he has cut himself off:

> 'What captivated my fancy was that I, Axel Heyst, the most detached of creatures in this earthly captivity, the veriest tramp on this earth, an indifferent stroller going through the world's bustle—that I should have been there to step into the situation of an agent of Providence. I, a man of universal scorn and unbelief ...' (pp. 198–9)

This isolation is imposed upon not only from without, but initially from within, from Heyst's latent compassion and acute, if dormant, sense of moral connectedness. His loan to Morrison and rescue of Lena result in the human involvements which he had pledged himself to avoid: 'I only know that he who forms a tie is lost. The germ of corruption has entered into his soul.' (pp. 199–200.) In spite of this he believes himself safe on his island with Lena: 'Nothing can break in on us here.' (p. 223.) He thus arrives at a most distinctly Conradian position: although human values have no metaphysical basis, they are nevertheless necessary to the business of 'hanging together': 'Truth, work, ambition, love itself, may only be counters in the lamentable or despicable game of life, but when one takes a hand one must play the game.' (p. 203.) Heyst continues to feel essentially alone, but must act as if he were not so.

But one can, of course, be outside the pale of human involvements in a number of ways. It is a major irony of *Victory* that Heyst's philosophical detachment is to be challenged by men whose analogous belief in the essential autonomy of human beings is only a psychopathic characteristic. Mr Jones, who 'depended on himself, as if the world were still one great, wild jungle without law' (p. 113), has a philosophical detachment that makes a tacit comment on Heyst's metaphysical stance. Jones's follower Pedro is literally what the revolutionaries of *Under Western Eyes* were figuratively, a creature of the jungle—only minimally human, with that fidelity to his master that links him more properly with watchdogs than with men. The third member of this unsavoury party is the manservant Martin Ricardo, who has his own attractive formulation of what it means for a man to be 'free':

> 'I follow a gentleman. That ain't the same thing as to serve an employer. They give you wages as they'd fling a bone to a dog, and they expect you to be grateful. It's worse than slavery. You don't expect a slave that's bought for money to be grateful. And if you sell your work—what is it but selling your own self? You've got so many days to live and you sell them one after another. Hey! Who can pay me enough for my life? Ay! But they throw at you your week's money and expect you to say "thank you" before you pick it up.' (p. 145)

What we are to witness is the opposition of two radically different versions of human autonomy: Heyst's isolated scepticism against the psychopathic amorality of Mr Jones and his peripatetic entourage.

But there is something gratuitous in this opposition, for Heyst, like Captain Anthony before him, has done nothing to bring his misfortunes upon himself. Yet both he and Mr Jones suggest an allegorical dimension to their conflict. Heyst calls Jones and his followers 'the envoys of the outer world. Here they are before you—evil intelligence, instinctive savagery, arm in arm. The brute force is at the back.' (p. 329.) Mr Jones, in reply to the demand that he 'define' himself, responds:

> 'In one way I am—yes I am the world itself, come to pay you a visit. In another sense I am an outcast—almost an outlaw. If you prefer a less materialistic view, I am a sort of fate—the retribution that waits its time.' (p. 379)

Thus we have in *Victory* the same tensions that underlie *Chance*: on the one hand there is the apparently irresistible need for a man to overcome isolation through love; on the other, the terrible fact that the universe is not indifferent, but hostile, to the affairs of humankind. Neither the union of Anthony and Flora nor that of Heyst and Lena can abide, the one destroyed by 'chance', the other by 'fate'—both of which are metaphysical principles not of neutrality, but of malignancy. But neither of the poles of this new tension is very adequately realized in the individual novels. Conrad had never written convincingly of romantic love, and his new belief in its importance is not accompanied by a greater capacity to portray it; thus we have a description of Lena's emotions as she is confronted by the lustful hotel-keeper, Schomberg:

> 'She was no longer alone in the world now. She resisted without a moment of faltering, because she was no longer deprived of moral support; because she was a human being who counted; because she was no longer defending herself for herself alone; because of the faith that had been born in her—the faith in the man of her destiny, and perhaps in the Heaven which had sent him so wonderfully to cross her path.' (p. 292)

This affirmation is nothing more than a string of romantic clichés.

The sentimental ethic of *Chance* and *Victory* is balanced by an emerging fatalism. Standing against the movement of a man towards a woman is the very nature of life itself, cruelly represented in *Victory* by Jones, Ricardo, and Pedro. Anthony's death is gratuitous; Heyst's is caused by the fact that Schomberg doesn't like him; thus the subtle ambiguities of Conrad's earlier works begin, in these novels, to be transformed into a relatively crude opposition between the sentiment of love and the kinds of bad luck that oppose it.

The ending of *Victory* confirms Heyst's belief that 'he who forms a tie is lost', although Heyst himself, at the last, seems to renounce it. As he goes to join the dead Lena in the blazing remains of his house, after the absurd debacle and multiple deaths of the novel's final scenes, he says to Davidson: 'Ah, Davidson, woe to the man whose heart has not learned while young to hope, to love—to put its trust in life!' (p. 410.) The terrible irony is that while this is an admirable enough emotion, life (as represented by Mr Jones) is not a very safe place in which to put one's trust. The Author's Note makes an attempt to straighten out the muddle, but its lucidity is no more than superficial:

> 'It is only when the catastrophe matches the natural obscurity of our fate that even the best representative of the race is liable to lose his detachment. It is very obvious that on the arrival of the gentlemanly Mr Jones, the single-minded Ricardo and the faithful Pedro, Heyst, the man of universal detachment, loses his mental self-possession, that fine attitude before the universally irremediable which wears the name of stoicism. It is all a matter of proportion. There should have been a remedy for that sort of thing. And yet there is no remedy. Behind this minute instance of life's hazards Heyst in his fine detachment had lost the habit of asserting himself. I don't mean the courage of self-assertion, either moral or physical, but the mere way of it, the trick of the thing, the readiness of mind and the turn of the hand that come without reflection and lead the man to excellence in life, in art, in crime, in virtue, and for the matter of that, even in love.' (p. x)

Victory (and *Chance*) are thus based on the opposition between what a man *rightly* wants and what the universe is prepared to allow him. Insofar as the catastrophe with which *Victory* ends does not appear to be the logical outcome either of Heyst's actions or of his beliefs, it might be maintained that this is a novel without those underlying moral tensions that characterize Conrad's earlier work.

In the novels from *An Outcast of the Islands* to *Under Western Eyes* (with the exception of *The Secret Agent*) a major question had continually recurred: what is it that a man should want? The answer, as we have seen, often involved recognizing that there were certain conflicts between what he wanted in and for himself and what he wanted in terms of a given social order. In the cases of Captain Anthony and Axel Heyst, however, the impulse to save and to cherish a lonely and helpless woman is quite explicitly endorsed. These are men who know what is right to do, though the universe may conspire against their doing it successfully.

Both novels have thematic structures that lend themselves interestingly to analysis, but both are (relatively) bad novels. Indeed, the tensions that sustain *Chance* and *Victory* seem to demand dramatization in melodramatic terms. Though such a conclusion may have been coming since the treatment of Decoud, nevertheless the key to this developmental view of Conrad lies in *The Secret Agent*, for it is in, and after, this novel that Conrad renounced a vision of personal autonomy in its positive sense. After *The Secret Agent* autonomy becomes a state that has to be transcended through love, whereas it had previously been felt to be a state of immense potential for evil (the corrosion of common value) *or* good (through its metaphysical clarity, and the values that may flow from that clarity). The apparently 'literary' defects of *Chance* and *Victory* (and most of the works after them)—their sentimental ethics, melodramatic plots, patches of slack writing—arise, if not because of this shift in Conrad's views about human life in general, then at least in conjunction with that shift. In *Chance* and *Victory* man comes to be less and less responsible for his own destiny. The universe takes over: it is a turbulent and capricious universe, but its workings are not so interesting as those of the human beings of Conrad's earlier novels, who had taken the responsibility (insofar as they knew what it was) for their own actions.

The Shadow Line (1917) is the last of Conrad's reasonably successful works, though it has about it some of the same strain that mars a similar story, 'The Secret Sharer' (1912)—most notably in its over-insistence on its major thematic dimension. Yet it begins in the spirit and rhetoric of that much earlier story, 'Youth' (1898):[8]

> 'Only the young have such moments. I don't mean the very young. No. The very young have, properly speaking, no moments. It is the privilege of early youth to live in advance of its days in all the beautiful continuity of hope which knows no pauses and no introspection.' (p. 3)

All three are stories of 'a man exclusively of sea and ships; the sea the only world that counted, and the ships the test of manliness, of temperament, of courage and fidelity—and of love.'⁹ Each recounts the manly overcoming of the rigours of that test through the virtues that Conrad called '*les valeurs idéales*'; and each has, if not a happy, at least a triumphal ending. As a group they have something of a prelapsarian quality, dedicated as they are (and as *The Nigger of the 'Narcissus'*, despite its pretensions to the contrary, is not) to that state of harmonious manliness that could once be found aboard ships. Cowardice and superstition are not banished from the world, but (what is more) overcome.

'Youth', which first introduces Marlow as a narrator, is a nice blend of the elegiac and ironic, as Marlow recounts his first experience as an officer, aboard the ill-fated *Judea*, with the motto 'Do or Die' on her stern: 'I remember it took my fancy immensely. There was a touch of romance in it, something that made me love the old thing—something that appealed to my youth!' (p. 5.) The voyage is one of those 'that seem ordered for the illustration of life, that might stand for a symbol of existence. You fight, work, sweat, nearly kill yourself, sometimes do kill yourself, trying to accomplish something—and you can't' (pp. 3–4). The remark is designed not so much to invoke the metaphor of the ship as microcosm, as to counterpoint the two prevailing interpretative modes of the narrative—the innocent and the experienced—and to do so from the start, so as to provide the right tonal balance for the ensuing action. For the problems raised by the last voyage of the *Judea* do not concern what to value, or how to go on valuing it. The sea into which it ingloriously disappears may be hostile, but it threatens only death, not that terrible corrosive disbelief that an imaginative man would reap from a contemplation of its hostility. The universe of Marlow's youth, then, has no psychic significance for him, for its alien qualities are not introjectible. Or, at least, not yet: the older Marlow, like his seasoned listeners, now knows his erstwhile pieties and romantic ideals for the 'illusions' that they were, and are—and can only regret their passing.

'. . . I remember my youth and the feeling that will never come back any more—the feeling that I could last for ever, outlast the sea, the earth, and all men; the deceitful feeling that lures us on to joys, to perils, to love, to vain effort—to death; the triumphant conviction of strength, the heat of life in the handful of dust, the glow in the heart that with every year grows dim, grows cold, grows small, and expires—and expires, too soon, too soon—before life itself.' (pp. 36–7)

But those illusions 'save' only when we are unaware that they are illusory.

The differences between 'Youth' and *The Shadow Line* are pertinent here, for they help to demonstrate the changes in the later Conrad. In the earlier story the innocence of the young Marlow, and its correlative conviction and courage, are balanced by the repeated incantation 'Pass the bottle' (itself both disillusioned and celebratory) of the mature Marlow, whose vision of his own past displays both its optimism and its wrong-headedness. In 'Youth' the older man's view of his own youth is the subject of the tale. Though this tension between innocence and experience survives in *The Shadow Line*, it does so only in an attenuated form.

The narrator of 'The Secret Sharer', like the young Marlow and the Captain in *The Shadow Line*, begins as an innocent, though the loss of that innocence is a slower and more conscious process than in the previous stories:

'Yes, I had my hands full of complications which were most valuable as "experience". People have a great opinion of the advantages of experience. But in that connection experience means always something disagreeable as opposed to the charm and innocence of illusions.' (p. 65)

To what extent this judgment is retrospective is unclear from the context, which is a problem inherent in the retrospective point of view. It is solved in a wholly convincing way by the introduction of passages from the Captain's diary of the time, which imposes a clear distinction between the remembering voice and the original lived experience. On board a becalmed ship, his crew prostrated, his chief mate sick to death with fear and fever, his essential supplies of quinine mysteriously ruined, the Captain has no question that the dreams and illusions of youth are irretrievably behind him:

'. . . as I emerge on deck the ordered arrangement of the stars meets my eye, unclouded, infinitely wearisome. There they are: stars, sun, light, darkness, space, great waters; the formidable work of the Seven Days, into which mankind seems to have blundered unbidden. Or else decoyed. Even as I have been decoyed into this awful, this death haunted command . . .' (pp. 97-8)

The mate, Mr Burns, believes the ship becalmed by the curse laid on it by its former captain; his new captain rejects this as superstitious nonsense, yet is himself given to a rhetoric suggesting not the indifference of the universe but its superhuman hostility: does man 'blunder' into the human predicament, or is he 'decoyed' into it? Though *The Shadow Line* rejects ghosts and their curses, more potent and yet more mysterious powers seem to lurk behind it: 'It appeared that even at sea a man could become the victim of evil spirits. I felt on my face the breath of unknown powers that shape our destinies.' (p. 62.) Why is the ship becalmed?—'only purposeful malevolence could account for it.' (p. 87.)

As *The Nigger of the 'Narcissus'* makes clear, the greatest danger at sea is too much free time, to think, to introspect, to contemplate one's condition. The malevolent powers of the Captain's tortuous imaginings are conjured rather than apprehended: his diary has the following entry: 'But I suppose the trouble is that the ship is still lying motionless, not under command; and that I have nothing to do to keep my imagination from running wild amongst the disastrous images of the worst that may befall us.' (p. 106.) To command, then, necessitates action, which in turn silences imagination. When the awaited breeze finally arrives only the Captain and Ransome, the cook with a heart disease, are (as it were) able-bodied. But Ransome works as if forgetful of his complaint, 'putting out his strength . . . for some distinct ideal' (p. 126), and the ship makes harbour. Once ashore he asks to be paid off, so as to enter hospital; at the close, the universal significance of this is carefully invoked: '. . . I listened to him going up the companion stairs cautiously, step by step, in mortal fear of starting into sudden anger our common enemy it was his hard fate to carry consciously within his faithful breast.' (p. 133.) With our knowledge of what has gone before, everything is here:

mortality, consciousness of it, and the heroism of keeping faith nonetheless. As Captain Giles says to his no-longer-young fellow captain: 'a man should stand up to his bad luck, to his mistakes, to his conscience, and all that sort of thing. Why—what else would you have to fight against?' (p. 132.)

It sounds like a creed, and it echoes through much of the late work, in unambiguous formulation. But the simple values invoked in fighting that good fight are not only too easily transgressed, but too easily recognized as artificial restraints imposed against our own egoism and tendency to despair. In his finest works, Conrad is unwilling to give up that creed—as E. M. Forster suggests—but equally unwilling to condemn unambiguously those who do so. Ultimately, the fighting of that fight resides in those attitudes of compassion, dignity, and honour that inform Conrad's attitude both towards his own work and towards his fellow man.

'My work shall not be an utter failure because it has the solid basis of a definite intention—first: and next because in its essence it is action (strange as this affirmation may sound at the present time), nothing but action—action observed, felt and interpreted with an absolute truth to sensations (which are the basis of art in literature)—actions of human beings that will bleed to a prick, and are moving in a visible world.

This is my creed. Time will show.'[10]

Notes

References to page numbers of individual works by Conrad are given in the text, and follow the pagination of the J. M. Dent *Collected Edition of the Works of Joseph Conrad* listed in the Bibliography. The pagination of this edition is identical with that of the Dent Uniform Edition (J. M. Dent & Sons, London and Toronto, 1923–28) and with that of Joseph Conrad, *The Complete Works* (Canterbury Edition, Doubleday, Page & Co., Garden City, New York, 1921–26). The following abbreviations are used in the Notes (see Bibliography for further details):

CPB—Conrad's Polish Background, ed. Najder
LBM—Joseph Conrad: Letters to William Blackwood and David S. Meldrun, ed. Blackburn
LC—Letters from Conrad, 1895–1924, ed. Garnett
LCG—Joseph Conrad's Letters to R. B. Cunninghame Graham, ed. Watts
LL, I ⎫—*Joseph Conrad: Life and Letters* in 2 volumes, by Jean-
LL, II ⎭ Aubry

The Bibliography also contains full bibliographical details of works by other authors cited in the Notes. References in the Notes are to first mentioned editions listed in the Bibliography.

Chapter 1 : Conrad's Moral World

1   Cf. Bernard Meyer, *Joseph Conrad: A Psychoanalytic Biography*.
2   *Under Western Eyes*, p. 67.
3   R. Curle, *The Last Twelve Years of Joseph Conrad*, p. 66.
4   Ibid., p. 133.
5   E. M. Forster, *Abinger Harvest*, pp. 152–3.
6   F. R. Leavis, *The Great Tradition*, p. 199.
7   I. Watt, 'Joseph Conrad: Alienation and Commitment', *The English Mind: Studies in the English Moralists Presented to Basil Willey*, p. 265.
8   *LL*, II, p. 34; 30 May 1906.
9   *LC*, pp. 172–3; 12 November 1900.
10 In Conrad's defence, it should be noted that this particular form of self-deprecation was one that he often used with strangers (Charles Cassé had written a warm article on Conrad in the *Figaro*, and Conrad was writing to thank him). Written from an assured position as a classic of English literature, his comment surely reflects that humility which often seems the most gracious response to the questions of men with whom one is not intimate. A look at the context of the remark indicates that Conrad was not talking about his opinion of the *value* of his works, or even their meaning, but was forcibly objecting to the naïve charge of 'Slavonism' that so plagued him. It is unlikely that Conrad's claim in this letter—'my claim to Westernism'—could be classified as an 'illusion'. (It is also worth remarking that Douglas Hewitt goes on, in his next paragraph, to quote one of Conrad's many helpful comments on his work.)
11 D. Hewitt, *Conrad: A Reassessment*, pp. 4–5.
12 In citing Conrad's references to his own work, I shall, like Douglas Hewitt, 'take comfort' from a passage in the letters, this time from one of 21 June 1924.
    'I think that an author who tries to "explain" is exposing himself to a very great risk—the risk of confessing himself a failure. For a work of art should speak for itself. Yet much could be said on the other side; for it is also clear that a work of art is not a logical demonstration carrying its intention on the face of it.' (*LL*, II, p. 344.)
13 Ibid., p. 54; 30 July 1907.
14 Ibid., p. 78; dated 'Wednesday' (1908).
15 Ibid., p. 204; 4 May 1918.
16 Ibid., p. 205; 4 May 1918.
17 A. Guerard, *Conrad the Novelist*, pp. 57–8.

18 Ibid., p. 58.

19 As Ian Watt notes, it is in Conrad's early letters that 'alienation is the pervading theme' (op. cit., p. 265).

20 Conrad told Garnett that he was 'in *intimate* correspondence' with Cunninghame Graham. *LC*, p. 117; 6 January 1898.

21 Although the letters are printed by Jean-Aubry, they have recently been published by C. T. Watts (*Joseph Conrad's Letters to R. B. Cunninghame Graham*), who has preserved the original punctuation, and made occasional changes in the dating of certain key letters. My references will thus be to Watts's edition.

22 *LCG*, pp. 56–7; 20 December 1897. On the same day Conrad was to write to Mme Angèle Zagórska, complaining: '*Les nerfs, les nerfs!* Uncertainty torments me. It is very foolish, no doubt—*mais que voulez-vous? l'homme est bête.*' (*LL*, I, p. 217.)

23 The phrase may apply to Kayerts in 'An Outpost of Progress', whose tongue sticks out irreverently after his suicide.

24 *LCG*, p. 65; 14 January 1898.

25 Ibid., p. 68; dated 'Sunday'. Watts suggests (p. 69) 23 February 1898. The immediate context makes it clear that Conrad's remarks are a response to his reading of 'The Impenitent Thief', an essay that Cunninghame Graham had just published, but the response quite clearly advances the dialogue as we have followed it.

26 Ibid., pp. 70–1; 31 January 1898.

27 Ibid., p. 103; 27 August 1898.

28 *LL*, I, p. 269; 8 February 1899.

29 T. Moser, *Joseph Conrad: Achievement and Decline*, p. 11.

30 *LL*, II, p. 185; 18 March 1917.

31 Zdzislaw Najder has suggested that these 'ideal' values are those of Polish romanticism:

> 'The values he wanted to see cherished—honour, duty, fidelity, friendship—were typically romantic and typically chivalrous, and it is only too obvious that we have to look for their origin to Poland, where the life of the whole nation was, for better or for worse, dominated by these very values . . .
>
> The influence of the particularly Polish romantic tradition can be clearly seen in Conrad's treatment of the problems of moral responsibility: his moral awareness is stated in social, not individual terms; in terms of duties and obligations, not in terms of conscience and self-perfection.' (*CPB*, p. 31.)

This is useful, but it ought to serve as a warning about the possible loss of perspective which biographical information can produce. It is certainly not true, for instance, that a complex novel like *Under Western Eyes* can be said to stress duties and obligations to society *rather than* to the self.

32 Hewitt, op. cit., p. 4.

33 Moser, op. cit., p. 15.

34 *LCG*, pp. 53–4; 14 December 1897.

35 Ibid., p. 70; 31 January 1898.

36 *The Nigger of the 'Narcissus'*, p. 6.

37 See the Author's Preface to *The Secret Agent*, p. xiii.

38 'Books', *Notes on Life and Letters*, pp. 8–9.

39 I do not wish to try to account here for this discrepancy. I have previously suggested that Conrad's vision of personal autonomy occurs most frequently in his early letters, while his assertions of social responsibility tend to come later—most fully after 1911. Although Conrad suggested that he was, by the time he began his writing career, a man of 'formed character', there is much evidence to suggest that his character developed markedly during his life as a writer. This development might briefly be characterized as a movement from the pessimism (and clarity) of the early letters, and their corresponding works, to the optimism (and frequent sentimentality and lack of clarity) of the later letters and autobiographies, and the corresponding late novels. The most persuasive account of this development is contained in *Joseph Conrad: A Psychoanalytic Biography*, in which Bernard Mayer argues that Conrad suffered a nervous breakdown in 1910 (the crucial factor being his break with Hueffer), and that his later thinking and writing shows a marked decline. Meyer speaks of Conrad, after 1910, 'turning his back upon his erstwhile scepticism, doubts, and introspection, and stepping forth resolutely as the cliché-ridden champion of solid virtue and duty with a capital "D".' (p. 222.) He suggests that this 'alienation from his own imaginative fancy after 1910 is discernible not only in his tales: it is also manifest in his retrospective comments on the earlier stories' (p. 241). I do not wholly agree with Meyer's account, both because Conrad had been a 'champion . . . of solid virtue and duty' well before 1910 (in *The Nigger of the 'Narcissus'*, for example) and because there is enough solidly satisfying writing (notably *Under Western Eyes*) after 1910 to cause doubts about such a radical split in Conrad's career. I do, however, recommend a close reading of Meyer's argument, particularly pp. 221–63.

40 'Anatole France', *Notes on Life and Letters*, pp. 33–4.

41 Moser, op. cit., p. 16.

42 *An Outcast of the Islands*, p. 273.
43 *Lord Jim*, p. ix.
44 *Nostromo*, p. xix.
45 *Under Western Eyes*, p. ix.
46 *LL*, I, p. 205; 27 June 1897.
47 *LC*, p. 216; 4 October 1907.
48 Preface to *The Nigger of the 'Narcissus'*, p. vii.
49 *A Personal Record*, p. 92.
50 Ibid., p. 93.
51 Matthew Arnold, 'The Study of Poetry', *Essays in Criticism*, Series II, London, 1915, pp. 2–3.
52 *LL*, II, p. 89; 6 October 1908.
53 *LC*, p. 23; 23 March 1896.
54 Ibid., pp. 282–3; 16 May 1918.

Chapter 2: *Almayer's Folly* to *Tales of Unrest*

1   For a full analysis of the textual history of *Almayer's Folly*, see J. D. Gordan, *Joseph Conrad: The Making of a Novelist*, pp. 35–54 and 112–35.
2   *A Personal Record*, pp. 9–10
3   Ibid., p. 68.
4   A short story, 'The Black Mate', was submitted to a competition held by *Tit-Bits* Magazine in 1884, but was rejected.
5   Conrad originally hoped to publish it in Unwin's *Pseudonym Library*; when it was rejected, the name 'Joseph Conrad' was equally unrecognizable.
6   It must be pointed out that the first of Unwin's readers of the manuscript was not Garnett, but W. H. Chesson. See *Conradiana*, Vol. IV, No. 2, pp. 5–15.
7   *LL*, II, p. 183; 14 March 1917.
8   *LL*, I, p. 237; 17 May 1898.
9   Garnett tentatively confirms Conrad's account of their meeting; *LC*, p. viii.
10 There is no doubt that it was begun well before Conrad remembered, for the meeting with Garnett took place in November 1894, while the letters indicate that 'Two Vagabonds' dates from the middle of August 1894. For the complete history of the transformation of 'Two Vagabonds' into *An Outcast of the Islands*, see J. D. Gordan, op. cit., pp. 189–98.
11 Regrettable especially to Conrad himself, who found himself thereafter classified, all too frequently, as an 'exotic' novelist—

a charge against which he was still hotly protesting when he wrote the Author's Note to *An Outcast* in 1919; see p. ix.

12 *LL*, I, p. 183; 28 October, 1895.
13 Guerard, *Conrad the Novelist*, p. 68.
14 Ibid., p. 79
15 *LC*, p. xii.
16 Dated either 29 October or 5 November 1894, as the heading says only '*Lundi matin*' (Yale Library).
17 In 'Lingard's Folly: The Lost Subject', Vernon Young maintains that the real subject of the Malayan trilogy should have been Lingard, but that only *The Rescue* has him at the centre. He holds, with Guerard, that 'Willems is never superseded as the novel's leading character' in *An Outcast*. He rather remarkably sees Willems as 'the striking creation of a complex, common man'. See R. W. Stallman, ed., *The Art of Joseph Conrad: A Critical Symposium*, p. 101.
18 A letter dated '*Samedi*', perhaps 18 August 1894 (Yale Library).
19 *LC*, p. 9; 12 May 1895.
20 Guerard, op. cit., p. 80.
21 Gordan reports that 'the death of Willems was the event towards which he had all the time been working' (op. cit., p. 105), but this does not necessarily prove that Willems's death can be regarded as the climax of the novel. Events, as Conrad said, are but accidents.
22 Moser, *Achievement and Decline*, p. 10. But Moser curiously fails to extend his insight to his consideration of *An Outcast*, for he virtually ignores Lingard in his discussion of the novel.
23 *LC*, pp. 14–15; 24 September 1895.
24 Conrad informed Garnett that he had considered the title *Idiots and Other Stories* for the volume, but had rather decided against it. See his letter of 14 August 1896; *LC*, p. 47.
25 'Karain: A Memory', p. 40.
26 An explicit statement of this perception occurs in each story: Karain says that 'I wanted peace, not life' (p. 42), after murdering Matara, and would have gone berserk had the English sailors not exorcized his personal demon; Susan, in 'The Idiots', tells her mother that in the afterlife she will find 'nothing worse than in this' (p. 76), and commits suicide; Kayerts, in 'An Outpost of Progress', is described thus: 'He found life more terrible and difficult than death' (p. 114), and he shortly hangs himself; Alvan Hervey, in 'The Return', finds that life seems to him 'perfectly intolerable' (p. 128), and leaves his wife to start anew somewhere; Arsat, in 'The Lagoon', plans to avenge

his brother's death, and in so doing sacrifice his own life, saying:
'I can see nothing—see nothing! There is no light and peace in
the world; but there is death—death for many.' (p. 203.)

27 The Author's Note to *Tales of Unrest*, p. vii. The heaviest part
    of the loot was, of course, 'Heart of Darkness'.

28 The theme of 'putting the tongue out' is found in the Cunning-
    hame Graham letters. See Chapter 1, p. 10.

29 As Conrad wrote of 'The Lagoon'; *LC*, p. 44; 5 August 1896.

30 Ibid., p. 47; 14 August 1896.

31 Author's Note to *Tales of Unrest*, pp. vii–viii.

32 As Conrad was writing the story 'The Lagoon', he mentioned
    to Garnett that his work was difficult for him: 'You see *the
    belief* is not in me—and without the belief—the brazen thick
    headed, thick skinned immovable belief nothing good can be
    done.' *LC*, p. 44; 5 August 1896.

33 J. Baines, *Joseph Conrad: A Critical Biography*, p. 190.

34 Moser mentions neither the episode of the sixpence nor the
    coda. He says that Karain in fact *remains* 'a slave of the dead';
    Moser, op. cit., p. 71.

35 Conrad's only other attempt at such a theme before 'The
    Return' was in 1896, in the fragment of a novel called 'The
    Sisters'.

36 *LC*, pp. 93–4; 29 September 1897.

37 See Chapter 1, p. 10.

38 Conrad refers to the story as 'the new gospel' in a letter to
    Garnett, whom he chastises for missing its symbolism. See *LC*,
    p. 120; 24 January 1898.

39 Ibid., p. 86.

40 Ibid., p. 92.

41 Meyer, *A Psychoanalytic Biography*, p. 125.

Chapter 3: *The Nigger of the 'Narcissus'*

1 *The Nigger* was completed in January of 1897.

2 *LC*, p. 60; 29 November 1896.

3 Ibid., p. 100; 11 October 1897.

4 Ibid., p. 118; 1 January 1898.

5 Arthur Symons wrote in praise of the descriptions in *The
   Nigger* and in Kipling's *Captains Courageous*, but added: 'What
   more is there? Where is the idea of which such things as these
   should be but servants? Ah, there has been an oversight;
   everything else is there, but that, these brilliant writers have for-

gotten to put in.' *Saturday Review*, LXXXV (1898), pp. 145–6.

6 *The Library of John Quinn*, New York, 1923–4, I, p. 170. A similar opinion is presented in a note 'To My Readers in America', in the post-1914 American edition of *The Nigger of the 'Narcissus'*, p. ix, and in a handwritten comment in Richard Curle's copy of the novel: *Richard Curle Conrad Collection*, item 26.

7 A full discussion of Wait's name as pun is to be found in Vernon Young's article 'Trial by Water', reprinted in R. W. Stallman, ed., *The Art of Joseph Conrad: A Critical Symposium*, pp. 108–20.

8 Several critics have suggested a parallel with Babo the Negro, who is used as an incarnation of evil in Melville's 'Benito Cereno'.

9 R. L. Stevenson's 'Thrawn Janet' (1878) also exploits the common belief that the Devil would appear as a black man: 'He was of great stature, an' black as hell, and his e'en were singular to see.' *Dr Jekyll and Mr Hyde*, London, 1966, p. 151.

10 *LC*, p. 52; 25 October 1896.

11 J. I. M. Stewart, *Joseph Conrad*, p. 62.

12 As the narrator disengages himself from his shipmates at the end of the story, he muses, 'Let the earth and the sea each have its own' (p. 172)—and it is quite clear what he means.

13 Guerard, *Conrad the Novelist*, p. 109.

14 This is also suggested by calling Wait 'a bladder full of gas' (p. 70), 'a cold black skin loosely stuffed with soft cotton wool' (p. 71), and a 'doll that had lost half its sawdust' (p. 72).

15 P. Kirschner, *Conrad: The Psychologist as Artist*, p. 109. He refers to the story as 'a social allegory of the self's awareness of mortality' (p. 102).

16 One of Conrad's favourite quotations (which he used as an epigraph to *Lord Jim*) was from Novalis: 'It is certain any conviction gains infinitely the moment another soul will believe in it.'

17 Singleton collects his wages, and signs his X, but we remember him reading *Pelham* (albeit slowly) on board ship. (Perhaps Conrad sometimes goes too far to establish his sea/land dichotomy?)

18 *LL*, II, p. 342; 7 April 1924.

19 *LL*, I, p. 200; 27 January 1897.

20 Quoted by Vernon Young, op. cit., p. 114.

Chapter 4: 'Heart of Darkness'

1 The story first appeared in *Blackwood's Magazine*, February–
April 1899.
2 *LCG*, p. 116; 8 February 1899.
3 Leavis, *The Great Tradition*, p. 203.
4 Ibid., p. 199.
5 Ibid., p. 200.
6 Although one cannot make the identification of Marlow with
Conrad absolute, the story is clearly based on Conrad's experiences in Africa: he refers to 'Heart of Darkness' as 'experience pushed a little (and only very little) beyond the actual
facts of the case . . .' (Author's Note, p. vii). He also imputes to
Marlow his own childhood desire to visit the heart of Africa.
7 The river is never named explicitly, but there can be no doubt
as to its identity.
8 Marlow had previously suggested that one can only resist the
call of the darkness through dedication to some task: 'What
saves us is efficiency—the devotion to efficiency' (p. 50); hence
the detailed accounts of daily work: pp. 50, 85, 87, 93–4, 97–8,
99, 117, and 149.
9 As he was writing 'Heart of Darkness', Conrad wrote to
Garnett: 'My fortitude is shaken by the view of the monster. It
does not move; its eyes are baleful; it is as still as death itself—
and it will devour me.' *LC*, p. 151; dated 'Good Friday', 1899.
10 Baines, *A Critical Biography*, p. 228.
11 This is not to deny that Kurtz is explicitly associated with evil,
as for instance in 'He had taken a high seat amongst the devils
of the land—I mean literally' (p. 116). What seems to me
important is that Kurtz's undeniable evil is seen as a result—
and probably a necessary result—of his freedom and of his
idealism.
12 Stewart, p. 84.
13 F. Nietzsche, *Beyond Good and Evil*, trans. R. J. Hollindale,
London, 1976, p. 50.
14 Conrad referred to himself as 'a mere animal' before his experiences in Africa.
15 *LBM*, p. 154; 31 May 1902.

Chapter 5: *Lord Jim*

1 The novel was first serialized in *Blackwood's Magazine*, October

1899–November 1900. First publication in book form took place later in 1900.

2   Conrad was later to admit privately that he had attempted to 'cram as much character and incident into it as it could hold. This explains its great length which the story itself does not justify' (Inscribed in Richard Curle's copy of the novel): T. J. Wise, *A Conrad Library*, 1928, p. 6.

3   Author's Note to *Lord Jim*, p. vii.

4   Ibid., p. viii.

5   *LC*, p. 172; 12 November 1900. Although the two parts of the novel are not formally divided in the text, it will be useful to refer to them in talking about the novel. Part I, then, runs to page 225, which seems to be a stopping point in both the action and in Marlow's mood of summing up ('My last words about Jim shall be few'). Pages 226–417 form Part II of the novel, and deal largely with Jim's experiences in Patusan.

6   A phrase repeated with tiresome regularity: see pp. ix, 43, 78, 93, 106, 224, 325, 331, 361, and 416.

7   Hewitt, *A Reassessment*, pp. 37–9.

8   Baines, *A Critical Biography*, p. 242.

9   On page 66, in answer to Marlow's assertion that 'It costs some money to run away', Brierly says 'Does it? Not always', with a bitter laugh. Marlow can only tell us that though the matter must have been 'of the gravest import', it had nothing to do with money, women, or drink. (p. 59.)

10   *The Nigger of the 'Narcissus'*, pp. 138–9.

11   Favoured by Dorothy Van Ghent, among other critics; see *The English Novel: Form and Function*, p. 230.

12   There is reason to suppose that this is what Conrad intended: 'A chance comes once in life to all of us. Not the chance to get on; that only comes to good men. Fate is inexorably just. But Fate is also merciful and even to the poorest there comes sometimes the chance of an intimate, full, complete and pure satisfaction.' A letter dated 18 October 1898; Pierpont Library, New York.

Chapter 6: *Nostromo*

1   For an extremely interesting study of the ways in which Conrad uses his shifts in time and point of view to further the thematic structure of *Nostromo*, see Guerard, *Conrad the Novelist*, pp. 175–95.

2 The entire time span of the novel seems to cover at least 27 years. C. B. Cox summarizes the action as follows: 'In brief, a period of fierce civil war is followed by the fifteen-year tyranny of Guzman Bento. After his death a period of at least twelve years and many governments elapses before Charles Gould reopens the mine. After about eight more years, very roughly, Sir John visits Sulaco, and eighteen months later the riots beak out.' *Nostromo* (*Notes on English Literature*), p. 17.

3 I will not pause here for the qualifications which ought to accompany a phrase like 'a better place in which to live'; indeed, one of the major questions with which Conrad is concerned is just what it is that man wants and needs in order to live a meaningful life.

4 In making this contrast, I will begin by summarizing the positions of two of the most distinguished Conrad critics, Robert Penn Warren and Albert Guerard. My references will be to Warren's essay entitled 'The Great Mirage: Conrad and *Nostromo*', from *Selected Essays*, pp. 31–58, and to Guerard's *Conrad the Novelist*.

5 Warren, op. cit., pp. 50, 54.

6 Guerard, op. cit., p. 189.

7 It is interesting to compare this thought, and the previous one of Dr Monygham, with Conrad's letter to Cunninghame Graham, dated Sunday, February 1898, which I have quoted on pp. 11–12.

8 Guerard, op. cit., p. 198.

9 Conrad refers to the novel as the history of 'events flowing from the passions of men short-sighted in good and evil' (p. xvii), in which Charles Gould is explicitly implicated; on p. 407, Conrad tells us that Gould 'suffered from his fellowship in evil' with the 'strange impotence' of the Provincial Assembly.

10 *LL*, II, p. 296; 7 March 1923.

11 The 'basic difference' between the Goulds is little more apparent to the reader than it is to Decoud at this point of the novel. It is not until the end of the novel that the real distinction between Emilia and her husband is clear. Decoud is at least implicitly aware of some difference between Emilia and Charles simply in his desire to deal openly and honestly with Mrs Gould.

12 It has been argued that Mrs Gould is far from the 'unequivocal heroine' (Guerard, op. cit., p. 191) that she may at first seem. In *Politics and the Novel*, Irving Howe suggests that Mrs Gould 'has sealed herself off in an enclave of disciplined suffering. The court she holds for the Europeans and a few chosen

"natives" is merely a mirror to her loneliness; the life of the country on which her comfort depends remains a secret forever closed to her. All Costaguanans, she admits, look alike to her—she means no malice, not even unfriendliness, yet how fatal an admission it nonetheless is. The rhythms of Costaguana are alien to her racial conventions, and because she cannot transcend these conventions—because she lacks the boldness of Mrs Moore in *Passage to India*—her life narrows into a ritual of controlled deprivation.' (p. 110)
This seems to make rather too much of Mrs Gould's isolation; the conditions imposed upon Costaguanan women—from which even Antonia suffers—limit the role of any given woman, particularly a foreign one. As Dr Monygham says of Mrs Gould, 'Costaguana was no place for a woman of that kind' (p. 576). Howe's suggested comparison with Mrs Moore is unconvincing. Ultimately, it might be argued, it does not matter that Mrs Gould's virtue is fugitive and cloistered, for *Nostromo* may well lead us to doubt that anything more is possible.

13 Giorgio Viola has several attributes in common with the brave and unselfconscious men who form the first group of characters of whom I have spoken. He differs from men like Don Pepé, Hernandez, and Barrios, in that he is explicitly dedicated to a political ideal, and also in that he is in no way implicated in the political action of the novel.

14 It might be useful to suggest that the change: Nostromo to Captain Fidanza, is paralleled by the related change: Costaguana to Occidental Republic.

15 The rifles are instrumental in the defeat of Montero; see p. 476.

16 The *Porvenir* becomes the major paper of Sulaco; see p. 478.

17 It is, for instance, the narrator who muses that 'Action is consolatory. It is the enemy of thought and the friend of flattering illusions. Only in the conduct of our action can we find the sense of mastery over the Fates.' (p. 66.) The narrator's Decoud-like scepticism is also clear in the remark that 'The popular mind is incapable of scepticism; and that incapacity delivers their helpless strength to the wiles of swindlers and to the pitiless enthusiasms of leaders inspired by visions of a high destiny.' (p. 420.)

18 Decoud's spirit is certainly close to that of the letters to Cunninghame Graham which I have quoted in my introduction. In his comments on Gould's tendency to idealize, his contempt for Holroyd and the materialism for which he stands, and his contemptuous seeking out of deceit and illusion, he speaks with

what Guerard calls a 'distinctly Conradian rhythm and rhetoric' (op. cit., p. 192).

In a letter to John Galsworthy, Conrad was to recommend a most Decoud-like theory of life:

'The fact is that you want more scepticism at the very foundation of your work. Scepticism, the tonic of life, the agent of truth,—the way of art and salvation.' (*LL*, I, p. 301; 11 November 1901.)

19 Leavis, *The Great Tradition*, p. 221.

20 Warren, op. cit., p. 39.

21 According to Guerard:

'The characterisation obviously belongs with those in which a writer attempts to separate out and demolish a facet of himself by proxy . . . To put matters bluntly: Conrad may be condemning Decoud for a withdrawal and skepticism more radical than Decoud ever shows; which are, in fact, Conrad's own.' (Op. cit., p. 199.)

22 Leavis, op. cit., p. 221.

23 In the Author's Note to *Nostromo*, which was written in the early 1920s, Conrad seems very much more sympathetic to Antonia than to Decoud, though he is still markedly identified with Decoud's 'levities' (p. xxii).

Chapter 7: *The Secret Agent*

1 The stories are published in the volume *A Set of Six*.

2 But it is a singularly ineffective shield; unlike his counterpart in *The Secret Agent*, this professor finally blows himself inadvertently to bits.

3 The anecdote related by Ford (who is not named, though it is most certainly he) served as the loose story line of the novel; the specific details of this, as well as Harcourt's phrase, may be found in the Author's Note to *The Secret Agent*, pp. x–xi.

4 Stewart, op. cit., pp. 174–5.

5 *LL*, II, p. 37; 12 September 1906. Conrad also expressed a great deal of dissatisfaction with *The Secret Agent* in a letter to Garnett dated 1 October 1907; *LC*, p. 211.

6 As Eloise Knapp Hay points out at some length in *The Political Novels of Joseph Conrad*, pp. 230–5.

7 See below, p. 140.

8 I do not mean to suggest that none of Conrad's other works makes use of this irony, for I have previously argued that both

Almayer's Folly and *An Outcast of the Islands* suffer to some degree from ironic undercutting of the protagonist. It is, however, in 'An Outpost of Progress' that this irony has a consistency of tone and purpose parallel to that in *The Secret Agent*. Douglas Hewitt has suggested (*A Reassessment*, p. 85) that the 'brutal and sordid farce' of 'Heart of Darkness' is similar to that of *The Secret Agent*, but the parallel with 'An Outpost of Progress' is surely more instructive, in that the farce in 'Heart of Darkness' is mitigated by the presence of Kurtz and his association with Marlow.

9 See, for instance, the Preface to *The Nigger of the 'Narcissus'*.
10 Leavis suggests that *The Secret Agent* and *Nostromo* are Conrad's best works (*The Great Tradition*, p. 242).

Chapter 8: *Under Western Eyes*

1 *Chance* was put aside due to lack of 'serious progress'. *LL*, II, p. 65; 6 January 1908.
2 Ibid., pp. 64–5. The de Flehve to whom Conrad refers was the Russian Minister of the Interior who was killed in 1904 by a student named Sasonov, who threw a bomb into his carriage. For a discussion of the historical context out of which Conrad drew several of the characters of *Under Western Eyes*, see Baines, *A Critical Biography*, pp. 370–2.
3 According to Jean-Aubry, Conrad had already completed the first part of the novel at the time that he wrote the above quoted letter to Galsworthy: there is a note 'done' in the margin of the paragraph outlining the theme up to the hanging of Haldin, and the words 'to do' in the margin of the following paragraph (*LL*, II, p. 65).
4 Conrad wrote to Sir Sidney Colvin: 'Russians . . . are born rotten.' *LL*, II, p. 198; 12 November 1917.
5 *Notes on Life and Letters*, pp. 83–114.
6 Baines, for instance, believes that Razumov is simply Conrad's 'mouthpiece' in this instance (op. cit., p. 364). But if this is the case, it must then follow that Razumov is right in betraying Haldin. The difficulty is that 'Unity' and 'Patriotism' in Razumov's Russian context are morally unjustifiable; Conrad had argued in 'Autocracy and War' that in the light of Russia's history 'the word Evolution, which is precisely the expression of the highest intellectual hope, is a gruesome pleasantry. There can be no evolution out of a grave.' (p. 99.) But he felt

equally strongly that revolution was also impossible in Russia: 'For the autocracy of Holy Russia the only conceivable self-reform is—suicide.' (p. 101.)

7   In Geneva he is later to reflect during the course of a conversation with Sophia Antonovna:

> 'As if anything could be changed! In this world of men nothing can be changed—neither happiness nor misery. They can only be displaced at the cost of corrupted consciences and broken lives—a futile game for arrogant philosophers and sanguinary triflers.' (p. 261.)

8   I have not had occasion to speak of Razumov's diary (in which all of this information is originally found) because it seems to me so little a factor in the narrative. Though not a particularly credible device (being of unbelievable duration and detail, and having been compiled in moments of stress so great that one cannot accept its validity), it doesn't seem to me to be offensively present, so I have chosen largely to ignore it.

9   Conrad was clearly concerned to maintain his artistic detachment sufficiently to create his anarchists more substantially than their counterparts in *The Secret Agent*. When Garnett accused him of abusing them out of a general hatred of Russians, Conrad rather testily replied:

> 'But it is hard after lavishing a "wealth of tenderness" on Tekla and Sophia, to be charged with the rather low trick of putting one's hate into a novel . . . Is it possible that you haven't seen that in this book I am concerned with nothing but ideas, to the exclusion of everything else, with no *arrière pensée* of any kind.' (*LC*, 249; 20 October 1911.)

On the other hand, it is quite clear from Conrad's comments in his Author's Note, as well as from 'Autocracy and War', that there were grounds for Garnett's charge.

10   Baines, op. cit., p. 363.

11   That is, when the teacher of languages reports the scenes through the medium of Razumov's diary, which has come into his possession.

12   Which is not to say that it *might* not come, or that it is fruitless to preserve a vision leading towards it. Certainly 'Autocracy and War' is informed by a vision much like that of Natalia Haldin:

> 'This service of unification . . . has prepared the ground for the advent of a still larger understanding: for the solidarity of Europeanism, which must be the next step towards the advent of Concord and Justice; an advent that, however

delayed by the fatal worship of force and the errors of national selfishness, has been, and remains, the only possible goal of our progress.' (p. 97.)

13 Guerard, *Conrad the Novelist*, p. 239.

14 As Conrad had argued in 'Autocracy and War':
    'The Russian autocracy as we see it now is a thing apart. It is impossible to assign to it any rational origin in the vices, the misfortunes, the necessities, or the aspirations of mankind. That despotism . . . seems to have no root either in the institutions or the follies of this earth.' (p. 98).

Chapter 9: Conclusion: *Chance, Victory, The Shadow Line*

1 *LL*, II, p. 146; 2 June 1913.

2 Baines, *A Critical Biography*, p. 380.

3 Author's Note to *Chance*, pp. viii–ix.

4 As noted by Guerard, *Conrad the Novelist*, pp. 262–3.

5 It isn't even clear that Marlow consistently believes in the workings of chance; or, if it is, it is incompatible with his belief that the 'Book of Destiny has been written up from the beginning to the last page' (p. 128).

6 Guerard, *Conrad the Novelist*, p. 264.

7 Crankshaw, *Joseph Conrad: Some Aspects of the Art of the Novel*, p. 132. Crankshaw, like Leavis, thinks *Chance* indisputably one of Conrad's greatest works.

8 The contrast between the stories is particularly constructive, since *The Shadow Line* was conceived as early as 1899, as a companion piece for 'Youth', entitled 'First Command'.

9 *The Shadow Line*, p. 40.

10 *LBM*, 31 May 1902, pp. 155–6.

Bibliography

I. The Writings and Letters of Joseph Conrad

Blackburn, W. (ed.) *Joseph Conrad: Letters to William Blackwood and David S. Meldrum*, London and Durham, NC, 1958.

Conrad, Joseph. *Collected Edition of the Works of Joseph Conrad* (in 21 volumes), J. M. Dent, London, 1946–65.

——. *Laughing Anne and One Day More* (two plays by Joseph Conrad with an Introduction by John Galsworthy), London, 1924.

——. *The Sisters* (An Unfinished Story, edited by Ugo Mursia), Milan, 1968.

Conrad, J. and Hueffer, F. W. *The Inheritors: An Extravagant Story*, London, 1923; repr. Boston, 1976.

——. *The Nature of a Crime*, London and New York, 1924.

Curle, R. (ed.). *Conrad to a Friend: 150 Selected Letters from Joseph Conrad to Richard Curle*, London and New York, 1928.

Garnett, E. (ed.). *Letters from Conrad, 1895–1924*, London and Indianapolis, 1928.

Gee, J. A. and Strum, P. J. (ed. and trans.). *Letters of Joseph Conrad to Marguerite Poradowska, 1890–1920*, London and New York, 1940.

Jean-Aubry, G. (ed.). *Lettres Françaises par Joseph Conrad*, Paris, 1930.

Najder, E. (ed.). *Conrad's Polish Background: Letters to and from Polish Friends*, London and New York, 1964.

Watts, C. T. (ed.). *Joseph Conrad's Letters to R. B. Cunninghame Graham*, Cambridge and New York, 1969.

II. Select Bibliography of Writings on Joseph Conrad

Allen, J. *The Sea Years of Joseph Conrad*, London, 1967; New York, 1965.

Baines, J. *Joseph Conrad: A Critical Biography*, London, 1960; New York, 1961.

Bojarski, E. A. 'Joseph Conrad's Sentimental Journey. A Fiftieth-Anniversary Review', *The Texas Quarterly*, Winter, 1964.

Bojarski, E. A. and H. T. 'Joseph Conrad: A Bibliography of Masters'

Theses and Doctoral Dissertations, 1917–1963', University of Kentucky Libraries, Occasional Contribution, No. 157, Lexington, Kentucky, 1964.

Bradbrook, M. C. *Joseph Conrad: Poland's English Genius*, Cambridge, 1942; repr. New York, 1965.

Conrad, Borys. *My Father: Joseph Conrad*, London and New York, 1970.

Conrad, Jessie. *Joseph Conrad as I Knew Him*, London, 1926; New York, 1925.

——. *Joseph Conrad and His Circle*, London, 1935; Port Washington, New York, 2nd ed. 1964.

Conradiana: A Journal of Joseph Conrad, Lubbock, Texas, 1968–72.

Cooper, C. *Conrad and The Human Dilemma*, London, 1970.

Cox, C. B. *Joseph Conrad: The Modern Imagination*, London, 1976.

——. *Nostromo* (*Notes on English Literature* Series), Oxford, 1964.

Crankshaw, E. *Joseph Conrad: Some Aspects of the Art of the Novel*, London and New York, 1936.

Curle, R. *The Last Twelve Years of Joseph Conrad*, London and New York, 1928.

Daiches, D. *A Critical History of English Literature*, Vol. II, London, 1963; 2nd ed., New York, 1970.

Fleishman, A. *Conrad's Politics*, Baltimore, Maryland, 1967; London, 1968.

Follett, W., *Joseph Conrad: A Short Study of his Intellectual and Emotional Attitude toward his Work and of the Chief Characteristics of his Novels*, New York, 1915.

Forster, E. M. *Abinger Harvest*, London and New York, 1967.

Galsworthy, J. *Castles in Spain and Other Screeds*, London, 1928.

Gordan, J. D. *Joseph Conrad: The Making of a Novelist*, Cambridge, Mass., 1940.

Graver, L. *Conrad's Short Fiction*, London, 1969.

Guerard, A. J. *Conrad the Novelist*, Cambridge, Mass. and London, 1958.

Gurko, L. *Joseph Conrad: Giant in Exile*, New York, 1962.

Hay, E. K. *The Political Novels of Joseph Conrad*, London and Chicago, 1963.

Hewitt, D. *Conrad: A Reassessment*, Cambridge, 1952.

Howe, I. *Politics and the Novel*, New York, 1957; London, 1960.

Hueffer, F. M. *Joseph Conrad: A Personal Remembrance*, London and Boston, 1924.

——. *Mightier than the Sword*, London, 1938.

James, Henry. 'The New Novel, 1914' from *Selected Literary Criticism*, London, 1963 (New York, 1964), pp. 358–91.

Jean-Aubry, G. *Joseph Conrad: Life and Letters*, 2 vols, London, 1927.

——. *The Sea Dreamer: A Definitive Biography of Joseph Conrad*, London, 1957.

Johnson, B. *Conrad's Models of Mind*, Minnesota, 1971; Oxford, 1972.

Karl, F. R. A. *A Reader's Guide to Joseph Conrad*, New York, 1960.

Keating, G. T. (comp.). *A Conrad Memorial Library: The Collection of G. T. Keating*, New York, 1929.

Kirschner, P. *Conrad: The Psychologist as Artist*, Edinburgh, 1968; Atlantic Highlands, 1974.

Leavis, F. R. *The Great Tradition*, London, 1948; repr. New York, 1963.

Lohf, K. A. and Sheehy, P. *Joseph Conrad at Mid-Century: Editions and Studies, 1895–1955*, Minnesota, 1968.

Megroz, R. L. *Joseph Conrad's Mind and Method*, London and New York, 1931.

Meyer, B. *Joseph Conrad: A Psychoanalytic Biography*, Princeton, New Jersey, 1967.

Morf, G. *The Polish Heritage of Joseph Conrad*, London, 1950; repr. New York, 1969.

Moser, T. *Joseph Conrad: Achievement and Decline*, Hampden, Conn., 1957; Oxford, 1955–9.

Mudrick, M. (ed.). *Conrad: A Collection of Critical Essays*, Engelwood Cliffs, NJ, 1966.

Newhouse, N. H. *Joseph Conrad*, London, 1966; New York, 1969.

Nowak, J. (ed.). *The Joseph Conrad Collection in The Polish Library in London*, London, 1970.

Palmer, J. A. *Joseph Conrad's Fiction: A Study in Literary Growth*, Ithaca, New York, 1968.

Richard Curle Conrad Collection, New York, 1927, item 26.

Rosenfield, C. *Paradise of Snakes: An Archetypal Analysis of Conrad's Political Novels*, Chicago, 1967; London, 1968.

Roussel, R. *The Metaphysics of Darkness*, Baltimore, Maryland; London, 1971.

Said, E. W. *Joseph Conrad and the Fiction of Autobiography*, Cambridge, Mass. and London, 1966.

Saveson, J. E. *Conrad, The Later Moralist*, Amsterdam, 1974; Atlantic Highlands, 1976.

Sherry, N. *Conrad and his World*, London, 1972; Levittown, 1974.

——. *Conrad's Eastern World*, London and New York, 1966.

——. *Conrad's Western World*, Cambridge and New York, 1971.

Stallman, R. W. (ed.). *The Art of Joseph Conrad: A Critical Symposium*, Michigan, 1960.

Stewart, J. I. M. *Eight Modern Writers*, Oxford, 1963; New York, 1975.

——. *Joseph Conrad*, London, 1968; New York, 1975.

Symons, A. *Notes on Joseph Conrad with some Unpublished Letters*, London and Fairfield, NJ, 1925.

Van Ghent, D. *The English Novel: Form and Function*, New York, 1953.

Visiak, E. H. *The Mirror of Conrad*, London, 1955.

Walpole, H. *Joseph Conrad*, London and New York, 1924.

Warner, O. *Joseph Conrad* (*Writers and Their Work* Series, No. 2), London and New York, 1950.

Warren, R. P. 'The Great Mirage: Conrad and *Nostromo*', from *Selected Essays*, New York, 1958, pp. 31–58.

Watt, I. 'Joseph Conrad: Alienation and Commitment', from *The English Mind: Studies in the English Moralists presented to Basil Willey*, Cambridge, 1964, pp. 257–78.

Wise, T. J. *A Bibliography of the Writings of Joseph Conrad (1895–1921)*, London, 1921.

——. *A Conrad Library: Collected by T. J. Wise*, London, 1928.

Woolf, Virginia. 'Joseph Conrad', from *Collected Essays*, Vol. I, London, 1966 (New York, 1967), pp. 302–8.

Zabel, M. D. *Craft and Character in Modern Fiction*, New York, 1957.

——. 'Critical Introduction' to *Under Western Eyes*, Anchor Books, New York, 1963, pp. ix–lviii.

Zyla, W. and Aycock, W. (eds). *Joseph Conrad: Theory and World Fiction*, Texas, 1974.

Index